This book is dedicated to William R. Powell

VYGOTSKY
in the
CLASSROOM

Mediated Literacy Instruction and Assessment

Lisbeth Dixon-Krauss
University of West Florida

Vygotsky in the Classroom: Mediated Literacy Instruction and Assessment

Longman, 10 Bank Street, White Plains, N.Y. 10606

Associated companies:
Longman Group Ltd., London
Longman Cheshire Pty., Melbourne
Longman Paul Pty., Auckland
Copp Clark Longman Ltd., Toronto

Production editor: Linda Moser/Professional Book Center
Development editor: Matt Baker
Cover design: Karin Batten
Compositor: Professional Book Center

Library of Congress Cataloging-in-Publication Data

Vygotsky in the classroom : mediated literacy instruction and assessment /
edited by Lisbeth Dixon-Krauss.
     p. cm.
  Includes bibliographical references and index.
  ISBN 0-8013-1590-5
  1. Language arts. 2. Language arts—Ability testing.
3. Learning, Psychology of. 4. Constructivism (Education)
5. Literacy. 6. Vygotskyii, L. S. (Lev Semenovich), 1896–1934.
I. Dixon-Krauss, Lisbeth.
LB1576.Y95 1996
372.6'044—dc20   95-9276
                                               CIP

1 2 3 4 5 6 7 8 9 10-MA-9998979695

Contents

CHAPTER 5   COLLABORATIVE LEARNING AND THINKING: THE VYGOTSKIAN APPROACH
Clara M. Jennings and Xu Di   **77**

CHAPTER 6   VYGOTSKY AND WRITING: CHILDREN USING LANGUAGE TO LEARN AND LEARNING FROM THE CHILD'S LANGUAGE WHAT TO TEACH
Marian Matthews   **93**

Preface

After seven years as a classroom teacher and a reading teacher, I was determined to find answers to the questions of how children learn to read, why some do not, and how to help teachers be more effective in their instruction. I knew that the key to teaching children is figuring out *what* and *how* they are thinking while the teaching and learning are actually happening. Teaching and learning occur in a social context as a dynamic process rather than as a preconceived one. Lev Vygotsky's work is based on this idea. The basic premise of his theory is that, if we want to study how children learn, to assess their potential to learn, and to improve instruction, we must analyze their performance and their thinking while they are engaged in learning activities. This is what effective teachers do daily.

Vygotsky in the Classroom: Mediated Literacy Instruction and Assessment is designed to help teachers think about, analyze, and make decisions on literacy instruction. It provides the conceptual framework and methodology to put these Vygotskian ideas into practice for classroom literacy instruction. Vygotsky's ideas have gained visibility among university teacher educators and researchers, but have not yet been explained and applied in a practical manner that allows teacher education students and practicing teachers to learn about and use them.

In this text, Vygotsky's ideas provide a cohesive conceptual framework and an operational model that teachers can use to integrate and apply the major current and future topics in literacy learning. These include whole language, emergent literacy, writing, integrating literature in content areas, collaborative learning, teacher decision making, technology as a tool for literacy development, and dynamic assessment for explaining children's diversity in and potential for literacy development. The chapters are written by teacher educators who have used the Vygotskian perspective to conduct research in authentic classrooms, design teaching and assessment techniques, and teach these techniques to their college and university teacher-education students.

CONTENT OF THE BOOK

Vygotsky In the Classroom contains two parts: Classroom Instruction and Classroom Assessment. In Part I, Classroom Instruction, major ideas of Vygotsky's theory are explained in the context of literacy instruction. A mediation model for literacy instruction is introduced and then used in each chapter to show how teachers can analyze students' literacy development during instruction and make decisions on the amount and type of teacher or peer support students need to move forward. Each chapter presents examples of authentic classrooms in which Vygotsky's ideas have been applied to a current topic in literacy instruction.

Part II, Classroom Assessment, applies Vygotsky's idea that assessment is dynamic and should occur while children are engaged in learning activities. This dynamic view of assessment is used to explain the diversity of children's literacy growth and to emphasize their potential for further development. Each chapter focuses on a current issue in literacy assessment including portfolio use, inclusion of children of diverse cultures and at-risk readers in classroom literacy activities, and using technology as a tool for enhancing the cognitive and social processes involved in students' literacy development.

SPECIAL FEATURES OF THE BOOK

This text contains the following special features:

- Explanation of Vygotsky's theory as a cohesive conceptual framework that teachers can apply to literacy instruction
- Opening each chapter, a classroom teaching context scenario that depicts how the literacy topic and Vygotskian principles apply to "classroom realities" that teachers encounter
- Reflection questions in each chapter that guide the reader in drawing connections between the theoretical principles on cognitive development and the current literacy topics and practices discussed
- A list of related readings for each chapter
- An operational model to guide teachers' instructional analyses and decision making
- Descriptions of how the theory and model have been applied in authentic classrooms
- Examples of how to analyze classroom dialogue and social interactions from authentic classroom settings
- Samples and analyses of children's writing

- Descriptions of teachers' perceptions about what they do during instruction
- Lesson framework examples for reading and writing instruction
- Dynamic assessment procedures
- Instructional strategies for inclusion of at-risk and culturally diverse students in classroom literacy instruction
- Examples of how to construct and use charts, surveys, conference notes, and portfolios for keeping records of students' progress

ACKNOWLEDGMENTS

I would like to thank several people who have contributed significantly to the success of this book. First, my appreciation goes to each of the chapter authors who share my interest in Vygotsky's theory; they have worked diligently to research his ideas, apply them to literacy instruction, and develop these manuscripts to share their expertise with teachers and teacher educators. I also thank Laura McKenna and Matt Baker of Longman Publishing for their continuous support and guidance in this project.

I offer a special thanks to William Powell, who has been a major influence on several of the contributors' research and application of Vygotsky's theory to literacy. I also thank Taffy Raphael for her contribution to the Book Club Program. I am grateful to James Wertsch, Bill Penuel, and their Russian colleagues on the Program Committee of the International Conference on L. S. Vygotsky and the Contemporary Human Sciences for allowing me to present my ideas on the mediation model for literacy instruction and to receive invaluable feedback while we were writing this book. I also thank the teachers and graduate assistants who worked with us in researching and applying our ideas in their classrooms: Tracy Danaher, Esther Gregory, Patricia Krauss, Laura Pardo, Bonnie Welch, Jeff Wright, and Deborah Young.

Finally, I express gratitude to my husband, Ron Krauss; my son, Michael Dixon; and my family, Rosalie Holt, Richard Holt, Bonnie Welch, and Linda McClanahan, for their support while I was working on this project.

On behalf of all the chapter authors, I thank the following reviewers whose thoughtful examination of the manuscripts provided us with guidance and support in this project:

Deanne Camp, Southwest Missouri State University

Patricia N. Chrosniak, LeMoyne College

Alan M. Frager, Miami University

Robert Gaskins, University of Kentucky

Christine H. Leland, Indiana University

Carolyn L. Piazza, Florida State University

Timothy V. Rasinski, Kent State University

Sharon Killingsworth Roberts, Iowa State University

Robert Rueda, University of Southern California
Timothy Shanahan, University of Illinois at Chicago
Lawrence L. Smith, Ball State University.

part I

Classroom Instruction

LEV SEMYONOVICH VYGOTSKY: BACKGROUND OF THE SCHOLAR/TEACHER'S LIFE AND WORK

Vygotsky's ideas have been a powerful force in educational practice in the former Soviet Union, but it is only during the past few years that his work has become an important influence on Western education. Most of this influence has been on the writings and research of psychologists in the areas of human development and learning. But Vygotsky was a teacher throughout his adult life, and he approached psychology through pedagogy (Moll 1990). His conception of human development has been described as a theory of education (Bruner 1987). The underlying theme throughout Vygotsky's work is the application of psychology to solving practical problems, especially in the area of education (Leontiev and Luria 1968).

A basic tenet of Vygotsky's approach to psychology is that human behavior is too complex to isolate, dissect, and study in a vacuum. It must instead be studied in the social and historical context within which it occurs; thus, this approach is *sociohistorical*. This introduction to Part I provides the context for understanding Vygotsky's work and its application to classroom literacy instruction.

Vygotsky's life is an interesting story. It gives us an appropriate background for understanding how the work of this Soviet genius, conducted more than 50 years ago, provides theoretical insights that are still useful today and suggests solutions that have become visions for the future of education and psychology (Blanck 1990). Vygotsky wrote no memoirs, but his history was reconstructed by Guillermo Blanck (1990) and Alex Kozulin (1986) through his family, personal acquaintances, and the writings of his colleagues.

BIOGRAPHICAL SKETCH

The Western world first came to know Lev Semyonovich Vygotsky when his final book, *Thought and Language,* was translated into English and published in 1962, 28 years after he died.[1] His research and writing career spanned only 10 years, from 1924 until his untimely death in 1934. During this brief period, he wrote more than 180 works (Blanck 1990). He spent most of his career at the Institute of Psychology in Moscow and the Ukrainian Psychoneurological Institute in Kharkov.

Vygotsky was born in 1896 in a small provincial town in Byelorussia Republic, located within the European portion of the former Soviet Union. He grew up in Gomel, a small town in southern Byelorussia, located next to the Republic of Ukraine and within the restricted territory, the Pale, where Jews were confined in Czarist Russia. Vygotsky's father, Semyon L'vovich Vygodsky, was a manager of the United Bank of Gomel, and his mother, Cecilia Moiseievna, was a licensed teacher. Lev was the second of their eight children. He was tutored at home and entered the public gymnasium at the junior high school level. He was gifted intellectually with exceptional speed in reading and an extraordinary memory.

Vygotsky entered Moscow University in 1913. He had a great love of the arts and humanities, and was active in theater, a connoisseur of poetry, and an aspiring literary critic. After graduating from Moscow University in 1917 with a specialization in literature, he returned to Byelorussia, where he spent the next seven years. There he taught language and literature to school children and adults in various schools and educational settings, logic and psychology at the Pedagogical Institute, aesthetics and art history at the conservatory in Gomel, and theater at a studio. He opened a psychology "clinic" and diagnosed learning problems and lectured on psychology of the arts and other topics in psychology, although he was never formally trained in these subjects.

Vygotsky entered professional psychology "impetuously, one may say in an onslaught" (Kozulin 1986, xiv), at the Second Psychoneurological Conference in Leningrad in 1924. Challenging the assembled seasoned behavioral scientists of the time, the young Vygotsky proclaimed that scientific psychology could not ignore the facts of consciousness. His presentation had such an impact that he was invited to join the Institute of Psychology of Moscow as a research fellow. Soon after his arrival in Moscow, Vygotsky met with Alexander Romanovich Luria and Aleksei Nikolaevich Leontiev to form the *troika*.[2] With Vygotsky assuming the leadership role, the three scholars began collaborating on organizing investigations and creating a new psychology. For the next 10 years, until his death from tuberculosis at the age of 38, Vygotsky played the leading role in developing Soviet psychology and its role in educational practice.

It is interesting to note the political, social, and educational context within which Vygotsky was working. The literacy rate in postrevolutionary Russia has been estimated at only about 30 percent (Downing 1988). A major focus of reconstructing Russia was the political campaign to eradicate illiteracy and integrate academics into the practical work activity of the citizens (Rosa and Montero 1990). Under Lenin's leadership, a national system of schools and teacher training was established. A preestablished curriculum was not imposed, and teachers were encouraged to create their own curriculum to meet the needs of students at the local level. This changed as Stalin gained control in the 1930s, and a closed national curriculum was imposed upon the schools. Following Vygotsky's death in 1934, his work was banned for 20 years during the Stalinist regime. It was then reissued in the Soviet Union in 1956.

OVERVIEW OF PART I

Vygotsky's approach to studying intellectual development in children involved using the **instrumental method** (Yaroshevsky 1989). Yaroshevsky explains how this method focuses on the child's (subject's) active use of language:

> The task with which the subject is concerned is the use of a ready-made sign system (not one he creates on his own) in communication, cognition or action in the surrounding world. (243)

Vygotsky's instrumental method included examining two important ideas about language and learning:

1. How children learn to use sign systems, primarily language, as *psychological tools* to communicate or share cultural meanings.
2. How using these cultural signs, language, affects the child's learning and cognitive development.

For Vygotsky, the most appropriate setting for studying how children's thinking develops is schools and classrooms within the context of instruction (Moll 1990).

Chapter 1 of this book begins with an explanation of the major ideas of Vygotsky's sociohistorical theory on cognitive development as they relate to literacy learning and instruction. These ideas are then related to three current movements in Western literacy instruction and learning: (1) constructivism, (2) emergent literacy, and (3) whole language. The chapter concludes with a description of a mediation model for literacy instruction designed to help teachers apply Vygotsky's ideas to literacy instruction. This model guides the teacher in making instructional decisions based on analysis of both how the students are learning printed language and how using printed language is affecting the students' learning and thinking.

In chapters 2 and 3, the mediation model of literacy instruction is used as a guide for designing and implementing classroom instruction from a Vygotskian perspective. Martha Combs presents specific strategies and lesson illustrations for sharing texts through reading, and creating texts through writing, with young, emerging readers and writers. In chapter 3, I explain how learning the more abstract systematic concepts, which Vygotsky labeled *scientific concepts,* develops children's conscious awareness and control of their thinking, and how integrating children's literature and literacy instruction with the content areas supports this concept development. I then provide examples of how to design, conduct, and manage integrated classroom instruction.

Chapters 4, 5, and 6 examine specific Vygotskian ideas that have been applied in authentic elementary school classrooms. In chapter 4, Susan I. McMahon describes a Book Club Program that was implemented in fourth and fifth grade classrooms. She shows how the program focuses on social interaction and students' use of oral and printed language to foster the development of their thinking and their literacy development. In chapter 5, Clara M. Jennings and Xu Di discuss how the social context of children collaborating with their peers on classroom literacy activities promotes their cognitive and affective development. They provide examples of how collaborative groups have been used in a first grade classroom and specific collaborative group activities for reading and writing. Marian Matthews explains in chapter 6 how teachers can integrate their observations of students with analyses of students' writings to determine their literacy and mental development. She describes the learner-centered classroom and the writing process approach within the context of authentic first and fifth grade classrooms.

Patricia Ashton concludes Part I with a discussion of the concept of activity that was introduced by Vygotsky and expanded by his colleague, A. N. Leontiev. She further explains the Vygotskian idea that children's thinking emerges in the context of activities that are embedded in specific social and cultural settings, especially in schools and classrooms. She expands on particular ways in which the language of school instructional activities affects the development of students' thinking, and then applies activity theory to literacy development and classroom instruction.

NOTES

1. Vygotsky's most popular work, *Myshlenie i rech,* was originally translated into English by Eugenia Hanfmann and Gertrude Vakar as *Thought and Language* in 1962. It was revised, edited, and translated again by Alex Kozulin in the 1986 publication. Kozulin notes that the title should be rendered in English as *Thought and Speech,* but he decided to retain the original 1962 translation, *Thought and Language.* In 1987 it was again translated by Norris Minick in *The Collected Works of L. S. Vygotsky,* Volume 1. The translator and editors of this volume decided to render the title as *Thinking and Speech* in order to make the translation true to Vygotsky's original intentions.
2. Vygotsky joined A. N. Leontiev and A. R. Luria as colleagues at the Psychological Institute in Moscow from 1924 to 1934. The three became known as the *troika* of the Vygotskian school. Although Vygotsky attracted many students and colleagues with his ingenious research agenda and lectures, Luria and Leontiev were the major developers of Vygotsky's ideas after his death. Luria continued with the cross-cultural research in Central Asia and other work on Vygotsky's theory, and Leontiev further developed Vygotsky's concept of activity.

chapter **1**

Vygotsky's Sociohistorical Perspective on Learning and Its Application to Western Literacy Instruction

Lisbeth Dixon-Krauss

SCENARIO

It is 3:00 on a Friday afternoon in late October 1994. As Mr. Miller, the custodian, peers through the doorway of the third grade classroom, he encounters a familiar, eerie sight. Ms. Holt appears to be in a trance. She is sitting at the front of the classroom casting a glassy stare out across the empty desks and tables. But in Ms. Holt's mind, the room is alive with bits and pieces of the past week's literacy activities.

Daniel has joined Michael, Kevin, and Jill at a table where they are rewriting a chapter of *The Courage of Sarah Noble* (Dalgliesh 1954) into a script for the play they will present to the class next week. Mark is reading his historical fiction composition to Eric. The rest of the children are working independently at their desks reading their self-selected books, writing character or chapter summaries in their literature logs, or composing their own historical fiction stories. Ms. Holt is recording notes in her conference log as she listens to Brian read the historical fiction book he selected for independent reading.

The clang of Mr. Miller's mop cart snaps Ms. Holt back to the present. Six weeks ago she had integrated language arts with social studies using a literature unit on historical fiction. As she surveys her conference logs and the students' literature logs, Ms. Holt notes the familiar trends: Three children in her class have successfully completed three historical fiction selections, 20 children have completed two books, and 2 will be finished with their selections by the following week. Because Ms. Holt had anticipated the problems these two students would have with their individual reading, she encouraged them to select the same book she was reading to the class during her daily read-aloud mini-lesson sessions. By the end of this final week of the unit, the children have learned several concepts about American history and about character and setting literary elements.

Now Ms. Holt must make a decision. She wonders, Where do we go from here? Do we work on another literature unit extending our focus on story characters to fables or tall tales? Should we move into a geography unit on Africa, bringing in African customs, folktales, art, and music? How do I continue to provide a high level of teacher assistance for my two students having problems with their independent reading and keep Daniel involved in the learning activities?

This scenario depicts a decisive shift that occurred in classroom literacy instruction in the past decade. The goal of literacy instruction has remained twofold: teaching students to read to comprehend and teaching students to write to convey their thoughts in print. But the means for accomplishing this goal, the classroom activities and the teacher's instructional decisions, have changed dramatically. Until the end of the 1980s, a basic skills perspective on literacy development was pervasive in American classrooms. In contrast, the teaching practices described in the previous scenario are driven by the social and functional view of literacy development that has gained momentum in the 1990s. This view is summarized by Harste (1990) as the belief that most of what a person knows about language is learned in the presence of others through use. It is this social and functional view of language that parallels L. S. Vygotsky's theory of development and that leads to its applications in classroom literacy instruction.

This chapter is an introduction to Vygotsky's work and how it can be applied to literacy learning and instruction. Some of the major concepts of his theory on human development and learning are explained. His concepts are then related to current movements and practices in Western literacy instruction. The chapter concludes with a description of a working model of classroom literacy instruction. This model is designed to be a guide for applying Vygotsky's ideas about development and learning to literacy instruction.

THE VYGOTSKIAN PERSPECTIVE

For several years after the English translation of *Thought and Language* in 1962, Western interest in Vygotsky focused on his work in psycholinguistics. A trail of Vygotskians can also be traced from the cross-cultural studies he and Luria initiated in 1931 and 1932 (Luria 1976, 1979) to those conducted by Michael Cole and his colleagues at the Laboratory of Comparative Cognition at the University of California, San Diego (Cole 1990; Scribner and Cole 1981). In the late 1970s, a broader range of Vygotsky's work was translated. Basic Vygotskian concepts such as *semiotic mediation, internalization, inner speech,* and the *zone of proximal development* began to surface on the American academic scene.

Vygotsky's primary objective was to create a unified psychological science by restoring the concept of consciousness to a field dominated by strict behaviorism.

The behaviorists viewed development as the individual's passive respo.
environment. For Vygotsky (1981) cognitive development was due to th
ual's social interactions within the environment. He found his explanation
sciousness in **socially meaningful activity;** that is, we know ourselves bec   σr
our interactions with others. In Vygotsky's words:

> The mechanism of social behavior and the mechanism of consciousness
> are the same. . . . We are aware of ourselves, for we are aware of others,
> and in the same way as we know others; and this is as it is because in re-
> lation to ourselves we are in the same [position] as others are to us. (Vy-
> gotsky 1978, 30)

Psychological Tools and Semiotic Mediation

We come to know ourselves and others through the mediation of psychological
tools. Like material tools that give us control or partial control over nature, **psychological tools** or signs give us control over our mental behavior. In his personal
notebooks of 1932, Vygotsky remarks that the analysis of signs was "the only adequate method for analyzing human consciousness" (cited in Wertsch 1980).

Vygotsky (1981) made a distinction between what he termed "lower, **natural
mental behavior**" and "higher, **cultural mental behavior.**" We share lower biological forms of mental behavior, such as elementary perception, memory, and attention, with animals. The higher forms of human mental functions, such as logical
memory, selective attention, decision making and comprehension of language, are
products of mediated activity. The mediators are psychological tools, or signs.

Signs give humans the power to regulate and change natural forms of behavior and cognition. For example, we make a note to ourselves as a sign to help us
remember to do something, and this note augments our natural ability to remember.
Through the mediating actions of mental tools, like the mnemonic device of a note
to ourselves, natural forms of behavior are transformed into higher, cultural forms
unique to humans. Vygotsky called this process **semiotic mediation.**

Pause and Reflect

Can you think of other examples of psychological tools or signs we use to
change or regulate our thinking?

Internalization

The direction of behavioral transformation of natural forms into higher cultural
forms is from external to internal; the behavior must exist socially before it can become part of the internal behavior of the individual (Vygotsky 1981). In his expla-

nation of Vygotsky's concept of internalization, Leontiev reflects, "consciousness is *co-knowledge,* as Vygotsky loved to say. Individual consciousness can exist only in the presence of social consciousness and language" (Leontiev 1981, 56).

Vygotsky's concept of **internalization** is the progressive transfer from external social activity mediated by signs to internal control. Vygotsky stated this concept of internalization in his general law of cultural development:

> Any function in the child's cultural development appears twice or on two planes. First it appears on the social plane, and then on the psychological plane. First it appears between two people as an interpsychological category, and then within the child as an intrapsychological category. (Vygotsky 1981,163)

With the concept of internalization, we can begin to see the prominent role education plays in Vygotskian psychology. Consider this example provided by Powell (1993): A student raises her hand to ask about an unfamiliar word. The activity is *object-regulated,* or controlled by the object (unknown word) the child is asking about. Enter the teacher, who interprets the child's raised hand as a gesture of a request for information—a communication. The child's activity now comes under another person's control, the teacher's control, making it *other-regulated.* The teacher offers a prompt using the context, word parts, letters, or sound characteristics. The child deciphers the word using this assistance and moves ahead in her reading. As a result of this experience, the child learns to direct her gesture to other adults rather than skip or ignore the objects (unknown words). The gesture becomes part of the student's mental repertoire, a sign she can use at will. It has become a psychological tool that is under the student's control. It is now *self-regulated.* External behaviors that were defined in part by the culture and internalized by the child can now function as mental tools for her.

Inner Speech

Vygotsky (1981) believed that lower mental behaviors are gradually transformed into higher ones through *social interaction.* He was especially interested in the transformational properties of human speech from its social origin to egocentric speech and later to inner speech.

> The word's first function is the social function, and if we want to trace how the word functions in the behavior of the individual we must consider how it functioned formerly in social behavior. (Vygotsky 1981, 158)

In Vygotsky's theory, language and thought develop along different lines (Vygotsky 1962). Language is a higher human behavior, whereas nonverbal thought (e.g., use of tools) is found among lower animals as well. Initially, a child's thought is nonverbal in the form of gestures, and her speech is nonintellectual in the form of babbling and crying. The child's first words are used socially, not as a verbal thought. By the age of 12 to 15 months, the lines of development of language and thought meet when the child begins to label objects in the environment (e.g., "da-da"). With continued social interaction, the child's vocabulary begins to increase rapidly, and "speech begins to serve intellect" (Vygotsky 1978, 42).

The function of speech is at first social, used for contact and interaction with others. As the child's social experiences accumulate, she uses external signs to help solve internal problems (e.g., she counts on her fingers to help her add sums). In language development, she talks out loud to herself in the form of egocentric speech. For Vygotsky (1962), **egocentric speech** is the "ingrowth" stage, the link between external social speech and internal thought. It shows that the child cannot fully differentiate the new thinking or self-regulating function of speech from its original social contact function (Wertsch 1980). Finally, a profound change occurs, and the external operations of egocentric speech turn inward. In addition to external social speech, language acquires a second, intellectual function and becomes the child's most important psychological tool for structuring thought. This soundless language for oneself is the concept Vygotsky called **inner speech.**

A direct parallel can be drawn between the early development of the ability to communicate through verbal language and the early development of the ability to communicate through printed language (Powell 1993). In the initial stage, reading occurs through social interaction, with the child and the parent or teacher pronouncing printed words together. As the student's reading experiences accumulate, she begins to internalize her knowledge of printed words, but she continues to use external oral signs in the form of "mumble reading" and "finger-pointing." Finally these external operations turn inward, silent reading begins, and printed language becomes a psychological tool for structuring thought.

Vygotsky's view on the role of speech in the development of the child's intellect differs from that of Piaget (Vygotsky 1962). For Piaget, inner speech preexists as a symptom of the child's egocentric thought. Social speech appears later when the child is able to take a less egocentric point of view and egocentric speech disappears. Piaget's position focuses on maturation whereby intellectual development becomes a prerequisite for learning. In contrast, Vygotsky (1962) argued that the developmental process moves from the social to the internal. In Vygotsky's view, learning leads development with the gradual internalization of intellectual processes that are activated through social interaction.

Pause and Reflect

Vygotsky claimed that intellectual development moves from the social (speech) to the internal (thought). Can you begin to draw some connections between his ideas on inner speech and monitoring or thinking about one's own thinking?

Concept Development

Vygotsky's ideas regarding concept development have received little attention in Western educational literature, but his view of concept development directly explains the link between his work on the sociohistorical approach to psychology and education. **Sociohistorical theory** in psychology deals with the social and cultural origins of development. For Vygotsky, the development of higher forms of mental processes in children occurs through their enculturation into society, through their education. Vygotsky's approach to psychology is based on pedagogy (Moll 1990).

> Instruction is one of the principal sources of the schoolchild's concepts and is also a powerful force in directing their evolution; it determines the fate of his total mental development. (Vygotsky 1962, 85)

In his studies on children's concept formation, Vygotsky extended his idea that mediating signs are used to master and direct the individual's thoughts. "In concept formation, that sign is the *word,* which at first plays the role of means in forming a concept and later becomes its symbol" (Vygotsky 1962, 56). Vygotsky described four stages of concept development in chapters 5 and 6 of *Thought and Language* (Vygotsky 1962, 1986). These stages of concept development are listed in Table 1.1. When the child begins to label objects in the environment, she groups them into random categories, or **heaps.** As her experiences in the world increase, she moves into thinking in **complexes.** During this stage, traits of objects are analyzed and concrete factual bonds or relationships among diverse objects are established through direct experience. The relationships established in these two early concept stages are unstable and shift with the child's attention to various objects and events occurring in the environment. At early school age, children enter the third stage of development, the stage of **potential concepts,** which lasts through adolescence. Abstract and logical bonds and relationships of fully matured **genuine concepts** emerge and are being formed during the stage of potential concepts.

Vygotsky's description of potential concepts provides an explanation of how children move from concrete thinking in spontaneous concepts to abstract thinking in scientific concepts (Vygotsky 1962). **Spontaneous concepts,** or **heaps** and **complexes,** are knowledge gained in a bottom-up manner through concrete, direct, and everyday experiences. **Scientific concepts** are abstract and systematized knowledge common to a specific culture and usually learned by its children during formal schooling. Scientific concepts are learned in a top-down manner because they are mediated by words instead of directly seen or experienced. In the transition from thinking in spontaneous concepts to thinking in scientific concepts, the

TABLE 1.1   Stages of concept development

Heaps	Random categories
Complexes	Concrete factual relationships among diverse objects
Potential Concepts	Transition from concrete, spontaneous to abstract, scientific concepts
Genuine Concepts	Abstract, systematized knowledge common to a culture

schoolchild's attention and memory become voluntary, logical, and guided by meaning (words).

Vygotsky (1962) stresses that scientific concepts are not passed down by the adult and absorbed ready-made by the child. They develop through use, through verbal interaction with an adult while the schoolchild progresses through the stage of potential concepts. As the child engages in verbal interaction, she develops the higher thinking abilities of awareness, abstraction, and control. The word functions as the thinking "tool." It is used by the child to center attention while she progresses through the process of **abstract synthesis,** which involves:

1. *abstracting* certain traits
2. *synthesizing* these traits
3. *symbolizing* them with a sign

For Vygotsky, this process of abstract synthesis becomes the main instrument of higher mental functioning.

Vygotsky's view of concept development provides some insight into the importance of vocabulary knowledge to reading comprehension. The reader who does not understand the important words that convey the meaning in a passage is not likely to comprehend the passage because she lacks the appropriate "tools" (signs) to engage in abstract synthesis during reading. Instructional activities such as pre-reading discussion, concept mapping, and webbing help children build the abstract bonds and relationships among the text concepts that are essential to its comprehension.

One of the reasons Vygotsky's view of concept development has received scant attention is that it is the most difficult to understand, especially the interaction that occurs between spontaneous and scientific concepts during school learning. In keeping with the Vygotskian perspective that mental development should be studied in the context within which it occurs, we can use a concept web lesson as a context for explaining this interaction between spontaneous and scientific concepts.

Building a concept web begins with extracting students' previously learned everyday knowledge (spontaneous concepts) by asking them to supply words they know about a specific topic. The teacher lists the words as they are supplied by the students. Through teacher-led discussion, common traits or relationships among these spontaneous concepts are abstracted. These relationships are then synthesized into a systematic representation of this knowledge (scientific concepts) in a visual diagram or web of the words for the students to see. Figure 1.1 is an example of a completed concept web on the topic of transportation. This systematized body of knowledge, represented in the concept web, restructures the spontaneous concept by:

- detaching it from the child's practical everyday experience
- representing it with a written symbol
- placing it within a position in a system of relationships, within a scientific concept

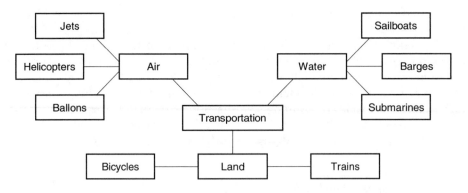

FIGURE 1.1 Example of a completed concept web on transportation

The concept web activity also provides us with an example of how the school-age child must use a concept before she has deliberate control over it and knows it as a fully developed scientific concept. This Vygotskian idea is in direct opposition to the traditional basic skills view that a child must learn a word before she can use it. From the Vygotskian perspective, the child would learn the word by using it.

Pause and Reflect

How does this idea relate to the practices of integrating reading and writing and encouraging the use of invented spellings of words?

The Zone of Proximal Development

The zone of proximal development is the most popular Vygotskian construct in Western education. It encompasses internalization, semiotic mediation, concept development, and all of his ideas previously discussed in this chapter. Vygotsky originally developed the concept of the zone in a critique of the use of individual IQ tests to assess a student's learning potential (Moll 1990; Vygotsky 1978, 1986). The zone of proximal development has become an important idea for clarifying the relationship between development and instruction.

According to Vygotsky, instruction both precedes and leads development:

> What the child can do in cooperation today he can do alone tomorrow. Therefore the only good kind of instruction is that which marches ahead of development and leads it; it must be aimed not so much at the ripe as at the ripening functions. (Vygotsky 1962, 104)

Vygotsky (1986) believed that good instruction is aimed at the learner's zone of proximal development. He describes the **zone of proximal development** as encompassing the gap between the child's level of *actual development* determined by independent problem solving and her level of *potential development* determined by problem solving supported by an adult or through collaboration with more capable peers (Vygotsky 1978). In order for the child to be operating within her zone of proximal development:

1. She must be engaged in an instructional activity that is too difficult for her to perform independently.
2. Her performance must be supported by an adult or capable peers.

Vygotsky's concept of the student's zone of proximal development has important implications for helping Western educators analyze classroom literacy instruction and assessment practices. His definition of the zone entails an *interdependent relationship between instruction and assessment.* In assessment, this zone concept causes us to rethink our position on the role of tests that measure students' independent literacy performance. The zone implies a need to design ways to evaluate students' performance *while they are engaged in actual instructional activities.* These assessment issues are discussed in the introduction to Part II of this book. In this section, the focus is on instruction within the zone of proximal development and the teacher's role in structuring a social context that provides guidance and support for students during instruction.

Instruction within the zone of proximal development begins with the Vygotskian idea that the path of learning is from social interaction to internalized independent functioning (Wertsch 1984). It is an ongoing progression from other-regulated to self-regulated performance. Social interaction provides the context for guiding the child's learning. During instruction, the teacher mediates or augments the child's ability to perform various learning tasks by providing guidance and support primarily through social dialogue.

James Wertsch and Michael Cole, two Western researchers, have translated and interpreted Vygotsky's concept of the zone of proximal development. Their work helps to further clarify how the teacher or adult provides support for the child's learning within the zone. Wertsch's work focuses on adult-child dialogue (Wertsch 1980). He uses the term **semiotic flexibility** to refer to the adult's shifts in speech that provide responses or directives to the child. These directives guide the child in creating understanding of the task and figuring out how to solve the learning problem at hand (Wertsch 1984). As the learning activity proceeds and the child gains more control, the adult's responses move from *very explicit directives* to *vague hints* and suggestions. Finally, the child is able to perform the learning task independently without any adult support.

Cole (1990) and his colleagues (Griffin and Cole 1984) stress some important aspects of Vygotsky's zone of proximal development that further clarify the role of the teacher during an instructional activity. The teacher provides support as the child develops novel, creative understandings and analyses during social interaction. The type of teacher support provided differs with various learning activities. Instruction within the zone does not follow a strict task analysis of levels of difficulty followed by the child's mechanistic stepwise progression through these task levels. Instead, the zone of proximal development encompasses several levels of tasks at once including both the previous steps and the next steps (Griffin and Cole 1984).

The teacher's role in supporting learning within the zone of proximal development involves three key elements:

1. *The teacher mediates or augments the child's learning.* She provides support for the child through social interaction as they cooperatively build bridges of awareness, understanding, and competence.
2. *The teacher's mediational role is flexible.* What she says or does depends on feedback from the child while they are actually engaged in the learning activity.
3. *The teacher focuses on the amount of support needed.* Her support can range from vary explicit directives to vague hints.

We can expand Powell's example of classroom instruction described in the section on internalization to demonstrate how the zone of proximal development can be applied to teacher prompting during classroom reading instruction. When the teacher interprets the child's raised hand as a request for information about the unfamiliar word and begins to provide support, the learning activity becomes other-regulated. The teacher offers this prompt: "Read the rest of the sentence and guess what word would make sense here." This is a *vague hint,* unless the word is clearly defined in the rest of the sentence or the student can abstract the word from the sentence context and fit it into her prior knowledge. If the child cannot identify the word, the teacher must supply a *more explicit directive,* such as drawing attention to a word part or isolating a letter or sound characteristic. With repeated attempts, the teacher gradually relinquishes support and the student learns to prompt herself. She learns the strategy (using context, word parts, letter-sound correspondences, etc.) to independently figure out unknown words, and the activity becomes self-regulated.

Pause and Reflect

Think of examples of prompts the teacher would use to help students learn context, word parts, or letter-sound strategies. How does the teacher decide which prompts to use?

Putting It All Together

To complete our understanding of the key ideas of Vygotsky's theory, we must synthesize them into a coherent, systematic theoretical perspective and begin applying them to classroom literacy instruction. Let us return to the opening classroom scenario and interpret it within the Vygotskian perspective.

Ms. Holt's theoretical perspective in the scenario is in tune with the types of literacy activities she provides for her class. We can see several of Vygotsky's ideas at work in Ms. Holt's classroom. It is obvious that she is planning her classroom learning activities with the social and cultural contexts of literacy in mind, and her children are learning printed language by using it as they read authentic literature and write their own compositions. We can see Vygotsky's ideas about semiotic mediation and the development of scientific concepts in the areas of social studies and literary elements. Ms. Holt is using the characters in the historical fiction stories to augment her students' understanding about people and life in the past. She is also recording notes and analyzing her students' performance while they are engaged in learning activities, focusing on how she must adjust her assistance to accommodate her students' zones of proximal development. Her theoretical perspective guides her in designing classroom literacy activities that require a high level of teacher-student and peer social interaction.

CURRENT PRACTICES AND
THE VYGOTSKIAN PERSPECTIVE

Vygotsky's work is particularly applicable to literacy development and instruction because of his emphasis on the role of language in development and learning. His emphasis on language and speech is apparent in both his early work on sign-mediated activity and his later work on socially mediated activity (Moll 1990; Minick 1987). For Vygotsky (1986), signs, (e.g., words) function as mental tools that enable humans to engage in the higher mental functions of voluntary attention, memory, and control. This is the word's secondary function: mediating human behavior. At the same time, the primary function of language and speech is social, for the purpose of communicating culturally established meanings.

In his later work on socially mediated activity within the zone of proximal development, Vygotsky emphasized that school instruction provides the social and cultural context for developing children's higher mental functions (Valsiner 1988). From a Vygotskian perspective, school literacy instruction could be described as sign-mediated activity nestled within socially mediated activity. During school literacy instruction (socially mediated activity), language takes on more advanced forms of its secondary function (sign-mediated activity). For Vygotsky (1986), learning printed language in school involves the child's developing a **conscious awareness** of the structure and use of language and speech. In school literacy instruction, the word becomes the primary object of study as well as a means of communication. The primary function of language remains communication, but the culturally established meanings communicated during school instruction are more abstract and systematized in the form of scientific concepts.

In Western literacy instruction, our knowledge, research, and practices have expanded and changed dramatically during the past several years (Harste 1990; Pearson 1993). We have shifted from a behaviorist view toward a focus on the individual's development, learning, and cognition. It is interesting to note that these changes have occurred at the same time that more of Vygotsky's work has been translated into English. Some of our changes can be traced to the efforts of Western psychologists and educators working within the Vygotskian perspective, and some cannot. Regardless of whether or not Vygotsky's work directly influenced these changes, it is now gaining more attention. His ideas are being incorporated into three important movements that are currently shaping the future of Western literacy education: constructivism, emergent literacy, and whole language.

Constructivist Learning

The most popular theoretical view in current literacy education is *constructivist learning* (Pearson 1993). In the **constructivist model of reading,** the reader draws on text information and prior knowledge to make inferences (Anderson and Pearson 1984) and actively *construct meaning.* From the constructivist perspective, the teacher's role in reading instruction is building the student's background knowledge and teaching strategies for using text cues and drawing inferences.

The most important contribution of the constructivist model to instruction is its focus on the learner's active participation in constructing meaning rather than passive acquisition of reading and composition skills and knowledge. The constructivist view of the student as an active participant in learning is consistent with Vygotsky's perspective. He explicitly stated his position that "passivity of the student is the greatest sin from a scientific point of view, since it relies on the false principle that the teacher is everything and the pupil nothing" (as quoted in Bozhovich and Slavina 1972, 165). Vygotsky's zone of proximal development enhances the constructivist perspective by adding the social context of learning. From a Vygotskian perspective, the teacher's role is mediating the child's learning activity as they share knowledge and meaning through social interaction.

Emergent Literacy

Emergent literacy is probably more consistent with Vygotskian theory than any other area of Western literacy research and practice. The term *emergent literacy* is derived from Marie Clay's work (Clay 1966) and from other Western researchers of the past two decades who have investigated what young children have learned about printed language prior to entering school (Sulzby and Teale 1991). Emergent literacy replaces the traditional idea of a brief stage of reading readiness just prior to formal instruction in learning conventional print.

Emergent literacy refers to a continuous period of young children's development; it includes all of their attempts to interpret or communicate using symbols, regardless of whether the symbols are print, scribbles, or pictures. Vygotsky also viewed written language development as a continuous, unified process. His theory emphasizes symbolic representation through speech used in play as well as early drawing. He states that "make-believe play, drawing and writing can be viewed as different moments in an essentially unified process of written language development" (Vygotsky 1978, 116).

Both the emergent literacy and the Vygotskian perspectives stress the cultural and social aspects of learning. During the emergent literacy period, children learn the importance of literacy because it mediates a variety of cultural activities in their everyday lives (Teale 1988). They also learn how to participate in socially organized practices involving the use of printed symbols (Sulzby and Teale 1991).

Vygotsky's concept of the zone of proximal development is evident in adult-child storybook reading. In storybook reading, the adult tailors the social interaction by **scaffolding** the reading activity to help guide the child's participation. As the storybook-reading activity progresses, the adult relinquishes more of the responsibility for creating the social interaction and comprehension of the text to match the child's increasing capabilities (Bruner 1986; Sulzby and Teale 1991).

The Western idea of **metalinguistic awareness** at the phonemic and word awareness levels is an important issue in emergent literacy. This, like emergent literacy, refers to the idea that children learn to reflect on language as they develop toward conventional literacy and parallels Vygotsky's theory that students develop a "conscious awareness" of the structure and function of speech and language as they learn printed language. Vygotsky's ideas about the zone of proximal development and scientific concept development during school instruction would extend the emergent motif to include the child's developing knowledge about printed language all the way through adolescence to maturity.

Whole Language

Vygotsky's ideas on language development, learning, and instruction complement whole language philosophy and procedures (McCaslin 1989). Vygotsky explained that speech "appears" to begin with individual words, but these one-word utterances often represent whole thoughts or whole sentences of meaning. Semantically, speech begins with the whole and is later differentiated into semantic parts or units (meanings of individual words) as the child's speech develops (Vygotsky 1986). This idea of language development implies that the child constructs her *understanding of language from whole to parts.*

In the whole language philosophy of literacy, the child's propensity for the acquisition of spoken language is applied to written language (Edelsky, Altwerger, and Flores 1991). Children in whole language classrooms become aware of print and its function through immersion in a print-rich environment that includes meaning-seeking opportunities rather than explicit skills instruction. The focus of instruction is communication and meaning, with the conventions of spelling and pronunciation initially assuming a subordinate role. As a result, the teacher in the whole language classroom tolerates many pronunciation and spelling "errors" during the child's early attempts to read or write sentences that are meaningful to him.

Vygotsky's social context perspective and his zone of proximal development have begun to inform and influence the whole language perspective on the role of the classroom teacher (McCaslin 1989). The role of the teacher as a mediator of student learning is consistent with the popular whole language roles, including the teacher as initiator and the teacher as a kid watcher (Goodman and Goodman

1990). Probably the most important influence of Vygotsky's work on the whole language movement is yet to come. Whole language teachers and teacher educators are asking important questions like *how* to provide a supportive instructional environment that focuses on social interaction (McCaslin 1989). This includes questions about the interplay among the learning tasks, the learner cues that inform teachers, and the type of supportive instruction needed to facilitate student learning.

Moving Forward into Instructional Mediation

Vygotsky's theory is both overarching and emerging in its application to Western literacy education. It spans the continuous period of oral and written language development from the time a child speaks his first word through adulthood. At the same time, the theory focuses in on instruction within a zone of proximal development beyond the learner's actual developmental level of performance. Vygotsky stresses the active nature of the learner who develops a "conscious awareness" of the structure of language by using it socially. However, "active learner" does not imply a passive teacher who overemphasizes discovery learning (McCaslin 1989). Instead, the teacher actively mediates the child's learning within the zone of proximal development through social interaction and collaboration.

A MEDIATION MODEL FOR LITERACY INSTRUCTION

The mediation model of literacy instruction (Dixon-Krauss 1994) is based on two principles derived from Vygotsky's ideas on language development and learning within the zone of proximal development. The first principle applies Vygotsky's view that the primary function of language is social communication. Literacy is a form of communication in which printed signs (words) are used to build shared meanings between the reader and the author. The second principle is the description of school literacy instruction as sign-mediated activity nestled within socially mediated activity.

In school literacy instruction, the teacher's role is to mediate shared meanings between the student reader and the text author or between the student author and the reader of the student's composition. The teacher does not simply pass text meaning on to the student reader or composition skills on to the student author. Instead, he provides support for his students' learning within the zone of proximal development as they collectively build bridges of understandings through social interaction. *Teacher mediation* is more than modeling or demonstrating how to do something. While the teacher is interacting with the student, he continuously analyzes how the student thinks and what strategies the student uses to solve problems and construct meaning. From this analysis, the teacher decides how much and what type of support to provide for his students.

The **mediation model for literacy instruction** is a dynamic, general framework that guides the teacher's decisions on planning instruction and his actions during instruction. It helps him sort out what he is doing and why he is doing it

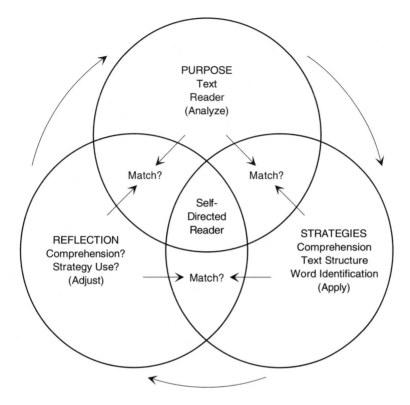

FIGURE 1.2   Diagram of the mediation model

while he and his students are actively engaged in the learning activity. The model is not a list of steps or a prescribed lesson plan. Rather, it is a dynamic working model because it both *guides* the social interaction and *evolves* through the social interaction occurring during the learning activity.

The mediation model can be applied to writing or most other school subjects, but it is explained here within the context of reading instruction. Figure 1.2 is a diagram of the model. The model begins with the goal of teacher mediation, which is stated in the center of the model. In reading, this goal helps the learner develop his own self-directed mediating system (learner self-knowledge) to become an independent, self-directed reader. The three circles represent the three components of the model: *purpose–strategy–reflection*. The teacher decision-making process proceeds through the components in a clockwise direction beginning with purpose.

The *purpose* depends on an analysis of characteristics that both the text and the reader bring to the reading activity. Text characteristics can include length, structure (informational, story, etc.), topic and related concepts presented, syntax, and vocabulary. Reader characteristics include the reader's knowledge about the type of text, the topic, the concepts and vocabulary, word recognition, and print decoding skills. The teacher analyzes the reader and text characteristics to decide what the reader needs to do to comprehend the text.

The text and reader analysis leads to selection of the *strategy* for helping the reader comprehend the text. Since there are a large variety of reading strategies available, grouping them into the following three areas helps the teacher match his strategy to his purpose: (1) comprehension strategies (prediction, sorting information, making inferences, etc.); (2) word identification strategies (context, phonetics, structural analysis, etc.); and (3) text structure strategies (story elements, main points or key concepts, dialogue, etc.). Once the strategy is selected, the teacher guides the student in applying the strategy and adjusts his support when needed.

Reflection focuses on analyzing whether the student is comprehending the text and on building the learner's self-knowledge through discussion. The discussion must include *both* the meaning derived by the student and how the student figured out this meaning. Having the student verbally reflect on how he used the strategies and figured out the meaning helps to build his conscious awareness of his own thinking. It also helps the teacher determine if there is a match between the purpose, strategy, and meaning derived by the student. If not, the teacher then reanalyzes the student/text characteristics to adjust the purpose, the strategy, or both.

To understand the dynamic nature of the model and how the teacher uses it to guide him during instruction, the model is explained in two examples using the context of prompting a student miscue during an oral reading activity. In these examples, the model components (purpose–strategy–reflection) are identified in parentheses to show how the teacher proceeds through the model. The teacher's adjustments to the amount of support he provides the student reader are also included in the examples.

EXAMPLE 1

The student is reading the following passage to the teacher:

> Ben opened the door and called his dogs into the house. The brown dog ran into the house and the *black* dog ran down the street.

The student miscues the word "black" and reads, "The brown dog ran into the house and the *brown* dog ran down the street." The teacher wants the student to self-correct his error (purpose) so he directs the student to reread (strategy) the sentence. This prompt provides a minimal amount of support to mediate the child's reading. The student rereads and miscues the word "black" again. At this point, the teacher identifies the student's need for a more explicit directive (reflection) to help him reason through the text meaning (purpose) by using his background knowledge to think about what the text means (strategy). He asks, "How can the brown dog run into the house and down the street at the same time?" The child responds, "I don't know," or "He just does 'cause it says so." The teacher analyzes the student's response (reflection) as follows: The child obviously cannot use the reasoning strategy. He needs more text information to derive the meaning. The teacher must now give more explicit support to help the student decode the word "black" (purpose). He remembers that this student often substitutes words with the same initial letter/sound as the text word. The student needs to attend to the ending sounds in the words, so the teacher's prompt focuses on decoding (strategy). He covers the *bl* and asks the child to say the word part "___ack," then he uncovers the *bl* and has the child blend together the whole word "bl-ack." The student rereads the sentence correctly. The teacher now has to decide (reflection) whether to return to the intermediate-level prompt and focus on building the child's reasoning through the meaning of the text (purpose) by asking, "Did the same dog run into the house and down the street?" or relinquish all support and let the student continue on with his reading.

This example shows the dynamic nature of the model and how it enables the teacher to make sound, on-the-spot instructional decisions. The decisions are based on specific teacher-selected purposes and strategies that match these purposes.

Pause and Reflect

Why did the teacher begin with minimal support (rereading prompt) and move toward a very explicit prompt (print decoding)?

A second example demonstrates how the mediation model is also a general framework providing for flexibility in teacher decision making within the context of his classroom reading instruction program. In this example, the teacher decides to focus on text structure because he has been working on literary elements with his class.

EXAMPLE 2

The child's miscue, "*brown* dog" instead of "*black* dog," occurs at the initiating event, and the following episodes in the story deal with mischief the black dog gets into because he ran away. The child needs to know that the *black* dog ran down the street in order to understand the logical progression of the story and connect the initiating event to the upcoming story episodes (purpose). Focusing on text structure, the teacher points to the word, reads it for the child, "the *black* dog," and asks the student to predict what might happen to the black dog who ran down the street (strategy). If the child responds with "I don't know" or his predictions deviate from the storyline, the teacher can adjust to a more explicit directive (reflection) to keep the student focused on connecting the initiating event to the upcoming story episodes (purpose). He then explains to the student that the dog might get into some trouble for running away, and asks him to read the story to find out what happens to the black dog who ran away (strategy). After the student reads the rest of the story, the teacher initiates discussion and analyzes (reflection) whether the student needs more directed reading lessons that focus on story structure (purpose).

The previous two examples show how the mediation model for literacy instruction is a dynamic general framework used to guide teacher decision making. The flexibility of the model makes it applicable to both the *specific* social interaction that occurs during instruction and the teacher's *general* classroom plan for literacy instruction. In the first example, the model guides the teacher's on-the-spot decisions during a 60-second segment of student-teacher social interaction during instruction. The second example extends the model to its use in guiding teacher planning decisions within the context of his classroom literacy instructional program.

CONCLUSION

Literacy instruction that reflects a social and functional view of language begins with the teacher's belief that most of what a person knows about language is learned through social interaction. Vygotsky's ideas provide the theoretical foundation to help teachers understand and apply the social and functional perspective of literacy development to classroom instruction.

The mediation model for literacy instruction reflects Vygotsky's ideas about instruction within the zone of proximal development. It guides the teacher in making instructional decisions by analyzing the student, the text, and the type and amount of mediation he needs to provide. The mediation model provides for a continuous process of literacy development because each episode of social interaction (purpose, strategy, and reflection) leads to a new episode and the creation of new zones of proximal development.

RELATED READINGS

Leontiev, A. N., and A. R. Luria (1968). The psychological ideas of L. S. Vygotskii. In B. B. Wolman (ed.), *The historical roots of contemporary psychology,* pp. 338–367. New York: Harper & Row.

Rogoff, B., and J. V. Wertsch (1984). *Children's learning in the "zone of proximal development."* San Francisco: Jossey-Bass.

Vygotsky, L. S. (1978). *Mind in society* (M. Cole, V. John-Steiner, S. Scribner, and E. Souberman, eds.). Cambridge, MA: Harvard University Press.

Vygotsky, L. S. (1981). The genesis of higher mental functions. In J. V. Wertsch (ed.), *The concept of activity in Soviet psychology,* pp. 144–188. Armonk, NY: Sharpe.

Vygotsky, L. S. (1986). *Thought and language* (A. Kozulin, ed.). Cambridge, MA: MIT Press.

chapter 2

Emerging Readers and Writers

Martha Combs

SCENARIO

Ms. Elliott is sitting in the rocking chair in the back of her classroom. Her kindergarten class is gathered around her, sitting on the rug and listening to her read the book, *The Napping House* (Wood and Wood 1984). She pauses to let the children share the story after reading the following page.

> And on that bed
> there is a granny,
> a snoring granny
> on a cozy bed
> in a napping house,
> where every one is sleeping.

EVAN: Look at that lady with her mouth open [pointing and giggling].

NOLAN: Yeah, she's yelling.

EVAN: She's not yelling! She's asleep.
See [pointing at the text], her eyes are closed.

NOLAN: [Doesn't respond to Evan's comment.]

Ms. Elliott analyzes the children's interactions, focusing her attention on Nolan, because she has noticed that his attention often wanders when she reads aloud to the class. Her questions are: Does Nolan understand that the woman, Granny, is sleeping? Will he be able to follow the story? How can I help him use the story language (sleep words such as "snoring") to follow the story's plot progression?

Young children should engage in reading and writing experiences that integrate language and action in a social context. It is in the social context of literacy activity that children are able to interpret their literacy experiences and internalize knowledge about reading and writing. It is also in this social context that the teacher will be able to make decisions about her role in mediating early school literacy experiences for emerging readers and writers. Assisting children's performance so that the learning activity leads their development should be the focus of instruction for emerging readers and writers.

As young children interpret the meaning of the literacy experiences in which they find themselves, learning opportunities must be provided that clearly demonstrate what we want children to do/know about literacy and then allow them to appropriate "rules" about reading and writing. In Vygotsky's view of learning, literacy experiences move from social interaction to internalized independent functioning through mediation of signs (Vygotsky 1981; Wertsch 1984). Literacy experiences are seen as "sign mediated activity nestled in socially mediated activity" (Dixon-Krauss 1994, 1). We see examples of such mediated learning as children move from observing bedtime stories read by a more knowledgeable other to participating in, even directing, the experience when they are familiar with the written language.

Opportunities must be provided for children to use the "rules" they appropriate independently, allowing them to regulate their own behavior as new literacy skills become part of their repertoire. The child who "reads" to herself or to a favorite stuffed animal has often internalized familiar text and strategies for "reading" from past literacy interactions with a more knowledgeable other.

The *social dialogue* that occurs during literacy interactions is a key factor in learning. The ultimate goal for a teacher of young children should be to provide the assistance, through social dialogue, that is necessary for children to move from other-regulated to self-regulated reading and writing.

In this chapter, the nature of assistance needed by emergent readers and writers as they move toward self-regulated behavior will be discussed against the backdrop of lesson illustrations. The assistance techniques presented are built on the *mediation model* discussed by Dixon-Krauss in chapter 1 of this book. Rehearsing a new text and assisted reading techniques are explained and illustrated using a children's literature selection. Techniques for shared writing and individual writing are then presented.

Before we continue, it will be helpful for you to be familiar with *The Napping House* by Audrey and Don Wood. This predictable children's book is used for the lesson illustrations in this chapter.

MEDIATED LEARNING

As explained in chapter 1, the mediation model is a model of *teacher decision making* that moves through a purpose–strategy–reflection cycle.

- **Purpose**—To determine your purpose you will need to analyze the characteristics of both the learner(s) and the text. Based on your text-reader analysis, you will identify an appropriate strategy for instruction.
- **Strategy**—The selected strategy will focus on:

    comprehension strategies,

    word-identification strategies, or

    text-structure strategies.

    As you guide students in applying the strategy, you will need to monitor and adjust the support you provide based on your interactions with students.
- **Reflection**—For students to become self-regulated, they must build self-knowledge about literacy processes. Through social interaction, you will determine the meaning that students derived from the strategy instruction and how they came to that meaning. Based on this reflection, a new cycle begins, with you reconsidering your purpose and strategy for instruction and making appropriate adjustments.

Because the mediation model is dynamic, you will probably move through this purpose–strategy–reflection cycle numerous times during a single lesson. As the teacher, you are key to the mediation of learning experiences for young children. The children's need to become self-directed learners should guide the instructional decisions you make.

WORKING IN TEXT WITH EMERGING READERS

During emergent reading activities, children will interact with texts that are both new and familiar. For children to build shared meanings with authors, texts must be accessible (Clay 1991; Holdaway 1979). Text that is accessible is within a child's **zone of proximal development** (Vygotsky 1986), which falls between a child's level of independent and her potential reading ability. Rehearsal and assisted reading are two techniques that can make text accessible to emerging readers (Combs, in press). When text is already familiar to readers, assistance techniques should be modified, focusing on specific strategies needed by individual children as they function at their level of assisted performance.

   The Napping House by Audrey and Don Wood (1984) is a text that can be accessible to emerging readers. In this chapter, *The Napping House* is used to illustrate suggested lesson frameworks. Being familiar with this children's book will provide support for your interpretation of what providing assistance to children entails.

When text is unfamiliar, an emerging reader can be supported by having a knowledgeable other rehearse the text before the listening or reading takes place. Assistance will enable emerging readers to interact with the text at a higher level than they would be able to do alone. This higher level of functioning will lead children's development as readers (Powell 1993). Assistance that you provide with new texts can become internal strategies or tools for later use.

Rehearsing a New Text

Rehearsal of text is a mediation technique that occurs *before* the reading of a text and provides children with explicit directives to make the text accessible. During a rehearsal you will essentially talk children through a text (Combs, in press). Rehearsal does more than merely make the story known; it also provides language that is needed to focus attention on important aspects of a text. When texts are unfamiliar, a more knowledgeable other leads the rehearsal, showing the emerging readers what they will need to think about as that text is read.

A rehearsal should:

- give a sense of how the author used important literary elements to develop the story (setting, character, plot);
- begin to build word meanings that will be essential for understanding and appreciating the text;
- highlight a strategy that will be useful in making meaning with the text; and
- generally help children have a sense of what they must do to interact with the text.

Determining Purpose.   The specific content of a rehearsal will depend upon the:

- demands of the selected piece of literature, and
- levels of performance of the emerging reader(s).

The first step in our text-reader analysis is to examine *The Napping House.* When we read it, we can recognize three important demands made by this text:

1. A cumulative plot pattern that builds tension toward a climax, then reverses the order of action as the plot moves to resolution.
2. The way the illustrator uses color to set the mood and to show the reader that the plot is moving past the climax and toward resolution.
3. The use of "sleep" words to describe most characters and the contrast of the "wakeful" flea.

Considering the way in which *The Napping House* is written and illustrated, we could focus children's attention on using the illustrations as a clue to understanding and interpreting plot and character.

Pause and Reflect

Why did we select using the illustrations as a clue to understanding and interpreting plot and characters?

The second step of our text-reader analysis is to consider the reader. To set a purpose for instruction, a child's zone of proximal development must be considered. This zone encompasses the level of actual development and potential development (Vygotsky 1986). Based upon past observations of children's independent reading performance, we must now think about the way children might handle *The Napping House* if they were to read the book independently. To "nudge" the children toward new understandings about reading, we want to provide assistance so that children can rehearse the text at a level that is just above where they function on their own.

Strategy Selection. Having completed the text-reader analysis, we now move to selecting the strategy for instruction. We know that the text will be read aloud after the rehearsal, so we consider carefully which strategies we want to prompt children to use. For *The Napping House,* we want to prompt children to use their "illustration" strategies to:

- anticipate and follow the cumulative plot, and
- help the words about sleep become meaningful as children think about characters' actions.

The rehearsal that follows shows how the teacher might talk emerging readers through *The Napping House,* making the text more accessible to them during the first reading.

LESSON ILLUSTRATION:
REHEARSAL FOR THE NAPPING HOUSE

Using the "Illustration" Strategy
Teacher says:

orienting/setting	The title of this book is *The Napping House,* because as the story begins, everyone in the house is sleeping. [Look at the first page of the book as you say this.]
illustration	Do you notice how everything in the picture looks blue, even the rain? The illustrator uses blue so you get in the mood for a story about sleeping.

"sleeping" words	The author uses different words about sleeping to tell what the animals are doing. Listen for those words. [Turn to the second page with Granny.]
plot order	The story begins with a snoring granny sleeping alone on a bed. The word "snoring" tells you that she is sleeping. [Turn page twice.]
characters	Then a dreaming child gets on the bed. "Dreaming" is another word about sleeping. [Turn page.]
	Next a dozing dog gets on the bed. What does "dozing" make you think of? [Turn page.]
	After that a snoozing cat gets on the bed. Which word is a "sleeping" word? [Turn page.]
	Then a slumbering mouse gets on the bed. Which word tells about a sleeping mouse? [Turn page.]
climax	Finally a wakeful flea gets on top of everyone. Does "wakeful" sound like a sleeping word? A change is coming in the story. Watch what happens. [Look hard to find the flea on top of the pile. Turn page.]
	That wakeful flea makes everyone wake up, one at a time, starting with the animal on top, the mouse. This is just the opposite of the way they went to sleep. [Turn page.]
color change	As each one wakes up, watch what happens to the colors. [Turn the pages showing each animal waking up and give the child a few seconds to notice the colors. Stop on last page.]
resolution	Did you notice how the animals woke up one by one? And as they did, the colors in the pictures got brighter, the rain stopped, and the sun came out. The illustrator was trying to show you that the story was coming to an ending, a happy ending.
strategy	You used the illustrations in this book to help you know things about the story. As we read the words in the book this time, use the illustrations to help you read. Think about the colors the illustrator used to show you what was happening in the story.
	As you meet each character again, how will you know they are sleeping? [Children should identify the "sleeping" words and the support of the illustrations.]

The rehearsal above helps prepare children for the reading of the text, making it more accessible. From this rehearsal we would move to an assisted reading of *The Napping House.* With support, children can attempt the suggested strategy of using illustrations to help with reading. The assisted reading should also give children the opportunity to anticipate plot order and use the "sleeping" words, both of which are supported by the illustration strategy.

Reflection. During the rehearsal, the teacher must carefully watch and listen to children's responses for a sense of how children are using strategies to interact and make meaning with the text. It is the feedback from children during this reading that will help the teacher know the usefulness of the rehearsal, the need for further attention to using strategies, and her role in providing assistance.

Pause and Reflect

Choose another children's literature selection and analyze it for three demands of the text. From these demands, decide which strategies you want to prompt. Can you now design a rehearsal for your literature selection?

Assisted Reading in Text

Assisted reading occurs when the teacher either reads text aloud for children or assists children as they read so they are able to perform at a higher level than when reading alone. For emerging readers, selecting text that is within their zone of proximal development is essential. Providing assistance that begins with very explicit directives and eventually becomes vague hints and suggestions, enables children to move from other-regulated to self-regulated activity (Wertsch 1985).

Children's level of actual development does not show all that children know. Emerging readers need to be placed in assisted learning situations that will allow the teacher to see what they are able to do with support. Assisted reading can show you where children are heading in their development.

The assistance provided depends on the type of mediation that will help children make the next step in their understanding of the reading process. Observations of children during past performances, both independent and assisted, should be used to inform decisions. Careful examination of the text to be read must become a consideration in planning the type of assistance.

Modeling and Guided Participation. Much of what proficient readers do in the process of reading cannot be observed by children. Therefore, techniques such as modeling and guided participation will be needed to support children's emerging understanding of print. **Modeling reading** includes the demonstration of reading behaviors with physical movements and verbal explanations. **Guided participa-**

tion incorporates modeling, but goes beyond it to include emerging readers in verbal interactions that provide feedback:

- to the teacher for adjusting support during strategy instruction, and
- to students in developing *conscious awareness* of their own learning.

Although both modeling and guided participation rely heavily on language to assist children with understanding the "rules" of reading, it is the "sign mediated activity nestled in the socially mediated activity" (Dixon-Krauss 1994, 1) of guided participation that offers real opportunities for assisted reading.

Several group instructional techniques can provide opportunities for modeling and guided participation with emerging readers. In this chapter we will examine two:

1. reading aloud
2. shared reading

We will consider the potential that each has to enable teachers to mediate literacy activities with emerging readers.

Assisted Read-Aloud.   In a mediation model, **assisted read-aloud** provides a responsive social setting in which emerging readers can provide feedback about their understanding of text-reader relationships and the uses of written language. It is also a natural follow-up to the rehearsal of *The Napping House*. At a listening level, children will be able to informally use their illustration strategy and understanding of "sleep" words to enjoy the story. The teacher's role as the more knowledgeable other must be a responsive one: being open to children's comments/questions and adjusting the pacing of the reading to the level of interaction that children desire and need. This is the children's opportunity to provide the teacher with feedback about their understanding of the strategy suggested by the rehearsal. How we respond to children during the read-aloud should be based on our observation of their interaction with the text, with the teacher and with each other.

Using *The Napping House* as an illustration, consider how reading aloud to children can provide assistance to emerging readers. As we consider the read-aloud dialogue, it may be helpful to look back at the rehearsal to remind us of what has already been introduced.

LESSON ILLUSTRATION:
***ASSISTED READ-ALOUD*—THE NAPPING HOUSE**

Using the "Illustration" Strategy
The teacher pauses after reading the following page aloud:

And on that bed
there is a granny,
a snoring granny

on a cozy bed
in a napping house,
where every one is sleeping.

EVAN: Look at that lady with her mouth open [pointing and giggling].

NOLAN: Yeah, she's yelling.

EVAN: She's not yelling! She's asleep. See [pointing at the text], her eyes are closed.

NOLAN: [Doesn't respond to Evan's comment.]

TEACHER: Look at the illustration again and listen to what the author says. [Teacher rereads.]

And on that bed
there is a granny,
a *snoring* granny . . . [emphasizing snoring]

[Teacher pauses to see if either of the boys, especially Nolan, picks up on the language of the text to clarify what the woman is doing.]

EVAN: My dad really snores when he sleeps [imitates the sound of his dad snoring]. [Comment shows understanding of snoring.]

NOLAN: Yeah, my dad snores too. [Could be imitating Evan's response.]

TEACHER: Nolan, when this granny is *snoring,* what is she doing?

NOLAN: Making noises when she sleeps. [Shows his understanding of the word.]

TEACHER: When you look at the illustration [pointing to illustration], how can you tell she is sleeping?

NOLAN: Her eyes are closed.

EVAN: Yeah, and she's snoring.

NOLAN: Yeah, she's snoring.

In this lesson illustration, Evan was immediately able to use the illustrations to interpret character, although he did not use "sleep" language from the text to support his comments. Nolan, however, appeared to need support to interpret the illustration before language ("snoring") would be helpful. Because the selected strategy focused on the use of illustration, the teacher drew the boys' attention back to the illustration and language of the text. Rereading, pausing to allow for thinking and comments, and then asking focused questions provided guided participation that allowed the boys to regulate their own understandings.

When Nolan did not respond to Evan's comment, the teacher decided she needed to know more about what Nolan was thinking, so she returned to the text. Since her strategy depended upon interpretation of illustration to support the understanding of plot and characters, she realized that she needed to assist Nolan in using the illustration before moving ahead in the story. Interestingly, on the next two facing pages of text, the granny still has her mouth open. After reading the text, the teacher paused, pointed to the illustration, and asked Nolan if he noticed what was happening. Nolan said, "She's still snoring."

In this illustration the teacher reflected on the feedback from the boys and used that feedback to adjust her purpose and strategy selection for the two boys during the lesson. Her decision to attend to Nolan's nonresponse by redirecting him to the text shows the type of adjustments that are made in a mediation model. Dynamic instruction and assessment take place when teachers mediate between readers, or in this case listeners, and text.

Assisted Shared Reading.   **Assisted shared reading** uses enlarged text, usually referred to as "big books," to model book orientation, directionality, and speech-to-print match (Holdaway 1979). Children are asked to consider the title and cover to predict possibilities. The text is then read aloud, with the teacher tracking the print as it is read. Discussion of the text during the reading is not always a part of the introductory activity. Children are usually encouraged to join in the reading when they are able, especially for highly predictable parts of the text. However, it is often not until repeated readings, when text is familiar, that guided participation is likely to be most effective. Using *The Napping House* as an illustration, consider the role of assistance in shared reading activities.

LESSON ILLUSTRATION:
ASSISTED SHARED READING—THE NAPPING HOUSE

Using the "Illustration" Strategy
A group of emerging readers reaches the climax in *The Napping House,* when the wakeful flea is added on top of the pile of characters sleeping on the bed. Because *The Napping House* has a cumulative predictable pattern, the children have had repeated exposure to the characters and their order.

The teacher leads the reading by pointing to text as she reads aloud:

> Can it be?
> A wakeful flea
> on a slumbering mouse
> on a snoozing cat
> on a dozing dog
> on a dreaming child
> on a snoring granny
> on a cozy bed . . .

The teacher notices that children join in the reading in various ways.

Examples
BAILEY: [Able to join in at the point that the pattern begins, but not certain of some "sleep" words.]
on a —— *mouse* [—— mumbles, not distinguishable]
on a snoozing *cat*

on a —— *dog*
on a —— *child*
on a snoring *granny* . . .

[Watches teacher point, looks at illustration when saying character name, emphasizes character.]

MARIE: [Pretends to be joining in; lip movements do not match syllables pronounced; appears to follow teacher pointing; does not look at illustration while teacher is pointing to text.]

The teacher realizes she is seeing at least two different levels of text reading among children in the group:

- Bailey and others: Are aware of pattern and illustration support, but uncertain of new "sleep" language.
- Marie and others: Do not use illustrations to support print, especially when teacher points to print; may not be aware of cumulative pattern.

Strategy Adjustment: Using Illustration to Support Character. The teacher rereads the page. This time she slows her reading/pointing slightly, and, as she points to the word for each character, she quickly points to the appropriate character in the illustration before pronouncing the character's name. The characters, depicted in the illustrations, are the most concrete, and most repeated, words for the children.

As the teacher rereads, she watches Marie to see if Marie follows her pointing and uses the illustration to help confirm the character's name. In the rereading, Marie does follow the pointing and "reads" the character name as the teacher points to the illustration.

Strategy Adjustment: Helping "Sleep" Language Become Meaningful.
The teacher adjusts further to support Bailey, and other children, who are struggling with the "sleep" words. As they turn the page in *The Napping House,* the text reads:

A wakeful flea
who bites the mouse,

The teacher decides to rehearse the text before reading it, using the illustration.

TEACHER: Is this flea sleeping [pointing to the flea]?

BAILEY: No.

TEACHER: This is a wakeful flea. He is awake. Let's read the words. [Points to words and reads text.] A w— [pauses] wakeful fl— [points to illustration] flea, who bites the m— [pauses, points to illustration] mouse,

BAILEY: [Attempts "wakeful," looks at illustration as if trying to recall previous discussion.]

MARIE: [Joins in on "flea" and "mouse," following pointer to illustration to confirm.]

Putting Both Strategy Adjustments Together. The teacher continues to rehearse individual pages, using the illustration to cue "sleep" language and character name, because the remaining text focuses on only one character on a page. The cumulative pattern is not repeated on each page, so children have less repetitions for benefiting from the teacher's rehearsal.

At the end of the reading, she asks the children to reflect on their participation in the reading.

TEACHER: What words in this story did you learn to read?

MARIE: I knew the animals.

TEACHER: How did you learn to read the names of the animals?

MARIE: I looked at the picture when you pointed.

TEACHER: Did the picture help you think about the word?

MARIE: Yes.

TEACHER: When I pointed to the picture, I was trying to remind you that sometimes pictures can help you think about the words.

Reflecting on the feedback from Marie, the teacher adjusted her purpose and strategy when the group reread *The Napping House* the next day. She pointed to text, cued the beginning sound of the "sleep" words and character names, but did not point to illustrations. She observed Bailey and Marie to see what strategies the girls used to support their reading of a familiar text.

Applying the mediation model, purpose–strategy–reflection, to literacy instruction with emerging readers can enable the teacher to be more responsive. The model focuses on assisting children, in a supportive social context, as they move from other-regulated to self-regulated learning.

CREATING TEXT WITH YOUNG WRITERS

Throughout their preschool years, children are forming concepts about written language. They observe print in their environment and see more knowledgeable others using print in a variety of ways. Most likely, they have experimented with print and produced writing of their own. Experiences with print support children's knowledge that:

- print is meaningful,
- print serves different purposes, and
- print must follow certain rules if it is to be understood by others. (Temple et al. 1993)

The way we think about writing is adult thinking, and often ...
writers, we are able to imagine the other participant, the audience, ...
teraction. Knowing the other participant creates a social context in th...
that influences his written interaction. Our knowledge of writing also...
skillfully use print as the medium for sharing meaning (Vygotsky 1981).

In contrast, emerging writers know very little about the abstract na ...e of writing. They can observe the production of print, but it is not clear to them what transpires in the mind of the writer concerning the writer's intent, audience, form, and voice unless the writer thinks aloud (Temple et al. 1993). Children's early experiences in writing must be based in social interaction, because it is through interaction with knowledgeable others that children will internalize the meaning of written language.

Pause and Reflect

Remember that Vygotsky described the development of speech and thought as moving from social to "inner speech." Can you draw some connections between his idea and the young child's ability to imagine an audience for her writing?

As a more knowledgeable other, the teacher will need to mediate children's learning. The mediation model, purpose–strategy–reflection, will guide the teacher's thinking as she engages emerging writers in constructing texts. The text-reader analysis conducted earlier to set purposes for instruction is now a text-writer analysis. The text, however, is the text to be created between the children and the imagined audience. Strategy will focus on composing/thinking, mechanics of writing, or form/function. Reflection continues to depend on the interaction between learners and a knowledgeable other.

Shared Writing Experiences

One method for creating text with children in individual or group settings is the **language experience approach** (LEA), in which a knowledgeable other serves as the recorder for children's dictation about a topic. LEA is typically used to create a text of children's language that will then be used for reading instruction. When LEA is used responsively, to model writing aspects of the writing process and as a guided participation to engage children's thinking, writing becomes a shared group writing experience. Shared writing experiences can focus on the construction of new text or an innovation on a known text.

Innovating on a Known Text. Did you ever learn about writing by looking at what another author had written and trying to imitate some aspect of his writing? If you did, you were innovating on that author's style. Children can learn much about writing if the teacher uses her knowledge to assist them in discovering the patterns that other writers use.

In *The Napping House,* what pattern(s) did the Woods use to tell their story? They used a cumulative pattern that added one character at a time and repeated all characters that came before. If we made a picture of this pattern, it would look like a set of stairs, going up and coming back down.

Pause and Reflect

We often find a cumulative pattern in folktales, which are told orally and by repetition get the point across. Do you know other writers who have used a similar pattern to tell their story?

Through assisted readings, children will build shared meanings with Audrey and Don Wood. The teacher can be a bridge for children's understanding when she helps children see patterns that could teach them about writing. After reading *The Napping House* in an assisted read-aloud or shared reading experience, the children can make a representation of each character. Using these representations, children can discover the Woods' pattern as they physically rebuild the story while the teacher rereads it. Once they have discovered the pattern, they can use it to write group stories with the teacher as the scribe. By innovating on the Woods' pattern, children add a new form to the possibilities they know of for sharing their ideas.

LESSON ILLUSTRATION:
SHARED WRITING EXPERIENCE

Innovating on a Known Text
A drawing of a bed is cut out and taped on the chalkboard. The children are gathered on the floor near the teacher. Cutouts of other characters are spread out on the floor. The teacher begins to reread *The Napping House.* A child places the snoring granny on the bed. Another child places the dreaming child on top of the snoring granny. As each new character is placed on top, the children begin at the bottom of the pile to "read" the story.

TASHA: This looks like an "adding" story.

TEACHER: What makes you think so?

[Teacher did not expect this comment, but decides to explore it to see if children can use the concept of adding to explore making a cumulative story.]

TASHA: When we read, we say a new person or animal and we add it on top of everybody else on the pile.

TEACHER: Can you think of something else that adds up? Something that keeps getting more and more until it's too much, then something happens to make it go back down?

[The teacher had thought of several examples of adding up, but waits to see what the children are thinking.]

BRAD: It's like our bus coming to school each day. More and more people get on at every stop till we get to school, then we all get off. [The teacher is really surprised by this observation and, because of children's reactions, decides to explore this topic.]

OTHERS: It gets too many people. We get squished . . .

TEACHER: Could we write to Ms. Popper [principal] and tell her what we think about the bus? Do you think we could tell our story the way that the Woods did?

TEACHER: How did the Woods begin their story?

> There is a house,
> a napping house,
> where every one is sleeping.

How can we change the story so Ms. Popper will know how we feel about the bus?

> There is a _____ ,
> a _____ _____ ,
> where every one is _____ .

TEACHER: What should we write? Think about what we want Ms. Popper to know.

TASHA: Bus. There is a bus—that's what we ride—a yellow bus.

TEACHER: What do you think? Does that tell Ms. Popper what we are thinking about?

BRAD: We should tell her that we get squished. That's what happens when everyone gets on.

OTHERS: Yeah. That's what happens. . . .

The story develops from there. The teacher guides the writing, helping the children consider the suggestions made and refocusing the children by asking them to keep the purpose of the story in mind.

Creating a New Text. Shared writing can also be used to compose a new text, helping children explore a particular aspect of writing. Shared writing can take any form that is appropriate to the intent of the message. It is best for emerging writers to clearly understand the intended audience. We can encourage the social interaction by refocusing children toward their audience as the writing takes shape.

LESSON ILLUSTRATION: SHARED WRITING EXPERIENCE

Creating a New Text—Mechanics of Writing

Following the birth of a new litter of guinea pigs, the children want to send announcements to other classes, inviting them to see the babies. We join the composing partway through. The teacher's intent with this writing is to help children write announcements, with conventional spelling, that other children will be able to read.

> *Come See Our Babies!*
>
> We have three new baby guinea pigs.
> Would you like to see them?
> You may come to our room at _____ .

TEACHER: How will we write *ten o'clock?*

GINNY: *T-t-t,* It starts with *t.* Ten, ten. *N,* I think.

TEACHER: [Writes the *t,* leaves a space, then writes *n.* Tries to assist Ginny with the vowel sound because Ginny has demonstrated an awareness of vowels in her journal entries.]

Ginny, say the word slowly, stretch it out like a rubber band to hear the sound in the middle [points to space between *t* and *n* on the chart].

GINNY: *T-e-e-e-n, e-e-e,* like *egg, e?*

TEACHER: [Writes *e* in space.]

Yes, ten is spelled *t-e-n.* How did you figure that out?

GINNY: It's like *egg,* and I know *egg.*

The group continues writing the announcement. As different children contribute, the teacher adjusts her support—where she places the letters and the clues she gives—to the knowledge of each child.

Shared writing offers opportunity for children to receive feedback about their thinking in writing. Children are also able to show the teacher what is internalized and how much support they each need within a group writing experience. The atmosphere should be relaxed so children feel free to share their thinking. The teacher should think aloud and encourage the children to think aloud, so that all children can share in the writing.

Individual Writing

Children will also want to explore with print, producing their own texts. Although children may be working on an independent piece, the context in which they are writing should be seen as a social context that supports their efforts to move from other-regulated to self-regulated learning. The teacher's assistance during independent writing will need to be responsive and within a child's zone of proximal development.

Daily independent writing opportunities must be provided if the teacher is to see children's actual development. These should include journals, clusters or webs, labels, lists, annotated drawings, "all about" stories, and other items. Shared writing is the teacher's opportunity to focus children's writing, while independent writing should be the children's opportunity to regulate their own learning with the teacher's support.

If children are free to interact during independent writing, many ideas for writing will be exchanged. Following the teacher's model, children will serve as knowledgeable others for each other, both coaching and providing support.

During independent writing, the teacher should walk around the room and listen for children who are puzzling over some aspect of writing. She must be able to quickly make a text-writer assessment and offer assistance that is within the child's zone of proximal development. This assistance will be focused on one of the writing components previously discussed:

- composing/thinking
- mechanics of writing
- form/function

CONCLUSION

The role the teacher takes as a decision maker in a classroom of emerging readers and writers will be the key to children's ability to engage effectively in literacy experiences. Teachers can use the mediation model to guide their decision making about the nature of assistance needed by young children in reading texts and in writing. Emerging readers and writers depend on responsive teachers to mediate written language experiences in the context of meaningful social activity.

RELATED READINGS

Clay, M. (1991). *Becoming literate: The construction of inner control.* Portsmouth, NH: Heinemann.

Holdaway, D. (1979). *Foundations of literacy.* Portsmouth, NH: Heinemann.

Mason, J. M. (1989). *Reading and writing connections.* Needham Heights, MA: Allyn & Bacon.

McGee, L. M., and D. J. Richgels. (1990). *Literacy's beginnings: Supporting young readers and writers.* Boston: Allyn & Bacon.

Sulzby, E., and W. H. Teale. (1991). Emergent literacy. In R. Barr, M. S. Kamil, P. Mosenthal, and P. D. Pearson (eds.), *Handbook of reading research,* Vol. II, pp. 727–757. New York: Longman.

chapter 3

Spontaneous and Scientific Concepts in Content-Area Instruction

Lisbeth Dixon-Krauss

SCENARIO

John, Steve, and Elise, in Mrs. Welch's second grade class, are looking for books to check out of their school library. Elise's older brother, Tim, who also happens to be in the library, sees them talking and strolls over to join in on the conversation.

JOHN: Here's a good one! It's called *Why Mosquitoes Buzz in People's Ears* (Aardema 1975). See this bump on my arm? I got a mosquito bite last night when I was out on the porch.

STEVEN: But that one has a lion and a monkey too. Mrs. Welch said we should find books about insects.

JOHN: So, a mosquito is an insect, and I want to see why they buzz in your ears.

ELISE: I found *Charlotte's Web* (White 1952). It's my favorite story. I saw it on TV last week.

TIM: I thought you were looking for books with insects.

ELISE: I am. Charlotte is a spider, and spiders are bugs.

TIM: Spiders aren't insects. Spiders are arachnids. They have eight legs.

ELISE: How do you know?

TIM: You learn those things when you get in fifth grade. It's called science.

These children are relating what they will read about in their selected books to things they know or real things that actually happened in their lives, and this is an important aspect of early literacy instruction. Their conversation also depicts how children's thinking develops from concepts learned through everyday concrete experiences to abstract logical concepts, and the crucial role school instruction plays in this development. Vygotsky (1986) explained this development as a movement from everyday *spontaneous* concepts to systematically structured *scientific* concepts.

During his final work, Vygotsky was particularly interested in the distinction between spontaneous and scientific concepts, and how the two interact to complement the development of one another in school learning. This chapter begins with an explanation of Vygotsky's idea of spontaneous and scientific concepts and how the two are integrated in school literacy instruction to form the student's zone of proximal development. It continues with a description of how integrating children's literature with the content areas can help teachers provide classroom instruction that is sensitive to students' zones. This includes using the mediation model described in chapter 1 of this text to design and implement classroom instruction within the Vygotskian perspective on scientific concept development.

SPONTANEOUS AND SCIENTIFIC
CONCEPT DEVELOPMENT

The basic theme of Vygotsky's work in cognitive development is his idea that the child's thinking develops through social interaction mediated by language (Vygotsky 1986). Words are the labels for concepts, but there is a qualitative difference between the concrete spontaneous concepts and the more abstract scientific concepts that a particular word can represent. Central to understanding Vygotsky's distinction between spontaneous and scientific concepts is his explanation of the differences in their histories of development and differences in the ways they are used for social interaction (Minick 1987). With this distinction in mind, we can begin to apply Vygotsky's idea of how the two are integrated to complement the development of one another in school literacy learning and instruction.

Spontaneous Concepts

Spontaneous concepts develop informally, growing upward as the child accumulates everyday direct life experiences. They begin to emerge when the young child, guided through verbal interaction with the parent, starts labeling objects and the spoken word becomes the means of communication (Vygotsky 1986). The everyday social interaction within which spontaneous concepts evolve focuses on *what* is being communicated. The purpose of the interaction is communication of concrete things, experiences, or events.

The child's spontaneous concepts develop apart from formal schooling and form the basis for her own intuitive theories of the world (Au 1990). In the children's library conversation, Elise's concept of *spider* illustrates the idea of spontaneous concepts. Elise has a rich understanding of the concept and a concrete realization of what a spider is in the real world, but her verbal definition of *spider* is vague and not yet logical or systematically structured.

Scientific Concepts

Scientific concepts differ from spontaneous ones because they are systematic in both their structure and in how they develop in children (Moll 1990). Scientific concepts are part of a culture's systematically organized bodies of knowledge usually associated with particular school subject areas, and they are learned by the child within a system of formal instruction through schooling (Vygotsky 1978, 1986). Because they are learned primarily through formal education and school instruction, scientific concepts are sometimes referred to as "schooled" concepts (Gallimore and Tharp 1990). Scientific concepts are not simply passed down by the teacher and absorbed ready-made by the child. Instead, their formation is worked out from the top downward through instruction in collaboration with the teacher or capable peers (Minick 1987).

Vygotsky stated that "development based on instruction is a fundamental fact" (Vygotsky 1978, 206). He explained that children become consciously aware of their thinking and gain deliberate voluntary control of it as their scientific concepts are formed during instruction. School instruction provides a special type of verbal interaction that awakens the child's ability to *consciously regard* and *voluntarily manipulate* concepts and their relationships. In the verbal social interaction of instruction, the word is not only the means of communication, but also the focus or the object of communication. Through instruction, the child's attention is directed to the semantic or logical meaning level of words and the relationships among them as the words are explained, compared, reflected on, and corrected.

Tim's concept of *spider* in the library conversation illustrates the conscious awareness in his thinking that is associated with scientific concepts. He has a logical, systematically structured verbal definition of *spider* that he can voluntarily access and use to explain and compare with other concepts. It is important to note that Tim's logical, systematically structured definition of spider (his scientific concept) would be meaningless if it were not preceded by a rich, concrete understanding (his spontaneous concept) of what a spider is.

Integrating Spontaneous and Scientific Concepts

Effective school instruction depends on the integration of scientific and spontaneous concepts, especially in the area of classroom literacy instruction. Spontaneous concepts provide the content used for explaining and defining the abstract scientific concepts, link the scientific concepts to the child's real experiences, and create the potential for understanding (Minick 1987). Scientific concepts, however, provide the structure for the child's spontaneous concepts to become logically defined, consciously accessible, and deliberately used.

In elementary school, children encounter two important transition points in learning printed language. Teachers can use Vygotsky's idea of integrating spontaneous and scientific concepts to help students proceed through these literacy developmental transitions.

The first transition occurs when the child enters school and begins to formally learn the abstract concept printed language. At this early stage of literacy learning, *spoken language* is the primary means of cognitive development, because the child has been using language orally to communicate concrete things and experiences. The child's printed language concepts emerge as she develops a conscious awareness of letter-sound patterns and the structure of printed words. This developing knowledge about the structure of print must be integrated with the child's existing knowledge of the function of language, which is to communicate or convey meaning. Research in emergent literacy supports the idea that children become aware of printed language and its function through immersion in a print-rich environment that includes meaning-seeking opportunities (Mason, Stewart, and Dunning 1986; Sulzby and Teale 1991).

The second transition point occurs after the beginning stages of reading when instruction shifts to an emphasis on reading content-area informational materials. At this point, children move from using spoken language to using *printed language* as the primary means of learning the abstract scientific concepts in the school subject areas. As Vygotsky (1962) stated, "When we impart systematic knowledge to the child, we teach him many things that he cannot directly see or experience" (86). Research shows that integrating children's literature into classroom subject-area instruction can be effective in helping students experience, interpret, and personalize the abstract concepts presented in the content areas (Krauss 1992).

Pause and Reflect

Can you think of some children's literature selections that would help students learn concepts related to: social studies? science? math?

DESIGNING INSTRUCTION TO INTEGRATE LITERATURE WITH CONTENT AREAS

Integrating literature with content-area texts helps teachers provide classroom instruction within students' zones of proximal development in an engaging way. Vygotsky explained that scientific concepts associated with content areas move the students' spontaneous concepts up to a higher level of awareness, control, and abstraction, forming a *zone of proximal development* that the student has not yet passed through. Student's spontaneous concepts lie within this zone; they emerge and are restructured through instruction (Vygotsky 1986).

Research shows that students' zones of proximal development related to reading development can range from two to four text readability levels beyond their current instructional reading levels commonly associated with basal reader instruction or their grade levels (Dixon, Stanley, and Powell 1984). Students can comprehend this more difficult material when the teacher or their peers mediate their performance by providing support in understanding the structure of the text and the difficult vocabulary and concepts it contains (Dixon 1986; Kragler 1991; Stanley 1986).

Content-area texts are usually assigned by grade level, (e.g., third grade social studies, math, and science textbooks). These materials are often difficult for students to read and comprehend because of their overly factual presentation of concepts, vast amount of information, and density of concepts (Anderson and Ambruster 1984). However, content-area textbooks are also an important resource for both teachers and students. They generally contain the essential subject matter students are expected to learn and are organized and structured to assist students in learning this subject matter. For these reasons, it is important for teachers not to simply abandon content-area texts or have more competent readers read the content texts orally so that underachieving students can be exposed to the content subject matter. Instead, the teacher needs to recognize the importance of supporting children in both learning to read the content-area texts and learning the information and concepts these texts contain.

Integrating children's literature with the content areas can help the teacher accomplish both these tasks. In a study of third-graders who were struggling with reading and comprehending the factual concepts presented in their social studies texts (Krauss 1992), the classroom teacher used children's literature and informational trade books to integrate her students' literacy instruction with a unit in their social studies text. After six weeks of the integrated curriculum, all her students showed improvement in both their social studies unit test and their reading and writing, but it was her underachieving students who showed the most improvement.

The mediation model described in chapter 1 can be used to guide our planning and implementation of a classroom curriculum that integrates children's literature into content-area instruction. With this model, the teacher's decisions on what and how to teach are based on students' learning of both the content subject matter and the thinking processes needed to learn this content.

Identifying Purposes through Reader-Text Analysis

Beginning with the purpose component of the model, the teacher conducts a **reader-text analysis** by understanding and mediating among the following three factors:

1. The informational nature of the content material
2. The student's developing thought processes (conscious awareness and deliberate control) needed to acquire and use this information
3. The personal knowledge contained in the student's spontaneous concepts.

Effective teaching with content materials begins with integrating factor 1, the informational and structural characteristics associated with the texts for particular subject areas, with factor 2, the thought processes students need to acquire and use this information in each subject area. With a clear understanding of these factors, the teacher forms book clusters (described later in this chapter) to guide her selection and use of appropriate trade books that will access and build on factor 3, the personal knowledge contained in students' spontaneous concepts.

Social Studies. Social studies texts are sources of information that present facts and ideas about various cultures. Although social studies texts are closer in content and structure to narrative-style books, the information is presented in a condensed form that often makes the concepts seem obscure or irrelevant. Literature can give children opportunities to elaborate on and personalize the information presented in social studies texts (Sanacore 1993). Literature translates large-scale events into human terms (Brozo and Tomlinson 1986), provides multiple examples for critical interpretations and different views of social issues and historical events (Spiegel 1987), and helps readers develop feelings of empathy and understanding for other cultures and different ways of life. (See chapter 8 of this text by Stanley.)

Both trade books and certain genres help students develop critical thinking when they question and compare multiple interpretations or sort out factual and fictional accounts of social studies issues and events (Wiseman 1992). Historical fiction helps students personalize and create rich understandings of past events as they grapple with the problems and choices people faced as well as the motives and perspectives of the people who lived during these events (Levstik 1990). Biographies and more colorful trade books, such as Jean Fritz's stories about Paul Revere, Teddy Roosevelt, and Ben Franklin, help children gain in-depth understandings of these characters who helped shape historical events. Books about people who live in different regions of the world and regional and ethnic folk literature add a human element to geography concepts and foster the development of understanding and appreciation for different cultures and ethnic backgrounds. Myths and legends, stories created by people from around the world to explain natural phenomena, can be used to integrate social studies and science concepts.

Science. The major obstacles to reading and comprehending science textbooks are the technical vocabulary, intensity of the information, systematic interrelationships among concepts, and precision in the stepwise directions to follow in experiments. Reading and learning in science especially highlight Vygotsky's idea of how spontaneous and scientific concepts are integrated through school instruction. Learning science material requires students to engage in a continuous process of accessing their prior world knowledge (spontaneous concepts), elaborating and expanding this knowledge, and organizing and restructuring it into systematic frameworks (scientific concepts). Conducting scientific experiments provides students with direct, concrete experiences for engagement in this developmental thought process, but it also requires reading and following explicit directions to complete a task.

Both nonfiction informational trade books and children's literature can provide students with elaboration of scientific concepts and extend their awareness of scientific phenomena. Nature, life cycles, and wildlife are common topics in children's books that can extend students' ecological awareness. Science fiction highlights the human, ethical, and moral issues related to humanity's rapidly increasing scientific and technological knowledge. Biographies of famous scientists show the individual effort required in scientific inquiry, and experiment books or even books of magic tricks provide concrete opportunities for students to practice following specific directions and to engage in their own scientific inquiry. Poetry can be a powerful resource for science instruction. Poems are subjective and imaginative interpretations of the world that can enrich the factual and objective explanations found in science subject matter.

Mathematics.   Three basic features of mathematics texts make them extremely difficult for children to read. First, they usually provide brief and concise explanations and directions for solving problems and many examples. This requires slow and careful reading of short segments of text. The second feature is specialized vocabulary that can be confusing. Words that children are familiar with, such as *factor* and *product,* can become ambiguous because they acquire multiple meanings when they are used in a math context. Third, students must deal with two symbol systems, oscillating between the verbal symbols of words and the mathematical symbols of computation. This is especially true when children are exposed to solving word or story problems.

Children's literature can help develop positive attitudes toward mathematics by capturing children's interest in it and helping them extend their mathematical investigations, relating them to authentic problems and experiences they can encounter in the real world (Tischler 1992). Counting books and concepts books can help illustrate ambiguous terms and new concepts. By writing responses to these books, children gain practice in using dual symbol systems as they summarize the concepts or explain the problem-solving processes they learned.

Literature.   Although narrative texts seem less difficult for children to read and enjoy than content-area texts, the organizational structure of stories is the most complex textual structure children encounter. Children's knowledge of story structure follows a pattern of development from preschool through the elementary school years (McConaughy 1980). From a Vygotskian perspective, children's concept of story develops from a concrete, disorganized (spontaneous) concept to an abstract, logical, and systematically structured (scientific) concept. For instance, we can see the young child's concept of story begin to emerge as a spontaneous concept linked directly to the concrete object (the book) when the parent finishes reading the last page of a storybook to the child, and the child reaches over and closes the book, responding, "The end!" At this point, the young child is displaying a rudimentary knowledge of story structure; she is beginning to understand that stories have a beginning, a middle, and an end. As the child gains more experience listening to and reading stories, primarily through elementary school instruction, she develops a more logical and systematic knowledge of story structural elements. The following is a list of the literary and story structure elements common to most narrative texts:

1. Characters: Usually animals or people.
2. Setting: Description of the location and time of the story.
3. Initiating Event: An action or event that introduces or sets up the problem.
4. Goal/Problem: The main character identifies a problem and formulates a goal to overcome the problem.
5. Attempt: Usually an overt action by the main character to solve the problem or attain the goal.
6. Outcome: Results of the attempt.
7. Reaction: Character's feelings about the outcome.
8. Resolution: Goal is met and the problem is solved, or goal is discarded.
9. Theme: The underlying message, moral, or recurring idea the author presents.
10. Style/Mood: How the author uses language to create emotions and images for the reader.

Effective teaching of literature begins with identification of stories that contain the structural elements appropriate for the students' developing concept of story. In the early primary grades, books with repetitive plots extend the child's concept of beginning, middle, and end of stories to understanding the idea that stories contain a series of attempts and outcomes for the main character. As students progress to the intermediate grades, matching the various genres to the literary elements is important. Experience in reading adventure stories and mysteries clarifies the logical progression of stories as children begin to understand how the initiating event leads to each outcome and how each attempt and its outcome are logically tied to the previous attempt. Historical fiction and tall tales provide more in-depth study of both setting and character analyses.

An important part of developing students' awareness of literary elements is helping them focus on the aesthetic stance. *Aesthetic stance* refers to what the reader is experiencing, thinking, and feeling (Rosenblatt 1991). The aesthetic stance leads toward developing students' understanding of mood, style, and theme. Theme is the most abstract literary element because it deals with the general truths about society and human nature conveyed in the story.

Book Clusters.   **Book clusters** are collections of fiction and nonfiction books related to the particular themes and concepts selected for topics of study (Crook and Lehman 1991). The teacher uses a book cluster to select and organize materials that relate content information to students' developing thought processes and to knowledge from their spontaneous concepts. Teachers in a single grade level or across two or three grade levels can collaborate in selecting their topics, subtopics, and concepts from their content-area texts, curriculum guides, or other professional resources. The subtopics identified are webbed around the topic, and the selected books are clustered around each subtopic. In order to accommodate the various reading abilities of students, it is important to include a wide range of difficulty levels in children's informational trade books and literature selected for each subtopic. A book cluster for a science topic, weather, is shown in Figure 3.1. With the purposes established and organized into a book cluster, the teacher continues through the model, selecting strategies that match the purposes.

Pause and Reflect

Look at the weather subtopics in Figure 3.1 (climate, conditions, water cycle). Can you think of some social studies, math, and literature concepts to integrate into each subtopic?

Strategies for Mediating Concept Development

Three types of strategies are particularly useful for mediating the development of students' spontaneous concepts forward into scientific concepts associated with the content areas.

- classification strategies
- monitoring strategies
- reader response strategies

First, **classification strategies** enable learners to access, elaborate, integrate, and use ideas and concepts by placing these concepts within systematically structured, organized bodies of knowledge. Second, **monitoring strategies** develop the students' conscious awareness and deliberate control of their thinking. Third, **reader response strategies** create shared understandings and meaning through social interaction.

Classification Strategies.   Classification strategies are designed to increase students' vocabulary knowledge by reorganizing concepts they already know to include new concepts, ideas, and information. This includes elaborating on the new concepts and integrating them into systematically organized bodies of knowledge by constructing graphic organizers.

Graphic organizers are visual diagrams that portray the relationships among concepts (More and Readence 1984). These diagrams can take a variety of forms, can be used as either a prereading or postreading activity, and can be used with either children's literature or content-area texts.

When used as a prereading strategy, graphic organizers provide students with a relational guide to the content information they will be reading. The most common

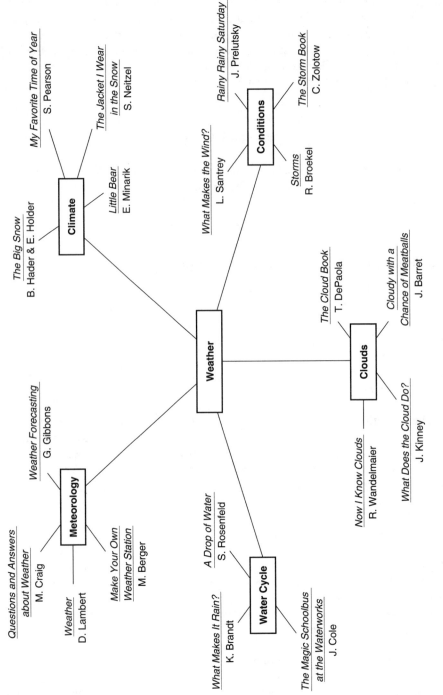

FIGURE 3.1 Book cluster of literature clustered by weather topics

Sight (eyes)	Taste (tongue)	Touch (skin)	Smell (nose)	Hear (ears)
people	sweet	soft	sweet	ringing
animals	sour	sharp	stinky	singing
things	salty	cold	salty	whistling
bright	strong	rough	smokey	talking
colorful	plain	dry	fresh	chirping
black and white		wet	damp	barking
words		hot		echoing
clear		hard		yelling
		smooth		loud
				quiet

FIGURE 3.2   Tree diagram of the five senses

prereading form is the *semantic web* described by Dixon-Krauss in chapter 1 of this book. The semantic web can also be used as a prewriting activity to help students access and organize their ideas on a writing topic as described by Matthews in chapter 6.

As a postreading activity, graphic organizers promote long-term comprehension of conceptual information because the information is systematically analyzed and organized to form the graphic display. The postreading graphic organizers displayed in Figures 3.2 through 3.4 were constructed by a third grade class. Figure 3.2 is a *tree diagram*. Important words from the text were selected and arranged hierarchically with subordinate concepts listed under the more inclusive (superordinate) concept. A *T-bar chart* is shown in Figure 3.3. The central concept of the selection is displayed at the top of the T. The children suggest, compare, and contrast examples and nonexamples of the concept. These contrasting examples are listed down the two sides of the stem of the T.

The *discussion web* (Alverman 1991) is a graphic aid used to help students see both sides of an issue before drawing conclusions. After reading the selection, students are paired to provide reasons for and against an issue. Two pairs are then merged into groups of four to discuss the webs of each pair and reach a consensus. Each group's consensus is then reviewed and compared in a whole class discussion, and each student writes an individual opinion on the issue. Figure 3.4 shows a discussion web of the third-graders' response to the story *Through Grandpa's Eyes*

Things to Do	Things *Not* to Do
Eat good food.	Eat junk food.
Get exercise every day.	Play videos or watch TV all day.
Get enough sleep.	Stay up late on school nights.
Wear clothes that fit the weather.	Forget your coat and umbrella.
Cover your coughs and sneezes.	Spread germs.
Wash hands before eating.	Eat with dirty hands.
Brush your teeth after you eat.	Don't clean your teeth.
Take a bath every day.	Got to bed dirty.

FIGURE 3.3   T-bar chart of staying fit

(Maclachlan 1989). Students supplied justification for and against John telling his blind grandfather that he switched the bedroom light on instead of off when he put John to bed. In this example, the class had been working on a social studies unit about elections and voting. The teacher concluded the discussion web with a class vote on whether John should tell his grandfather that he had left the light on. The results were 6 yes votes and 18 no votes.

Monitoring Strategies.   Monitoring strategies are designed to make readers actively think about the text information and control their reading behavior. This can include pauses during reading to sort out main points and summarize information, self-directions for finding the source of information needed to comprehend in the text, and prediction. Study guides, discussion, and written summaries are techniques used to sort and summarize text information. The Question-Answer-Relationship (QAR) method helps readers identify the information source as the readers' prior knowledge, the text, or both. (See chapter 9 by Kragler for a discussion of QAR.) Prediction is a strategy that can be used with both narratives and content-area texts.

FIGURE 3.4   Discussion web of *Through Grandpa's Eyes*

Yes		No
So he wouldn't have to get out of bed to do it himself.		John may have hurt Grandpa's feelings.
John couldn't sleep with the light on.	**Should John have told Grandpa about the light?**	It was an excuse to get up.
So John could go to bed faster.		Maybe it was hard for Grandpa to do.
So John wouldn't get cold by getting out of bed.		John could sleep with the light on.
Grandpa could learn from John.		Grandpa couldn't see it anyway.

The most common monitoring strategy is **prediction,** pausing during reading to make a hypothesis about what might occur in the upcoming text. Prediction can help to develop readers' knowledge of story structural elements when the teacher poses prediction questions appropriately within narratives. In the primary grades, predicting between the attempts and outcomes helps to develop young readers' conception of plot development. As children develop a more complete concept of story structure, predictions should highlight the logical connection of the initiating event to the outcome. For example, when reading *Goldilocks and the Three Bears,* the teacher would stop when Goldilocks comes upon the cottage in the woods and ask, "What might happen to Goldilocks if she enters this cottage?" It is important for teachers to exercise moderation in the use of prediction questions within a particular story. Each time students are asked to stop and predict, story reading is disrupted, which could interfere with students' comprehension or interest in the story.

Prediction strategies used with content-area learning usually include accessing students' prior information on a topic and determining reading purposes. The *K-W-L* model (Ogle 1986) is a strategy that begins with discussing and listing what the students *know* about the topic and predicting what they *want* to learn about it. After the text is read, students recall information read by listing what they *learned* from their reading. Figure 3.5 is a K-W-L chart composed by the third-graders when they read *Johnny Appleseed* (Kellogg 1988).

Reader Response Strategies.   Reader response begins with the idea that shared meanings between the reader and the text author occur as an individual's personal meanings are evoked during reading. These meanings can be *efferent,* dealing with

FIGURE 3.5   K-W-L chart of *Johnny Appleseed*

K What You *KNOW*	W What You *WANT* to Learn	L What You *LEARNED*
He took a lot of journeys.	Is he still alive?	His mother and brother died when he was two.
He was nice.	How old was he when he died?	He made friends with the Indians.
He liked apple trees.	Why does he wear a pan on his head?	He was born September 26, 1774.
He died 220 years ago.		He was 70 years old when he died.
He loved the forest animals.		He carried his pan on his head so his hands would be free.
His real name was John Chapman.		There are many legends about Johnny Appleseed.
Everywhere he went he planted apple trees.		

acquiring information, or *aesthetic,* dealing with ideas, feelings, or experiences (Rosenblatt 1993). When readers share their individual meanings or unique interpretations of texts with others, similar interpretations or common understandings emerge.

Reader response activities allow students to create individual, unique interpretations or to create similar interpretations and share common meanings. Reader response activities can be designed around traditional media for sharing meanings such as art projects, drama, creative writing, and literature response journals. Electronic media can also be used for students to create TV or radio broadcasts or computer interaction. (See chapter 11 of this book by Peters.)

Organizing and Evaluating Instruction through Reflection

When teachers integrate literature and the content areas to provide instruction within students' zones of proximal development, organizing and evaluating instruction are continuous, interdependent processes. The following two factors are crucial for guiding teachers in accomplishing these tasks:

1. Organizational tools for gathering information.
2. Organizational patterns for implementing instruction.

Organizational tools are used to gather evaluation information on students' performance while they are engaged in learning activities as well as information contained in the products they produce from these activities. From an analysis of this information, the teacher creates and/or adjusts her organizational patterns for classroom instruction according to the amount and type of support her students need.

Organizational Tools. **Organizational tools** are record-keeping devices used by the teacher and/or students to provide information about what the students have learned, what the students are learning, and what the students need or want to learn next. These records can be maintained by the teacher, the students, or both. They are usually kept in the forms of charts, notes, or students' written products.

A *status of the class survey* is a weekly chart listing students' names vertically and with boxes corresponding to the days of the week across the top. At the beginning of each day, the group or individual learning activities the students will be doing are recorded for each student and posted in order to help keep students "on track" when they are working individually or in groups without direct teacher assistance. They can also be used by the teacher to track an individual student's progress.

Individual entries in learning or *literature logs* provide a written record of the student's development in both content-area concepts and literary elements. For example, in a social studies class, a description or analysis of a historical fiction character could include the motives or perspective of the character who lived during a particular time in the past. Individual or group written products such as graphic organizers or K-W-L charts provide information on students' progress in concept development, monitoring their own thinking or the shared or individual meanings students create.

Student-teacher conference logs are records maintained by the teacher to provide information on specific areas of reading (comprehension, word recognition, etc.), content-area concepts, or writing. During an individual conference, teachers can listen to students read and discuss their reading, their content-area materials, or their literature and learning logs. Group conferences and teachers' recorded observations during group activities can also be used to record information on individual students' performance in these areas when they are engaged in social interaction with their peers.

Organizational Patterns.   **Organizational patterns** for instruction can include individual, paired, group, or whole class activities. Teachers use these patterns primarily to adjust the amount of social interaction and assistance students need for various learning activities. In deciding which organizational patterns to select, the teacher begins with the purpose factors, including analysis of the informational nature of the texts or literature and the thinking process required, and matches these factors to the appropriate learning strategies. She then selects an organizational pattern for the learning activities to implement these strategies based on the amount and type of social interaction needed to facilitate her students' performance. *Efficiency* is a key factor in deciding which organizational pattern to select.

A class **mini-lesson** (Atwell 1987) is a most efficient organizational pattern used to increase teacher support for the entire class, a portion of the class, or an individual student. In designing the mini-lessons, the teacher selects literature or informational trade books from her book cluster for a daily read-aloud session with the class. Any of the graphic organizer classification strategies, monitoring strategies, or literature response strategies can be implemented in the read-aloud session. For example, the teacher can work on a literary element such as character by leading a class discussion and composing a class composition on one of the characters from the story she reads aloud. When one or two students are struggling with reading their individual self-selected books, the teacher can use their books for the class read-aloud and discussion to facilitate their independent performance with the material. The read-aloud can be audiotaped to provide further support for these students when they later read their book independently.

Student pairs and small groups provide students with opportunities to support each other in creating shared meanings through reading and responding to literature and informational texts. Working in small groups to create graphic organizers, K-W-L charts, or literature response activities provides more opportunities for each student to engage in discussion than whole class activities do. Paired reading, followed by discussion and dialogue journal-writing about the book read, facilitates students' word recognition, use of comprehension strategies, and written reflections on the story's or book's content (Krauss 1995). These organizational patterns also allow the teacher to circulate and collect information while her students are actually engaged in the learning activities.

Pause and Reflect

An important part of evaluating instruction is making decisions on which organizational tools will be appropriate for the various organizational patterns you use. Can you match the organizational tools we discussed with the organizational patterns? Can you think of other examples of organizational tools?

CONCLUSION

This chapter has explained a key idea of Vygotsky's work on how learning and the development of the child's thinking are integrated through school instruction. Vygotsky (1978, 1986) explained this development in terms of how a zone of proximal development is formed when the student's everyday, concrete spontaneous concepts are restructured into systematic, abstract scientific concepts during school instruction.

The mediation model was used as a framework for helping teachers design and implement classroom instruction to put this Vygotskian idea into practice. Children's literature was used to integrate students' spontaneous concepts with the scientific concepts of the content subject areas. In each component of the purpose–strategy–reflection model, the teacher's instructional decisions focused on analyzing both the students' learning of the content subject matter and the development of their thinking processes needed to acquire and use the content.

RELATED READINGS

Gallimore, R., and R. Tharp. (1990). Teaching mind in society: Teaching, schooling, and literate discourse. In L. C. Moll (ed.), *Vygotsky and education: Instructional implications and applications of sociohistorical psychology,* pp. 175–205. Cambridge, MA: Cambridge University Press.

Krauss, L. D. (1992). Whole language: Bridging the gap from spontaneous to scientific concepts. *Journal of Reading Education* 18: 16–26.

Rosenblatt, L. (1993). The literary transaction: Evocation and response. In K. E. Holland, R. A. Hungerford, and S. B. Ernst (eds.), *Journeying: Children responding to literature,* pp. 6–23. Portsmouth, NH: Heinemann.

Tompkins, G. E., and L. M. McGee (1993). *Teaching reading with literature: Case studies to action plans.* New York: Merrill.

Wiseman, D. L. (1992). *Learning to read with literature.* Boston: Allyn & Bacon.

chapter 4

Book Club: The Influence of a Vygotskian Perspective on a Literature-Based Reading Program

Susan I. McMahon

SCENARIO

It is the first week of the new semester, and Mr. Baker has decided to divide his fourth grade class into literature discussion groups. He had watched Ms. Jackson use this arrangement successfully with her class: Her students were genuinely interested in their reading, each student had more opportunity to participate in book discussions, and their reading and thinking skills were growing as they were able to bring their own background knowledge into the discussions.

Today he begins by having the groups make predictions about their books. But as Mr. Baker surveys his class groups, he sees disaster: Most of the groups are discussing the game they played at PE, several students are writing notes to one another, and only one group is discussing their book. At the end of the day, Mr. Baker reflects on what to do about his literature groups. He decides to try the groups again, but this time he will require that they turn in a written response following the discussion.

The next day Mr. Baker encounters the same problem. Only ten papers are turned in, and most of the students did the same things during group discussion: write notes or talk about PE. At the end of the day, Mr. Baker again reflects in search of a solution. Should he scrap the entire idea? How did Ms. Jackson design and maintain her classroom program to make it work?

In the first chapter of this book, Dixon-Krauss identifies four key aspects of Vygotsky's ideas related to both the role of language on the development of thought and the role of the adult in a child's learning: (1) the zone of proximal development, (2) semiotic mediation, (3) concept development, and (4) internalization.

Since these ideas have relevancy for literacy instruction across grades, educators considering reform in traditional literacy teaching must examine these beliefs so that instruction facilitates growth in higher-order thinking.

When my colleagues and I designed the *Book Club Program* for upper elementary children (McMahon, Raphael, and Goatley, in press; Raphael and McMahon 1994), we made these principles the basis upon which to develop the key components: reading, writing, community share, and book club. Further, we stressed the importance of the role of more knowledgeable others within a context fostering literacy development for two reasons. First, we saw the teacher's instructional role as key to student learning. Second, we believed that students could act as more knowledgeable others for their peers. Therefore, we designed a program in which the teacher's instructional role was central and in which the children could interact sufficiently to help each other.

Once we had constructed a design for the literature-based reading program, Book Club, we began a collaborative intervention with two elementary teachers in urban elementary classrooms: one fifth and one fourth/fifth grade split. We collected data in these classes for two years. The students described in this chapter were from a fifth grade classroom during either the first or the second year of the project. These groups were selected and observed two or three times a week, audiotaped on days they were observed, videotaped occasionally, and interviewed several times. Examples of their reading logs and discussions are included here to explain how Vygotskian principles are applied to classroom instruction.

This chapter begins with a description of the role of the knowledgeable other as related to the zone of proximal development, and evidence of students fulfilling this role is provided. In each of the subsequent sections, the key aspects of Vygotsky's ideas discussed in chapter 1 are reviewed, then connected to the Book Club Program. Examples of student work or discourse are provided in a theory-to-practice application of each Vygotskian principle.

THE ZONE OF PROXIMAL DEVELOPMENT AND THE ROLE OF MORE KNOWLEDGEABLE OTHERS

A Vygotskian perspective on learning does not assume that children will naturally learn on their own. Instead, it assumes they need someone more knowledgeable who plans and guides learning. The appropriate point for teaching is related to what Vygotsky called the zone of proximal development. In Vygotsky's words, the **zone of proximal development** (ZPD) is "the distance between the child's actual developmental level as determined by independent problem solving and the higher level of potential development as determined through problem solving under adult guidance or in collaboration with more capable peers" (Wertsch 1985, 67–68). In other words, the ZPD is that area in which children can achieve a goal with the support and guidance of a more knowledgeable other. Thus, the ZPD is defined by both the child's level of development and the form of instruction, and it can be determined by how the child seeks help, how she uses various aspects of her environment, and how she asks questions. This information enables the knowledgeable one to tailor instruction for the learner.

Instruction must proceed ahead of development, much as a scaffold precedes the building of a house, providing temporary and adjustable support. In interactions between parents and their children, the parent is continually assessing the child's progress. In the case of the classroom, it is essential for either the teacher to be this knowledgeable other or for her to identify other students who can assume such a role. The teacher who considers the ZPD arranges the environment and creates a **scaffold** so that the learner is able to attain a higher or more abstract perspective on the learning task. The child benefits from the consciousness awareness of this **more knowledgeable other,** who understands the learner's current capabilities, the end goal, and the means to help the learner reach it.

Bruner (1989) elaborates on Vygotsky's ideas about the ZPD by identifying two important conditions that must be present for successful learning.

1. Learner must be willing to try.
2. Teacher must provide a scaffold.

The teacher cannot provide instruction on concepts associated with literacy if the child refuses to read or write. In addition, the teacher must provide a scaffold that narrows the task sufficiently for the learner. This task must not be too easy, nor must it be too difficult. As noted in chapter 1, (1) teachers mediate learning through social interaction, (2) their roles remain flexible, and (3) their support should be based upon the student's needs. The teacher focusing on literacy instruction must understand the learner's writing, reading, and response processes to plan instruction appropriately. Key to this is sufficient opportunities for language use to reflect thought.

ZPDs and the Role of Knowledgeable Others in Book Club Classrooms

In many forms of classroom instruction, the teacher's opportunities to monitor student thinking are severely limited. For example, written work is often confined to single-answer responses to questions on worksheets, and oral language is restricted to responding to teacher-generated (Edwards and Mercer 1987), text-based (Anderson et al. 1985) comprehension questions. Such instructional designs do not allow students multiple opportunities to use language in a variety of ways so that the teacher can monitor their growth in higher-order thinking. Instead, language use is controlled, restricting learners' language use and teachers' abilities to build instruction on what children already know.

To help the teacher successfully determine a student's ZPD and plan lessons accordingly, the Book Club Program provided the teacher regular opportunities to monitor student thinking. The purposes of teacher monitoring included determining children's interests in the hope of helping them engage in reading and establishing their instructional needs. In a book club classroom, the students regularly write their responses to texts and discuss their ideas in small groups. This allows the teacher more occasions to monitor students closely by reading their written responses and hearing their ideas during small-group and total-class discussions. Further, the teacher also provides more modeling and scaffolding for individuals, for groups, and for the entire class through daily instruction. Teacher modeling and scaffolding help students develop personal responses and essential reading skills and strategies, such as predicting, summarizing, and developing vocabulary. Although instruction that fosters such an interaction between student learning and teacher instruction is clearly valuable, it is not limited to the teacher's role. All her efforts occur within a social context in which other students participate. With her prompting, peers help one another in their literacy development whenever possible.

Pause and Reflect

Can you think of some ways Mr. Baker could have structured and supported his students' discussion groups rather than simply requiring a written assignment?

Since the teacher's role as knowledgeable other for all students pervades the entire program, the subsequent sections of this chapter provide an explanation of how various student work enables the teacher to assess the students' literacy development related to the key Vygotskian principles. At the same time, because the role of knowledgeable other is not limited solely to the teacher, the student-led book clubs provide all students time and opportunity to help one another construct meaning related to the texts they read. The next section focuses on students acting as more knowledgeable others.

Theory to Practice: Students as Knowledgeable Others

In our classroom study, one obvious way students acted as more knowledgeable others for their peers emerged as some students struggled with participating in a student-led discussion. Since in traditional classrooms the teacher controls all interactions, some students struggled when they realized they suddenly had the authority to lead discussions. In such situations, students who better understood the expectations and strategies for group conversations provided support.

The following transcript is of a book club early in the school year. All transcripts in this chapter are written in ways that try to capture as closely as possible the actual language students used. This includes slang, dialectical representations, and repeated words. In the following interaction, Crystal provided a scaffold for Trenton as he struggled to express his ideas.

CRYSTAL: Okay, what do you think? What did you write in your log?

TRENTON: I wrote, "No."

CRYSTAL: Why?

TRENTON: Because they don't have no cars.

CRYSTAL: Oh yeah, and what else?

TRENTON: What would we do without cars? They ain't got Nintendo. They have wooden spoons. We have silver spoons. Um, they have wooden floors. We have classic floors. Um, um, they have a whole bunch of trees and I don't want a bunch of trees in front of my house. They got snakes out there and stuff.

CRYSTAL: And that's why you think you wouldn't want to live in her time. [September 17, 1991]

Before this meeting, the teacher had asked students to respond in their logs to the question, "Would you like to live in the same time period as Winnie?" (Winnie is the main character in *Tuck Everlasting* [Babbitt 1975]). Trenton's one-word response, "No," did not foster any extended conversations in book club and revealed that he saw the log entry as a school task, not as a tool to help him express his thinking in discussions. Faced with little to discuss, Crystal asked him to elaborate on his answer ("Why?" "Oh yeah, and what else?"). These questions prompted Trenton to further share the ideas he had related to the prompt and the text because Crystal took the initiative for providing the support he needed to express his ideas. Further, she probably accepted that role because her teacher gave instruction on how students could help one another participate in student-led discussions, and modelled how to refer to the text or their logs when confusion arose. In this case, Crystal's efforts appeared to be successful because Trenton elaborated on his thinking. To imply students were always successful in their attempts to help one another, however, would be misleading. Providing instruction within the learner's ZPD is not easy. Experienced classroom teachers know that peers can sometimes be the least helpful and may even create additional problems if they are not prepared to provide appropriate feedback, as the next section of transcript demonstrates. (The brackets indicate that both girls are speaking at the same time.)

CRYSTAL: [Predict what you think is going to happen next.]

CAMILLE: [Predict what you think is going to happen next.]

LATRICE: Huh? (clearly perplexed)

CRYSTAL: [Predict what you think will happen next.]

CAMILLE: [Predict what you think will happen next.]

LATRICE: I don't want to.

CRYSTAL: What do you think will happen next?

CAMILLE: Predict. What do you think will happen next?

LATRICE: I think . . .

CRYSTAL: What do you think? What do you think the sheriff is going to do?

Latrice was a new student in the class on the day of this book club meeting, so she was having significant problems participating in student-led discussions. Both Crystal and Camille tried to provide support as Crystal had done earlier with Trenton, but Latrice seemed confused ("Huh?") and resistant ("I don't want to."), resulting in her failure to participate.

Consideration of Bruner's (1989) ideas helps explain this failure. First, he argues that the learner must be willing to try. As the transcript reveals, it is possible that Latrice did not want to participate in the group discussion. If she was not motivated, her peers could not facilitate her understanding of the process. Second, Bruner states that the knowledgeable other must structure the support appropriately depending on the learner's ZPD. In this case, perhaps Crystal and Camille were not doing this. Both girls knew what it means to predict and to participate in book club. However, they do not reveal enough about either of these concepts to communicate them well to Latrice. Therefore, because of either Latrice's lack of motivation or Crystal's and Camille's lack of appropriate scaffolding, this effort failed, demonstrating how students cannot always fulfill the role of knowledgeable other in ways that are helpful. This emphasizes the need for the teacher to *monitor peer interactions continually to determine further instruction and support.* Although peers can act as knowledgeable others in a classroom, the teacher's role continues to be paramount in fostering student literacy growth.

SEMIOTIC MEDIATION

Vygotsky (1978) argued that the manipulation of signs and symbols led to the development of higher-order thinking. That is, the ability for logical memory, selective attention, decision making, and language comprehension resulted from experience in manipulating signs and symbols within a social context. The more opportunities learners have to use signs and symbols to construct and communicate meaning, the greater will be the development of their higher-order thinking. Although many such signs are a part of human activity, one major manifestation is language; in Western cultures, higher-order thinking associated with language use is heavily dependent on literacy. Therefore, instruction must provide learners multiple occasions to use language and signs to construct and communicate meaning.

Semiotic Mediation as Part of the Book Club Design

When we designed the Book Club Program, we wanted to expand elementary children's daily experiences with language in terms of both the amount and the kinds of interactions in which they participated to strengthen their literacy capabilities. Therefore, we decided that children needed extended opportunities to read, write, and discuss the texts they were reading.

Reading. In many classrooms, reading is bounded in terms of the kinds of texts children read and the amount of time they spend reading. What they read is frequently limited to texts required by the curriculum without consideration of the students, interests or prior knowledge. Often these texts are basal stories, frequently written to teach reading, and as such they contain constrained language with limited vocabulary (Goodman et al. 1988). In addition to limitations on what students read, the time provided for reading is measurable in terms of minutes per day (Walmsley and Walp 1989).

With these issues in mind, our first commitment was to reading and using texts that were written to convey meaning, since they provide better models of language use for learners than texts written to facilitate reading instruction. Further, we wanted the texts to relate to students' interests and be sequenced in ways that would help build student knowledge bases. For example, students selected from a number of books grouped by similarities, such as genre or setting. Such sequencing facilitated students' abilities to build on their own interests and prior knowledge, to make connections across texts, and to increase their own knowledge of literary elements, such as themes, genres, characterization, and/or assorted settings.

Finally, we required that students have extended periods of time each day devoted to interacting with texts. That is, for a minimum of 15 minutes each day, children read books. This reading occurred in a variety of ways, such as reading aloud or silently, with a partner or alone, or having the teacher or a peer read aloud for the class. By designing a program with these considerations for reading instruction, we were incorporating multiple opportunities for students to interact with texts in which authors had organized language in a variety of ways to convey meaning.

Writing. In addition to considering Vygotsky's ideas for requirements of the reading component, we outlined minimal standards for writing. Instead of one-word or short answers to comprehension questions, every student was expected to write extended text related to their reading every day. For this aspect of the program, we included several genres, all of which were intended to expand student language use for a variety of purposes. They wrote daily in their *reading logs*. Periodically, they developed their ideas further on *think-sheets*. Finally, they occasionally wrote more *extended texts,* following a complete writing process of drafting, revising, and publishing.

Most frequently, students wrote responses to a teacher prompt in their **reading logs.** These prompts varied from open-ended questions such as, "What did you read today that you would like to share in book club?", to more focused questions related to the teacher's instructional goals such as, "What do you think will happen next in the story?" Students also had the opportunity to respond to the teacher's prompt in multiple formats, providing additional means through which to manipulate symbols conveying meaning to others. That is, they could draw something related to the text or construct a concept map to convey their responses. In addition to the teacher's prompts, students always had the opportunity to include additional responses in their logs.

The second format we adopted for written responses involved **think-sheets** (Raphael and Englert 1990), which provided very specific guidance toward a predetermined goal. For example, if we wanted students to critique a book, we designed a sheet with questions helping them to record and organize their ideas (Figure 4.1). Students generally used these sheets as part of a synthesis activity after having completed a book or series of books.

The think-sheets often led to the third type of writing in the program, which required more **extended texts,** such as the writing of a book critique or a comparison paper. These were more polished papers eliciting student thinking about broader issues. The overarching goal for all three formats was for the teacher to include time every day for children to engage in extended written activities that allowed them to use language in a variety of ways to construct their own meaning.

Discussion. Finally, we needed to devote attention to the learners, use of oral language in the classroom. To this end, we designed two different contexts in which children discussed daily the texts they had read and ones they had written: community share and book club. The first of these, **community share,** was a total-class, teacher-led activity. For this aspect of the program, either the teacher or the students identified topics for discussion. The purpose was to provide a forum in which the entire class could discuss issues related to the texts and in which the teacher could monitor student responses to identify topics for instruction for individual students, small groups, or the entire class.

Book club consisted of small, student-led discussion groups that met every day and were guided by the students' log entries. While the teacher circulated and monitored the discussions, students decided on the issues they wanted to discuss related to the texts. Both community share and book clubs were designed to provide students with opportunities to express their own thoughts orally before an audience who was expected to respond to the ideas presented. However, because of the small size, book clubs were more likely to be the forums in which a greater number of children were able to communicate.

With a design that included daily opportunities for students to read, write, and discuss texts written to convey meaning, we felt we had addressed, at least in part, the need for children to have multiple experiences manipulating signs and symbols associated with language.

Pause and Reflect

Reading, writing, and discussion provide opportunities for students to manipulate signs and symbols. Can you think of some other methods for providing students with opportunities to use signs and symbols?

NAME: _____   DATE: _____

Stepping Out Book "Critique"

I plan to critique (plot, character, or setting?): _____

_____

What are some things the author did well?:_____

_____

_____

_____

_____

_____

_____

_____

_____

What are some things the author could do to improve the story?:_____

_____

_____

_____

_____

_____

_____

_____

_____

FIGURE 4.1   Think-sheet for critiquing a book

Theory to Practice: Semiotic Mediation

Since reading, writing, and discussion were included every day, there were multiple examples of students' use of language to convey their thinking. However, this section provides an example of how drawing demonstrated students' meaning and how the teacher, as knowledgeable other, considered these drawings as she assessed each student's literacy development and planned further instruction.

Frequently, the teacher encouraged students to represent through a drawing a section of the text they had just read. She also encouraged them to share these drawings with their book club. After reading the first chapter of *Sadako and the Thousand Paper Cranes* (Coerr 1977), Bart and Chris illustrated their ideas and revealed their choice of topic to represent: warfare. Bart's drawing represented a plane dropping a bomb on a carnival (see Figure 4.2) and illustrated his initial focus on weapons and death.

FIGURE 4.2 Bart's representation of *Sadako and the Thousand Paper Cranes*

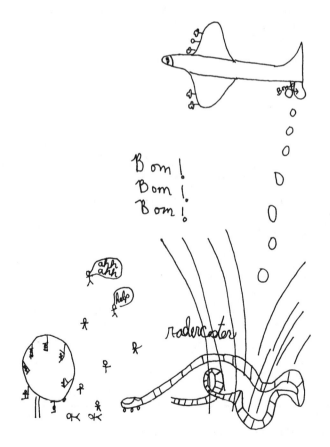

As the teacher examined this drawing, she noted several aspects that helped her consider further instruction for Bart. First, the drawing revealed little evidence that Bart questioned the idea of war or its outcomes. In his drawing, there is no evidence of pain, suffering, or death. Many small, faceless figures fall soundlessly to their death, looking exactly like people standing on the ground. Second, this representation raised questions about the meaning Bart was constructing from the book.

The first chapter of *Sadako and the Thousand Paper Cranes* refers to the Peace Day Carnival, a commemoration for those who died during the bombing of Hiroshima and Nagasaki. It also mentions Sadako's grandmother's death resulting from the bombing; however, there is no reference to a bombing of a carnival. Bart's drawing revealed that he connected the word "carnival" to his own experiences as an American child—that is, a place with rides and large crowds having fun. He joined this prior experience with "carnival" to the references in the first chapter to the Peace Day Carnival and the bombing of Hiroshima to illustrate the meaning he was constructing from the text.

As the knowledgeable other, the teacher assessed through Bart's drawing that he had learned to use his own values and prior experiences to construct meaning from texts. This was a strength that she could help him build upon. At the same time, this had two implications for future instruction. First, the teacher needed to scaffold Bart's constructed meaning so that he understood the author's intent to communicate the horrors of war. Further, she needed to help Bart build his knowledge of Japanese culture in the 1950s as it contrasts to U.S. culture in the 1990s. She had to consider this information as she planned further instruction for Bart and his peers.

Chris's illustration demonstrated other instructional decisions the teacher needed to make. When assigning this log entry, the teacher directed the students first to write or draw in their logs, and later suggested they share their representations with one another. After several minutes without drawing or writing, Chris looked over at Bart's drawing then completed his own, which resembles Bart's (see Figure 4.3).

Frequently, the sequence of students' work may be unclear, but in this instance, the teacher noted that Chris began drawing after Bart had almost finished. Therefore, she knew it was originally Bart's idea to illustrate the bombing of the carnival and concluded that Chris had followed Bart's lead. This led to several issues she needed to consider for instruction within Chris's ZPD.

Bart had constructed a meaning inconsistent with the events in the text. The teacher knew that either Chris had constructed exactly the same inconsistent meaning (which was highly unlikely) or that he appropriated Bart's interpretation without question, knowledge, or consideration of the fact that it did not match text events. Each of these items needed further attention in the future to help plan instruction for Chris. First, she needed to provide additional support so both boys' constructed meanings more closely matched the intent of the author. Second, regardless of the specific reasons Chris's drawing resembled Bart's, she knew that Bart had influenced Chris, so she wondered whether Chris was either less comfortable or less capable of representing his ideas through drawing. Therefore, she de-

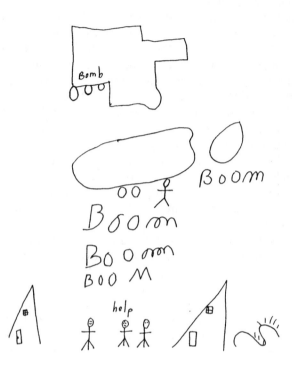

FIGURE 4.3 Chris's representation of *Sadako and the Thousand Paper Cranes*

cided to monitor this relationship as it related to Chris's constructions of meaning and provide support for Chris's independence as necessary.

Thus, the teacher examined what both representations revealed about each boy's meaning construction related to the text and dispositions about war so that she could plan future instruction to facilitate growth through their individual ZPDs. These representations were just one example of the semiotic mediation that revealed the meanings students were constructing and enlightened the teacher as to her role as knowledgeable other.

Before proceeding to the next section of the chapter, it is important to summarize the book club discussion that resulted as the boys shared their drawings. Bart began by sharing his drawing and laughing at the people in it, causing the other students to laugh as well. Bart's mediation of the language use in book club led to a humorous tone that prevailed throughout, causing the group to spend more time discussing these two drawings than those of the other students. Further, Bart and Chris presented a united front—both shared similar representations and dispositions toward war. The next section of the chapter includes a discussion among this same group, four weeks later, that reveals how their conceptions of war generated a much more serious stance and how the boys developed different concepts of war leading to opposing positions.

CONCEPT DEVELOPMENT

Vygotsky argued that higher-order thinking occurs as the result of enculturation into society through education. Learners do not simply internalize concepts as presented by an adult. Instead, they consider new ideas as they relate to existing knowledge, constructing their own knowledge base. However, they need to make these constructions visible for other's reactions before they can internalize the conventions and knowledge of the culture. When others respond to the ideas, participants must consider how these compare to their thinking. This process is continuous as the learner develops higher-order thinking and demonstrates what Vygotsky meant when he claimed that thinking developed through social interaction.

Concept Development in Book Club

Vygotsky's ideas related to conceptual development help us understand that it is essential to provide learners with multiple opportunities to express their ideas and to receive feedback. Providing single-word answers on a worksheet or answering questions that test only factual recall of text information limits learners' abilities to develop higher-order thinking. To foster greater conceptual development, book club provided a variety of means through which students revealed their developing thought in both written and oral forms. As already mentioned, students read, wrote, and responded orally to the texts and the ideas presented every day. Further, both teacher and peers provided feedback on ideas, causing students to reassess, refine, and strengthen their constructed meanings. The entire daily process was designed to foster student development of concepts related to higher-order thinking. As the next section demonstrates, Bart and Chris developed different concepts of war, which led to their adopting very different stances.

Theory to Practice: Concept Development

During one unit at the beginning of the first year, children read, responded to, and discussed three books set in Japan during World War II: *Sadako and the Thousand Paper Cranes* (Coerr 1977), *Hiroshima, No Pika* (Maruki 1982), and *Faithful Elephants* (Yukio 1988). At least two of these authors, Maruki and Yukio, have adopted a pacifist stance toward war and hope that their books will lead children to question warfare. As their initial drawings demonstrated, Bart and Chris constructed very similar drawings that seemed to ignore the serious effects of war. Further, they led their book club group in a humorous discussion about what happened when Japan got bombed. Four weeks later, however, even though they had read the same books, responded in similar ways (written or drawn responses to prompts), and discussed them during community share and book club, the boys had adopted very different concepts about war:

BART: I wrote about survival too and I wrote about Japanese. I was speaking about Japanese people and their culture. That's what I was really thinking about. But I wrote . . .

CHRIS: [Unclear; talking too softly to pick up, but he seems to be disagreeing with Bart.]

BART: I know, I know, but I was thinking, if you can't bomb Americans . . .

CHRIS: It's war. They bombed us and we bombed 'em back.

BART: I know, but still . . .

CHRIS: [Says something the tape doesn't pick up.]

BART: Yeah, but if Japan bombs, uhm, a part that's not, uhm, if Japan, this part, we don't have the right to go back and bomb them. Two wrongs don't make a right.

CHRIS: Japan bombed Pearl Harbor.

BART: I know, but still . . .

CHRIS: Americans had to go bomb them back.

BART: It doesn't make sense to go back and bomb them. That's like President Bush . . . He gets a mistake, like really, if they, if they make a move on us, we have a war. Two wrongs don't make a right. That's wrong. I would saying run me over, if they do something . . .

MARTISSE: Bomb them back.

LISSA: No!

BART: No! Just *leave,* leave it. Just leave.

LISSA: Let it be. [Book Club Transcript, October 23, 1990]

This discussion occurred four weeks after these students had begun reading about Japan during World War II and after the drawings discussed above. Unlike their initial stance, in which Bart influenced Chris's response and both boys saw humor in discussing war, they appeared more serious during this discussion, adopting opposite stances.

Bart began by expressing concern for the Japanese people, their culture, and Americans who were also living in Japan. This response demonstrates his continued ability to make connections between his life and the text. Bart is one-quarter Japanese and had visited relatives in Japan the previous summer. This personal relationship to the people and culture undoubtedly had an effect on his stance, even though it was not reflected in his initial drawing or related comments. Further, he compared the events in World War II to then-current events. During October 1991, when this discussion occurred, conditions between the United States and Iraq were escalating and resulted in the war in the Gulf. These students were discussing this situation during social studies and displayed significant interest, since many of their family friends and relatives were being sent to the Gulf.

At the same time, Chris adopted an opposite stance, responding that the United States had to retaliate for the bombing of Pearl Harbor and revealing that he seemed to be less influenced by Bart than he had been previously. Even though Chris seemed hesitant and uncertain, as evidenced by his soft-spoken comments, he was rejecting Bart's perspective to voice his own. The boys, debate and the connection to current events caused other students to become involved, each taking opposite stances. Martisse argued that retaliation is necessary ("Bomb them back.") while Lissa agreed with Bart ("No!" "Let it be.").

This particular section of a lengthy discussion about war is significant when considering students' development of the higher-order thinking that Vygotsky described. Decisions about whether or not to engage in war are never easy, and debates rage continually about which circumstances warrant such actions. To debate the issues by taking a stand and supporting it requires participants to have developed concepts related to the issues. This discussion seems to indicate that these students had made progress in this area. Their first drawings and the related conversation in book club conveyed a humorous, childish stance toward bombing, revealing a lack of understanding of the serious consequences of war. In contrast, their conversation four weeks later revealed more depth in their understanding of the complexity of the issues. Although they still had much to learn about the issues, as well as argumentation and support, they appeared to have developed more sophisticated ideas related to war.

Bart's and Chris's conceptual development as evidenced in this discussion may be due to many factors, including current events and students' personal connections to the texts. At the same time, book club, with its adoption of Vygotskian principles, provided them with texts to read and an arena in which to express their constructed meanings and developing responses, to hear differing opinions, and to adjust their thinking as they chose. Further, the teacher continually monitored their thinking as they revealed it in their writing and discussions so that she could provide the necessary modeling and scaffolded instruction in terms of:

- the required skills and strategies associated with literacy development
- their personal responses
- their constructed meanings compared to text events

This undoubtedly led to the higher-order thinking Vygotsky described and, it is hoped, to internalizing the values and concepts they read about and heard voiced in their discussions.

INTERNALIZATION

Vygotsky (1978) suggested that individuals are guided by their own mental processes as they participate in social acts, but these processes are influenced by social experiences. He argued that mental functions begin on a social, or **interpsychological,** plane, then move to an inner, **intrapsychological,** plane, a process he called **internalization.** The social reality of the individual in groups plays a major role in determining how the internal plane functions. This internalization is not a process of copying the external reality of a social interaction on some preexisting plane. Instead, it is a process in which the internal plane of consciousness is formed.

Pause and Reflect

Think about how these children's interactions on the interpsychological plane shaped the development of their individual concepts of war. Consider the effects of both their classroom context and their cultural contexts.

Internalization and Book Club

If we consider an elementary classroom using the Book Club Program, one in which students responded daily to literature in both written and oral forms and in both large and small discussion groups, this concept of the role of a social plane in internalization becomes clearer. The more opportunities learners have to interact with others through language, the greater the number of occasions for feedback, leading to reconsideration of their thinking. Book club provided several social planes on which students interacted with the goal of eventually internalizing the language as part of their thought development regarding reading and responding to texts: (1) reading logs, (2) community share, and (3) book clubs. Although each was designed to fulfill this role, discussions, both in community share and book clubs, revealed this process more readily.

By planning time for children to participate in discussions, teachers give learners two opportunities: first, to express their developing ideas related to texts for others' responses; and second, to see and hear the teacher and peers respond to texts, revealing alternative constructed meanings and struggles they may have in communicating their ideas. All of this facilitates the students' development of thought.

The Book Club Program included both large- and small-group discussions every day to provide forums for such social interactions. Community share facilitated internalization because the teacher could monitor these discussions and all students could, at least in theory, participate. However, time and class size limit how many children can talk during large-group discussions, constraining individual language use. Further, some children are less comfortable talking in large groups. Therefore, Vygotsky stressed the need for learners to participate in smaller groups in which they not only can hear the ideas of other students, but can also share and receive feedback on their own ideas. The book clubs provided a context with optimal learning opportunities in which students practiced interactions they saw the teacher model but which reflected their own ideas. In book club, more students had time and opportunity to express their constructed meanings, the connections they were making between the texts and their experiences, and their responses to other students' ideas. Such occasions enabled greater chances for participation on an interpsychological plane and for eventual internalization to occur.

Theory to Practice: Internalization

Because internalization refers to a thought process that is not visible to others, and because such evidence may emerge only after several interactions across time, it is not possible here to include specific examples from book club to demonstrate how internalization may have occurred with individual students. However, the previous examples in the chapter do illustrate how these students interacted during student-led discussions, how they responded to texts, and how some of them changed their thinking about war after having read, written about, and discussed books. For example, Crystal and Camille seemed to have internalized *how* one contributes during a book club discussion. Bart and Chris seemed to have internalized perspectives on war different from the ones they had initially voiced. Although no one knows exactly what these children were thinking, each of these examples seems to support the idea that internalization occurs through meaningful interactions monitored by a more knowledgeable other and carried out within the learner's zone of proximal development.

CONCLUSION

In this chapter I have reviewed the key aspects of Vygotsky's ideas as outlined in the first chapter. I then connected them to the Book Club, a literature-based reading program designed for elementary classrooms, and provided examples from the program to illustrate how children's responses provide valuable information for instruction and support the success of such a program. Although Book Club is a successful example of the implementation of instruction grounded in Vygotskian ideals, there are many other possible approaches. Educators need not try to imitate one program but, instead, do as we did with Book Club: Consider what Vygotsky emphasized, then design a program that incorporates his key principles and fits well within a given educational context.

RELATED READINGS

Anderson, R. C., E. H. Hiebert, J. A. Scott, and I. A. G. Wilkinson. (1985). *Becoming a nation of readers: The report of the commission on reading*. Washington, DC: U.S. Department of Education.

Bruner, J. (1989). Vygotsky: A historical and conceptual perspective. In J. V. Wertsch (ed.), *Culture, communication, and cognition*. New York: Cambridge University Press.

Raphael, T. E., and S. I. McMahon. (1994). "Book Club": An alternative framework for reading instruction. *Reading Teacher* 48(2); 102–116.

Walmsley, S. A., and T. P. Walp. (1989). *Teaching literature in elementary school* (Report Series 1.3). Albany: State University of New York, Center for the Learning and Teaching of Literature.

Wertsch, J. V. (ed.). (1985). *Vygotsky and the social formation of mind*. Cambridge, MA: Harvard University Press.

chapter **5**

Collaborative Learning and Thinking: The Vygotskian Approach

Clara M. Jennings and Xu Di

SCENARIO

In a first grade classroom, 25 children are clustered in five different groups. Each group has five members, circling around a desk-island. Mrs. Gregory, their teacher, has just read the story *Jim and the Beanstalk* (Briggs 1970) to the children and has asked each group to take a different episode from the story and re-create it.

The children read, talk, discuss, and write together. The class is very lively and busy, with laughter and heated debates. Finally it is time to share the results.

Ashley's group selected the episode where Jim first encountered the giant. In the story, the giant thought that Jim was Jack. Ashley's group wrote:

> Jim peeked through the window and then through a window in the door. Then, he decided to knock on the door. The giant was so old that he could not hear Jim's knock. Jim knocked again, but the giant did not hear him. So Jim took a brick and threw it into the door which made a very loud noise. The giant opened the door and was so blind that he could not see Jim. "May I touch you?" asked the giant. "Yes," said Jim. When the giant touched Jim, he said, "Are you the boy with yellow hair?" "No, my hair is brown," said Jim.

What the child can do in cooperation today he can do alone tomorrow. (Vygotsky 1962, 104)

Cooperation or collaboration, to a large extent, makes up the backbone of Vygotsky's theory. Taking the human social context into consideration, Vygotsky highlights the significance of this element in teaching and learning. Any analysis of Vygotsky's works should include an in-depth examination of these central concepts.

This chapter explores the following questions: What is Vygotsky's notion of collaboration? What are the reasons for and power of collaboration? What are the benefits for students as well as teachers? And finally, how exactly can this approach be applied and implemented in everyday classrooms?

COLLABORATION AND COGNITIVE DEVELOPMENT

To fully understand the notion of Vygotsky's ideas on collaboration, it is necessary to take a close look at the rationale behind his theory. (See chapter 1 by Dixon-Krauss.) The significant role of collaboration results from Vygotsky's fundamental beliefs concerning human psychological processes. According to Vygotsky,

> The mechanism of social behavior and the mechanism of consciousness are the same . . . We are aware of ourselves, for we are aware of others, and in the same way we know others; and this is as it is because in relation to ourselves we are in the same [position] as others to us. (1979, 1)

Vygotsky claimed that human development is relational. It consists of internal consciousness as well as external behaviors, cognitive processes as well as social ones. Social context and other human beings play a vital role in the cognitive growth of the individual. Vygotsky highlighted one aspect that has been left out by Pavlov, Skinner, Piaget, and other psychological theorists: the *social origin* of psychological ideas. In Vygotsky's own words, "In the instrumental act, individuals master themselves from outside—through psychological tools" (1981, 141).

To describe the interrelationship of the outside and the inside—the social and cognitive processes—Vygotsky used the term **zone of proximal development.** This refers to the area between a child's *present actual level* of functioning (what a child does without help or support) and his *potential performance level* (the level at which a child can perform with help and guidance). The tools used to reach this goal are interpersonal and intrapersonal dialogues, or **collaboration.** As Kozulin (1993) points out, Vygotsky's approach "required that the topology of semiotic means of mediation should be complemented by the topology of the overt and inner dialogue in which culture acquires its psychologically individual form" (xxxvi–xxxvii).

The role of the second topology in the human cognitive process consequently demands changes in educational practice. It emphasizes the interaction between the teacher and the child, the children and the adults, and among children themselves. The interactions require a holistic and meaningful search for knowledge in which everyone has an active part. These interactions include the highly logical and abstract dialogue, as well as "spontaneous dialogue" from both teachers and learners. This dialogical characteristic of learning, described in Vygotsky's theory, inevitably leads to the notion of collaboration and cooperation. Without social interaction, meaning of context and content would not exist. At the same time, the means and the transference from the unknown to the known would disappear. Internalization and learning would never occur. In this sense, collaboration, derived from Vygotsky's theory, serves as a powerful vehicle of socialization in human psychological development.

Vygotsky's research extends the use of oral language as both a means of communication and a tool for mediating thinking (Vygotsky 1962). Social interaction leads to more advanced cognitive development in the area of academic achievement (Slavin 1983). Providing opportunities for children to interact with others forces them to think and to communicate about their thinking. Vygotsky (1976) stressed the contribution of play to cognitive development. For example, in looking at the levels of children's growth toward maturity, Vygotsky identified play as a key factor in causing them to move from one level of development to the next. Children must interact physically and socially with an object in order to be able to conceptualize and express ideas about it, which, according to Vygotsky, is how their thinking transforms from concrete to abstract. Through children's play, teachers can determine what children understand and assess what the next step might be. If the interaction with the adult or a more capable peer focuses appropriately on the child's zone of proximal development during the process, then achievement can occur.

For children, collaborative learning can have a positive effect on their cognitive development. Vygotsky (1962) stated that language and all other learning are centered in social interactions. He further stated that not only does collaborative learning influence literacy acquisition, but all types of cognitive development are enhanced by interacting with others in the children's environment. That is, children gradually come to know and understand the content knowledge that others in their environment know and understand. Vygotsky argued that children's cognition can benefit from interaction with more experienced members of their culture if the level of interaction falls within the range between what the child can do independently and what can be done with guidance from someone more advanced.

A **collaborative group** refers to a group of students with varying abilities working together to solve a problem or complete a project. In any heterogeneous group of children, there will be an opportunity for a more capable child to assist a child who is academically less able (Vygotsky 1962; Duffy and Roehler 1993). In fact, collaborative groups are designed to encourage children to help and support their peers in the group rather than compete against them. As previously stated, this idea is based on the assumption that the perceived value of academic achievement is raised when children are all working toward the same goal. The classroom becomes a *community of learners* in which children are engaged in activities that facilitate the development of all elements of communication (reading, writing, talking, and listening). Therefore, children should be given the opportunity to work comfortably with a wide range of children in order to acquire social and cognitive skills in playing, working, and learning.

Vygotsky's theory of collaboration has great significance, both theoretically and practically, for education in terms of teaching and learning. First, it extends the horizon of education by integrating the social dimension into teaching and learning. Consequently, education becomes much more complex, humane, exciting, and challenging. Education no longer remains primarily in the traditional cognitive domain as merely individual pursuits. It turns into a web of related individual growth in a larger social context. Second, Vygotsky's idea builds a strong connection between cognitive development and social and affective development. Therefore, it presents a more realistic and complicated picture of human development and growth as a whole.

These characteristics are largely what distinguish Vygotsky's theory from the well-known theories of other theorists such as Skinner and Piaget. Vygotsky's theory surpasses both Skinner's and Piaget's approaches by extending education beyond controlled experiments and beyond the traditional focus on individuality. Instead of developing his approaches through lab testing, Vygotsky's approach starts exactly where the real world is: in authentic social interaction. Unlike Skinner's theory, which focuses primarily on behaviors, the external end result or product of education, Vygotsky's theory, like Piaget's, includes the whole process before, during, and after each product. And while Piaget's approach focuses primarily on the cognitive dimension of learning and growth, Vygotsky's approach encompasses the social and affective dimension as well as cognitive development. As a result, Vygotsky's theory portrays the bigger picture of teaching and learning, captures the collective wisdom of thoughts and actions, and more closely represents reality and its complexity.

Pause and Reflect

Consider the statement "Vygotsky's approach encompasses the social and affective dimension as well as cognitive development." Think of some ways that teachers can structure classroom literacy instruction to include all three dimensions—affective, social, and cognitive.

THE BENEFITS OF COLLABORATION
FOR TEACHING AND LEARNING

The benefits of collaboration can be grouped into two categories: benefits for children and benefits for teachers. Organizing children into collaborative groups affects their cognitive and affective development but can also have a positive effect on teachers.

The Effects of Collaborative Groups
on Children's Development

To observe how collaboration benefits children in the classroom, we will visit a real classroom that uses Vygotsky's approach. We can return to Mrs. Gregory's first grade class to see how the other four groups re-created their episodes of *Jim and the Beanstalk* (Briggs 1970).

SCENARIO

Armond's group selected the episode in the story where Jim measured the giant's head with a measuring tape to have a wig made for him. Armond's group wrote:

> Jim did not have a way to measure the giant's head, so he took a sheet off the giant's bed and cut it into strips, tied them together and took a magic marker and wrote numbers on the long strip. "Lie on the floor so that I can measure your head to see how big your wig must be", said Jim. After the giant was on the floor, Jim stacked several chairs on top of the other. He then placed the sheet strip underneath the giant's head and holding on to one end of the sheet strip, he climbed to the top of the chairs to measure the giant's head.

Nichole's group chose the part in the story where the giant received his eyeglasses. The story says that "the giant began reading rhymes to Jim." Nichole's group wrote:

> The giant was so excited that he ran to the window and looked out and saw a big white cloud. "Who gave the painters permission to spray my house with white paint?" said the giant. Then he ran to the door and screamed, "Get away and leave my house alone!" screamed the giant. He ran back and said to Jim, "I don't want my house painted. I liked it the color it was."

Sarah's group selected the part of the story where Jim was at the dentist's office. The story states that "the dentist worked all night and in the morning the teeth were ready." Sarah's group wrote:

> The dentist's office was too small to make teeth big enough for the giant. So first the dentist had to decide where he could work. Appearing to be thinking by scratching his head several times, Jim said, "make the teeth outside behind your shop." "Thanks, the teeth will be ready in the morning," said the dentist.

The final group chose the section of the story where the giant wrote the note to Jim. John's group wrote:

> Finally, when Jim hit the ground, he said "Wow, what a day!" But no sooner than he hit the ground a note landed beside him. The note said, "Thanks Jim. You have been a great help to me. Please come back to visit me another time. A Friend, The Giant."

All groups wrote versions that were quite different from the episode they had selected from the story. Mrs. Gregory encouraged each child to interpret his own perception of the new episode, conceived and written by the group, by drawing illustrations of the episodes.

Cognitive Development.   As children were encouraged to meet the various challenges involved in creating the narrative in collaborative groups and drawing their own individual pictures to accompany the narrative, they made the transition described by Vygotsky (1986). The written language of children developed through a process of shifting from re-creating the story with the assistance of peers to internal drawings that made the learning real to each child. Once the groups had written the new story elements, Mrs. Gregory assisted the children in putting all the pieces together to make a new story. During the writing process, all the children contributed to the thinking that went into the final selection.

Mrs. Gregory's children gained much from working together toward a common goal: to create ideas together. In achieving this goal, they engaged in brainstorming sessions that produced all kinds of exciting adventures, and used very complex vocabulary to write narratives. As the children talked, their social talk began to focus more on each other's thinking than on the content of the material. The children also went beyond the original goal of thinking and writing together to illustrating the episodes.

Collectively, the children wrote a new story as a group project and made decisions based on consensus building. Dewey (1910, 1916) claimed that students can only learn to live in a democratic society if their education provides them with actual experiences of democratic decision making and problem solving.

Organizing children into collaborative groups for the primary purpose of selecting, reading, and analyzing good children's literature is a productive way to get children excited and enthusiastic about reading for pleasure. Educators of young children have recognized for some time that children's literature, if used frequently and properly, contributes to children's cognitive and affective development. Stories also encourage productive thinking among children and provide teachers with insight into their thinking process (Jennings and Terry 1990). Good literature is an excellent catalyst for creative and critical thought, leading children to wonder, to dream, and to imagine.

Ennis and Ennin (1985) define **critical thought** as reflective thinking focused on what to believe or think. The social interaction with literature that children experience in collaborative groups forces them to strive to analyze arguments, look for valid evidence, and reach sound conclusions. This grouping arrangement in a classroom fosters critical thinking as students gain confidence in their ability to draw their own conclusions and express them to others.

Creative thinking is the mental process by which an individual creates new ideas or recombines existing ideas (Gallagher 1985). Creativity must be nurtured in an environment where new ideas are encouraged, valued, and discussed freely without fear of a judgmental peer or adult. Creative thinking is enhanced as children react to questions and solve problems that promote divergent responses among themselves. Collaborative groups provide this kind of environment, and good literature provides the content tool for instruction, which Vygotsky (1962) believed could be the fate of the child's total mental development. Literature can be the means through which children develop a positive self-concept about learning and thinking.

Children's exploration of various types and forms of literature enhances their ability to use effective oral and written communication skills. When children interact with each other about good literature, they have opportunities to listen to and make modifications in their own language in order to be better understood by others. Leontiev (1981) refers to this process, in reference to Vygotsky's concept of internalization, as "individual consciousness," which he claims can exist only in the presence of social consciousness and language. By listening to and internalizing what others have to say about a book in literature study groups, children learn to recognize and value the positions of others.

By using literature study groups, children have the opportunity to engage in shared inquiry, thereby discovering for themselves certain meanings in the literature and learning that they must support their views with facts and evidence from reading. According to Rothlein and Meinbach (1991), having the opportunity to participate in group shared inquiry helps develop critical thinking skills, encourages divergent answers, models an inquiry style of learning, provides a framework for classroom discussion, helps children interpret what they read, and promotes independent and reflective thought. This philosophy is supported by the Vygotskian approach to thinking in that it challenges children to move from their actual development to their potential development with the support of capable peers.

Ellis and Whalen (1990) propose four reasons why collaborative learning is far more effective than individualistic or competitive structures for increasing students' achievement and promoting their cognitive growth. First, embedded in the idea of collaborative learning is what cognitive psychologists call "thinking out loud." In order to learn, children need the opportunity to think and talk about what they are doing. As they talk, they hear themselves, and others learn to recognize that which they understand or do not understand. Talking out loud helps children clarify their own thinking about thinking. Second, in collaborative groups, children are more focused on achieving the task, and thus spend much more time on the task in groups than they would working individually. Third, the group situation forces children to engage in more higher-order thinking skills, such as application, analysis, synthesis, and evaluation, rather than operating continually at the knowledge and comprehension levels. In fact, Vygotsky (1986) described the zone of proximal development as encompassing the gap between the child's actual development and his potential development. The child must have the opportunity to engage in an instructional activity that is too difficult for him to perform independently, and thus his performance must be supported by capable peers in collaborative groups. The group environment can challenge children to perform at the maximum level of their potential development.

Affective Development.   As children work in collaborative groups, they acquire social skills, such as listening to others, taking turns, contributing ideas, explaining oneself clearly, encouraging others, and criticizing ideas rather than others. For example, during the literature response activity for *Jim and the Beanstalk* (Briggs 1970), the children in Mrs. Gregory's first grade class listened attentively to what others had to say and made each other feel like vital contributors to the discussions.

In many cases, the contribution made by one child prompted a thought in another child, which automatically encouraged the child who had the original thought not only to feel good about what he had said, but also to move to a higher level of thinking. As the children in Mrs. Gregory's class came to realize that the others welcomed their contributions, they began to view themselves as competent learners who were valued by their peers. Finally, the children were highly motivated doing the activities because they had the joy of winning and success, whether they were high- or low-achieving students.

Collaborative learning promotes children's acceptance of differences, whether those differences result from ethnic backgrounds or from handicaps. Slavin (1984) and Sharan (1984) also report that collaborative groups improve race relations among children. By working together and participating in multiracial teams, children often choose others from their own heterogeneous group as friends on the playground and in other social settings (Johnson and Johnson 1984). Children learn to accept each other's contributions toward the completion of the group task. When children are allowed to participate in collaborative learning, the classroom becomes a community of learners actively working together to enhance each other's knowledge, proficiency, and enjoyment.

Finally, cooperative learning promotes the development of children's self-esteem. Johnson and Johnson (1984) attribute this effect to a relationship between cooperative engagement with peers and basic, unconditional self-acceptance. Children also "like the teacher better and perceive the teacher as being more supportive and accepting of them academically and personally" (Johnson and Johnson 1984, 22).

The Effects of Collaborative Groups on Teachers

To observe how collaborative groups benefit teachers, we will once again visit Mrs. Gregory's first grade class. After giving the children their assignment and dividing them into groups, Mrs. Gregory carefully watched as each group plunged into action. She noticed that John in Nichole's group seemed to be distracted, and she quickly walked over to talk to him. It happened that John was excited about his friend's birthday party that evening. Mrs. Gregory kindly talked to John to refocus his attention on the task, then moved around to help others as needed. While observing the children at work, Mrs. Gregory got a better sense of how each child was progressing with the lesson and decided to make a few adjustments to her lesson plan for the rest of the class.

Pause and Reflect

Refer to the mediation model at the end of chapter 1. Can you identify the model components—purpose–strategy–reflection—in the description of Mrs. Gregory's teaching decisions?

The scenario just presented illustrates that the advantages of Vygotsky's collaborative approach benefit not only students but teachers as well. An examination of Mrs. Gregory's interaction with the children in class reveals some of the most obvious benefits that result from the change in class structure. For example, by assigning the children collaborative group activities, Mrs. Gregory was able to break away from the traditional authoritarian teaching style that many philosophers and educators have condemned but found difficult to replace in the classroom. Teaching with Vygotsky's approach becomes a guided active pursuit rather than a forced passive submission to teaching. Teaching and learning in Mrs. Gregory's classroom tended to be interactive and dialectic, and it is an excellent example of the mediation model as discussed by Dixon-Krauss in chapter 1 of this book.

At the same time, the collaborative groups offered Mrs. Gregory a solution to a problem that has haunted educators for years—that is, how to meet each individual child's needs in an overcrowded classroom. With a variety of activities at different levels and a range of learning interaction going on simultaneously, the collaborative groups made teaching and learning more interesting and challenging for Mrs. Gregory. The collaborative groups provided children with choices and avenues to match learning to their interests and developmental levels, and therefore made the teacher's goal of serving *all* the children both manageable and attainable.

A collaborative classroom setting not only improved the learning environment for children, but also changed the environment for Mrs. Gregory as well. She did not have to bear the pressure of "knowing it all" and "doing it all." Instead, she could share the pleasure and stimulation of human interaction with the children. During this process, she did not need to focus completely on the text or the content of teaching, but rather could pay attention to the children, getting to know each one individually, checking and monitoring each one's learning process, and providing needed assistance.

Collaborative groups allow teachers more time to collect data about a child's interests, ability to get along with other children, and social relationships. Having this information about each child before assigning her to collaborative groups is crucial to avoiding cliques of children assigned to the same group. Duffy and Roehler (1993) identify the following four ways that teachers can collect information on a child:

1. Daily observations
2. Questionnaires to solicit children's interests and attitudes
3. Talking to children
4. Sociograms

This information benefits the teacher's lesson planning and teaching and also stimulates and promotes the teacher's professional development and growth, which is an important aspect of improving the quality of education.

Collaborative groups reduce the amount of time teachers need for keeping children focused on the learning task. Since organizing children in collaborative groups enhances both their social and cognitive skills, the teacher's role is *nondi-*

rective. She can spend more time activating children's prior knowledge about the subject matter content. In addition, she can devote more time to helping children make connections between the text and their own experience, another book, or a movie, to help make the content more meaningful. Teachers can go beyond the textbook and encourage children to be creative and help them see the relevance of the concept in meaningful ways (Jennings et al. 1992). They can spend time coaching and supporting the children's efforts as they work in the collaborative groups. For example, having a teacher who prompts, shares, enjoys, and confirms children's discoveries soon causes them to feel successful in learning. This is supported by Vygotsky's (1986) zone of proximal development theory.

The previous discussion is by no means an exhaustive list of the advantages of collaboration for learning. The power of collaboration does not reside only within a classroom setting between children and a teacher. In terms of Vygotsky's social interaction and context, collaboration can also be effective among teachers, parents, community members, researchers, and administrators.

IMPLEMENTATION OF COLLABORATIVE LEARNING STRATEGIES

As powerful as Vygotsky's notion of collaboration is for teaching and learning, the full benefits of his approach can only be made possible when it is consciously and creatively implemented in the classroom. The real success of any theory relies largely on the results of its implementation.

How exactly can we adapt Vygotsky's collaborative approach to our educational practice to enhance the quality of teaching and learning? To many educational practitioners, Vygotsky remains a foreign figure, and his approach a mere theory in research or a university curriculum. It is a challenge for educators to transplant his theory, which was developed in a rather different social context and interactions, to education in the United States, where individuality is perceived to be one of the most sacred of human rights. To other educators, collaboration does not seem to ring any new note or pluck any new string. For years, group activities and projects have been more or less part of U.S. education. What are the nuances of Vygotsky's approach? How is it different from what has been done in our classrooms? To address all these questions, we will examine the collaborative learning strategies according to Vygotsky's notion of collaboration. The following examples and discussion can serve as stimulation for further thoughts and actions.

Literature Study Groups

Collaborative groups established for the purpose of analyzing children's books are referred to by Smith (1986) as *literacy clubs*. For example, children can select various bibliotherapy books for consideration of how societal and developmental issues are treated. Such books, for example, could be about gender roles, race, old age, death, special needs, or divorce.

The following are examples of collaborative activities for a literacy club divid- ede into groups of five children by gender.

1. Give each group of children two lists: one of occupations you believe are primarily male, and one of occupations you believe are primarily female, with each occupation ranked by salary level and prestige. Ask the groups to decide which jobs they feel are available to women and which ones are available to men and to mark them accordingly. Compare the lists from the male groups with the lists from the female groups. Discuss the results with the students.

2. Have children read *My Mom Travels a Lot* (Beaver 1981). In this story, the young narrator's mother has a job that requires a lot of traveling. There are advantages and disadvantages for the little girl: She likes going to the airport to see her mother off, but she does not like getting only her fa- ther's goodnight kiss and the fact that her mother must sometimes miss an event, such as a school play. The T-bar chart in chapter 3 can be used to contrast the various advantages and disadvantages.

3. Have children discuss the book, noting the different story elements such as setting, characters, episodes in the plot, and conclusion.

4. Have children discuss the book by comparing the occupation of the woman in the book to the occupations selected. List similarities and differ- ences.

This activity not only helps children understand the elements of story structure but also allows them to engage in the analysis, synthesis, and evaluative levels of thinking about the story elements. The children also gain the experience of working together to arrive at a solution to the problem presented in the literature selection.

Progressive Reading

Collaborative groups can also be given a reading/writing social studies assignment that uses the "progressive dinner" concept, in which people eat a five-course meal at five different houses. The following example shows how this strategy, which uses reading, process writing, and oral discussion, can be applied:

1. Select five books all relating to the same topic or theme—for instance, va- cationing in Hawaii. Materials for the lesson include artifacts (mau- mau/clothing, curbing, crown of flowers [lei], ono treat, model of a canoe, picture of girls Holoholo dancing, kukui nuts, string of dried nutmeats, sand coconuts, etc.) or other materials made by the children. To activate their prior knowledge ask the children what they know about Hawaii and what kinds of things people do there. Divide the class into five groups and select a child in each group to be the recorder.

2. Introduce the reading activity as a collaborative reading/writing assign- ment and require that all the children participate in the reading assign-

ment. Have one child in each group read the book to the other children. After the book is read, have the group brainstorm and write down words or ideas (*prewrite*) about vacationing in Hawaii.

3. Review the words and ideas with the whole class, categorize them, and organize them into a concept web with at least five major areas. Have each group select a different concept or idea from the web.

4. Have each group select from among the artifacts at least one object that relates to the concept/idea for which they will develop a story. After eight minutes, have each group rotate to another table, continue to develop the ideas started by the other group, and begin to write (*draft*) a story.

5. After eight minutes, have the children rotate to another table and *revise* (add, delete, or reorganize) the story written by the other group.

6. After five minutes, have each group of children move to another table and *edit* the story for mechanics (spelling, grammar, etc.). The children should create a final copy.

7. Finally, have the children move to their original table, look at the object, and share reactions.

Using collaborative groups in this manner provides opportunities for children to get involved physically and socially with the content, thereby creating deeper understanding of the topic.

Learning Teams

Learning teams have become very popular in recent years. Slavin (1983, 1990) advocates several variations of learning teams. In *Student Teams Achievement Division* (STAD), the teacher presents the information to the total class; as a follow-up, students in groups of four or five practice applying the skills learned from the information the teacher presented. With the *Teams-Games Tournaments* (TGT) approach, the children work together to prepare one another for the task. *Team Accelerated Instruction* (TAI) collaborative learning is combined with individualized instruction in a form of team tutoring. In *Cooperative Integrated Reading and Writing Composition* (CIRWC), pairs of students are assigned to encourage and support each other in their reading, thinking, and writing efforts.

The following scenarios illustrate the CIRWC approach used in Mrs. Gregory's first grade class. In that class, the pairs of children were known as "reading friends." Mrs. Gregory was working with a small group in reading, and the other children were working in pairs.

Sara and Anthony: Sara was reading the story *Sylvester and the Magic Pebble* (Steig 1987) aloud to Anthony. Anthony was listening very attentively and following along with the pictures as Sara read.

Queida and Kneita: These girls had just completed reading *Why Mosquitoes Buzz in People's Ears* (Aardema 1975). Queida was summarizing the story for Kneita.

In the midst of Queita's summarization, Kneita interrupted and said, "This is an African story. How can there be mosquitoes when there is no water in Africa? Do the people have mosquitoes in Africa? My father is from Africa, and he never told me that they had mosquitoes." "No, stupid," said Queida. "There are no mosquitoes in Africa. This is a make-believe story."

Clearly, Kneita and Queita's story discussion went far beyond the teacher's expectations for the paired reading assignment. Kneita got involved by using the knowledge she already had about mosquitoes, and both children moved to the application level of thinking.

Another form of learning teams is **peer tutoring,** in which a higher achiever or an older child tutors a lower achiever or a younger child. This may occur with children in the same classroom or from different classrooms. Both the higher achiever and the lower achiever benefit from working together. The lower achiever benefits from modeling and interacting with the higher achiever, whereas the higher achiever learns how to be tolerant and understanding of individual differences. He learns to respect others for who they are and what they are able to do. While learning to organize and teach what he knows, he also learns to reflect on and monitor his own thought processes.

Jigsaw

Helping children develop the feeling of being experts on some piece of information is important. The *jigsaw* approach (Aronson 1978) is another collaborative group arrangement for use in classrooms. This strategy allows each small group to be responsible for a particular part of the assignment.

For example, following a social studies lesson on "People from Around the World," the assignment is to create an exhibit that will communicate to parents the content learned in the unit. The teacher divides the class into groups of five children. Each group is given a different set of people on which they must prepare a presentation for the exhibit. The presentation, for example, might be a short paper and a collection of artifacts to show the culture of that group of people, such as their customs, clothing, foods, and so on. Regardless of each group's results, the presentations are all graded equally, because each group is an expert in its own right.

Discussion

For decades, teachers have grouped children homogeneously or heterogeneously for instruction. *Homogeneous grouping* means dividing children into smaller groups for instruction after they have been evaluated as having similar levels of competence, primarily in reading and mathematics. *Heterogeneous grouping* means dividing children with varying levels of competence into small groups for instruction. No matter how children are grouped for instruction in the classroom, teachers should consider each learning episode and the optimal learning form for each child. There are times in every classroom when teaching the whole class is appropriate. Organizing children into small heterogeneous collaborative groups, however, is preferred.

The focus of collaborative groups is to facilitate interaction patterns or the social dynamics that occur within groups. Collaborative groups are characterized by positive **goal interdependence:** The children work together to achieve a goal, and each group member is accountable for the end results of the task or project. This organizational structure is supported by Vygotsky's (1962) zone of proximal development by helping children perform at the level of their potential development with the assistance of a more capable peer. Dewey (1916) claims that children learn the meaning of living and working in a democratic society by having experiences in the classroom with the democratic process. Collaborative groups may be assigned by the teacher or initiated by the children, and are used primarily for developing positive attitude goals about thinking and learning. Collaborative groups are temporary groups assigned to do a specific task, such as creating a literature-response activity to a certain story, a position paper on a particular issue, or a different ending to a story.

CONCLUSION

While developing and analyzing his theory of human interactions in a social context, Vygotsky mapped out the complexity and power of collaboration for teaching and learning, as well as for development of the individual and the society. By so doing, he turned a common occurrence in human society into a powerful tool for education and social reform, and provided a valuable alternative for teaching and learning practices.

As Vygotsky's theory becomes more popular and scholars and educators begin to use it in the classroom, it is important for us to realize that successful implementation of the collaboration approach does not reside in a singular or "correct" form. As Vygotsky's theory indicates, learning requires "consciousness" and "behaviors" from individuals as well as from the community. *All* members of the society are part of learning.

It is also important to add a word of caution. As Miller (1990) wisely points out, "One can become entrapped within collaborative assumptions just as easily as within individual assumptions" (103). It is collaboration in its fullest form, not the shallow imitation of grouping or pretended cooperation, that carries vigor and power. Consequently, it is imperative that all teachers strive for a deep understanding of the role collaboration can play in education.

RELATED READINGS

Ellis, S. S., and F. S. Whalen. (1990). *Collaborative learning: Getting started.* New York: Scholastic.

Hill, S., and T. Hill. (1990). *The collaborative classroom: A guide to co-operative classroom.* Portsmouth, NH: Heinemann.

Slavin, R. E. (1990). *Cooperative learning: Theory, research and practice.* Englewood Cliffs, NJ: Prentice Hall.

Tudge, J. R., and P. A. Winterhoff. (1993). Vygotsky, Piaget, and Bandura: Perspectives on the relations between the social world and cognitive development. *Human Development* 36: 61–81.

Vygotsky, L. S. (1976). Play and its role in the mental development of the child. In J. Bruner, A. Jolly, and K. Sylvia (eds.), *Play: Its role in development and evolution.* Middlesex, Eng.: Penguin Books.

chapter 6

Vygotsky and Writing: Children Using Language to Learn and Learning from the Child's Language What to Teach

Marian Matthews

SCENARIO

Dr. Matthews and her graduate assistant, Susan, enter Mrs. Mabry's first grade classroom, where they will conduct a study on children's writing development. They pick up the children's writing folders, take them to a table in the back of the room, and begin reviewing the children's writing samples collected over the past week. They begin with Emily's writing sample, shown in Figure 6.1 (see next page).

They record notes about Emily's writing, describing her knowledge about story structure, punctuation, and other print concepts. Then they move on to Carl's sample, shown in Figure 6.2.

Susan turns to Dr. Matthews and asks, "What does this mean? How do we analyze this one?"

By using children's writing, teachers gain unique opportunities to understand what children already know and what they are ready to learn, both about writing and about a multitude of other areas. The previous two texts written by children in Mrs. Mabry's first grade class provide dramatic examples of these children's understandings.

In the first story, Emily shows us that she clearly understands sequence and also that she may know something about the importance of leaving the ending to the imagination. In addition, we know that she is ready to learn more about how to use periods at the end of sentences because she has experimented with them and uses them mostly in appropriate stopping places, even though she frequently wrote "and." Once she is taught to leave out the conjunctions, she will probably understand that she has to use capital letters at the beginning of her sentences, since she

One day thar was a tre.
and on that tree thar was
a nest. and in that nest
thar was a ege and in
that ege thar was
a chick. and dawn
on the grawnd thar
was a hoter. and in
his hand thar was a
gon.

FIGURE 6.1 Emily's writing sample
One day there was a tree. and on that tree there was a nest. and in that nest
there was a egg and in that egg there was a chick. and down on the ground
there was a hunter. and in his hand there was a gun.

Tuesday March
12 1991 MOM
I am going
go on razing
my hand

FIGURE 6.2 Carl's writing sample
Mom, I am going to go on raising my hand.

used a capital letter correctly at the beginning of this story. She may also be ready to learn how to spell "egg" and "there," since her spellings of these words are consistent throughout her piece.

The second example is more problematic. We immediately see the spelling and syntax errors Carl has made, but more important, what does he mean?

The only way to understand the meaning of Carl's statement is to reflect on what has been happening in the classroom. Throughout my observation of him in this classroom, I noticed that during group meeting times, his teacher, Mrs. Mabry, did not usually call on him, even though he always waved his hand excitedly to answer any question she might ask. When I asked her about this, Mrs. Mabry said that she had not been calling on Carl because he "always knows the answer" and she wanted to give the students who were a little slower a chance to respond to her questions. Although this had not been directly explained to Carl or his classmates, they knew that it was happening. Carl, therefore, wrote a note to his mother, who will be visiting the class on parent visitation day, that he is going to go on raising his hand even if the teacher never calls on him.

Through classroom observation, listening to children, and reading their writing, teachers can learn much about their students. They can develop deep understandings about their stories and how those stories affect their learning and their understanding of the world around them.

OBSERVING CHILDREN: A VYGOTSKIAN PERSPECTIVE

The teacher's understandings can be informed by what Vygotsky and his research associates discovered about children and language. Their research was based on close observation of children involved in tasks the researchers had set up. Not only did they observe the children at work, but they also questioned them about what they did in order to learn the children's understandings of the tasks.

The researchers' hypotheses were not completely established before they began their experiments. "Hypothesis and experiment—these two poles of one dynamic whole . . . developed and grew side by side, promoting each other" (Vygotsky 1986, 209). In other words, they did not have specific answers in mind before they started and did not use their research, as has traditionally been done, to test those preestablished answers. Instead they used their research to help them form questions, a few answers, and then even more questions.

Pause and Reflect

Consider the *mediation model* discussed in chapter 1 with the analysis of these two writing samples. Can you see ways in which the reflection component causes us to continuously rethink and adjust our purposes and strategies?

This kind of research is essential for effective classroom instruction. All teachers have questions as they begin their work, and good teachers consistently ask themselves how individual children learn best. To answer this question, we can draw from Vygotsky and his associates' research methodology and apply it in classroom literacy instruction. (See, for example, Vygotsky's description of their work on egocentric speech in young children [1986, 227–235].) This includes closely observing children involved in their daily tasks and minutely documenting what they say and do while engaged in these tasks. We need to ask the children what they think or feel about what they are doing in order to grasp their understandings of their learning. Once we know what the children understand, we can adapt the tasks to meet their learning needs.

To understand how children learn, we must become close observers of both the children and ourselves, carefully documenting what they and we do as we go about our everyday work. We must also question them and ourselves about what we do so that we truly understand what it is we are seeing. This is considered a **reflective understanding** of the teaching and learning process. Mrs. Mabry's awareness of what she was doing in relation to Carl may have been initially heightened when she read Carl's text, "I am going go on razing my hand." She might have wished to question Carl after she read his sentence to see what he meant, and then she might have changed her own behavior by calling on Carl more often or by explaining what she was doing so that Carl could understand why he was not being called on.

HOW WE CAN ADAPT VYGOTSKY'S RESEARCH TO WHAT WE DO IN CLASSROOMS

Vygotsky emphasized the importance of understanding the history of child behavior in order to understand the present development of the child. This includes not only general child behavior and developmental stages but also the histories and developmental patterns of individual children. According to Vygotsky (1978), "learning and development are interrelated from the child's very first day of life" (84). Vygotsky emphasized how important it is to know each child since every child's individual development is a complex and uneven process. A child's development is based on his own biological capabilities and the environmental factors inherent in his life. Every child has his own adaptations to the impediments he encounters.

Vygotsky identified several areas of general development in speech and thinking and then discussed the development of written language. He described how young "children solve practical tasks with the help of their speech, as well as their eyes and hands" (1978, 28). This is particularly applicable to children in the primary grades, especially pre-kindergarten through second grade, who must be allowed to talk in order to think and solve problems. Children who are silent in such an atmosphere may either be advanced developmentally (they have internalized their egocentric speech and thinking) or they may be delayed in using this important thinking and problem-solving tool. Knowing the children's histories (their stories), closely observing their behavior, and talking with them about what they do (making their thinking visible to us and to them) help us create the deepest understanding of an individual child's learning needs.

Also necessary for understanding the cultural development of a child is the idea that "an interpersonal process is transformed into an intrapersonal one" (Vygotsky 1978, 57). In other words, what a child does first on a social level, he will later do on an individual level. This concept helps us understand what Vygotsky described as the zone of proximal development (Vygotsky 1986), which clarifies the need for instruction that acknowledges the child's emerging or potential development determined by what the child can do when engaged in learning under adult guidance or peer collaboration. When we make use of this understanding of how a child develops and learns, we ensure, as Vygotsky suggests, that the children in our care will interact extensively with the people in their environment and work in cooperation with their peers.

Vygotsky noted that "learning is not development; however, properly organized learning results in mental development and sets in motion a variety of developmental processes that would be impossible apart from learning" (1978, 90). He also stated that "the only 'good learning' is that which is in advance of development" (89). Since learning and development are so intertwined in a child, we cannot teach strictly from a predetermined curriculum, which by its very nature cannot meet the needs of each and every child in the classroom. It is incumbent upon us to determine the individual learning needs of children in our classrooms if we are to provide for their continued mental development. The idea that what we do in the classroom might somehow affect a child's mental development is a far more important concept than the generally accepted notion that, in any one year, a child either learns or does not learn what we teach. It is imperative, therefore, that all classrooms be **learner-centered.** In learner-centered classrooms, meaningful writing is emphasized, and the child's perspective is of paramount importance.

Meaningful writing must be learner-centered. As Vygotsky wrote, "The turning points at which a general principle becomes clear to the child cannot be set in advance by the curriculum" (1986, 185); instruction must occur at the *"optimum moment"* (187). From their students' writing, teachers can easily learn what those turning points, or **optimum moments,** are and use their understandings about their children's needs (also generally demonstrated in their writing) to teach them what they need to know next in their *"curve of development"* (185).

For instance, in this fifth-grader's response to what he read in *The Secret Garden* (Burnett 1938), we learn quite a bit about what he is able to do in response to literature and his understanding about this story in particular:

I feel bad for Mary because she was just like a piece of junk to her Mem Sahib. It is kind of strange that all of the Aha's left Mary in the house alone. I think Mary could be a nice person but she just wants to keep her reputation of being a sour puss and brat. I think that Mr. Crane is just like

Mary, trying to keep his reputation of being a sour puss and a snot. You can tell that she was almost giving up her reputation when the lady was telling her about Mr. Crane and his wife. I think that Mary and Mr. Crane will become good friends.

We see that Charles is engaged in the story and can *identify with the main character*. He understands exactly why both she and Mr. Crane behave badly. He knows how to compare and *contrast characters* by showing how Mary and Mr. Crane are alike, and he is able to *make accurate predictions*. None of these types of responses were specifically required by the teacher for the writing that Charles did, but emerged naturally in the work because Charles already has these rather sophisticated abilities.

In contrast to Charles's response is this piece his classmate wrote about *The Girl Who Owned a City* (Nelson 1975):

I don't like this book much because it is boring. Kids that walk into houses and take whatever they want is a pretty dumb thing to read about.

James is not engaged with the story he has chosen to read, but his teacher must probe a little deeper to discover why. Perhaps he just does not understand the premise of the story: that all the adults in the world have been killed in some kind of holocaust and that the children must try to live as best they can. Or perhaps he just hates the story. In Mrs. O'Brien's fifth grade classroom, the students are allowed to abandon books they do not wish to finish so long as they "give the book a chance." Mrs. O'Brien will determine what she needs to do to help James so that he can give the book a chance. He may not be ready, in his development, to understand the science fiction premise of the book, and may need a more realistic book to read. Or he may have missed in his reading what the book said about the holocaust. Mrs. O'Brien may help him directly or encourage him to discuss the book with other students who have read and enjoyed it. No matter which strategy she selects, the teacher in this learner-centered classroom will keep track of what happens in those discussions so she knows what James needs to do next.

Pause and Reflect

Return again to the mediation model. Note the reader-text analysis (purpose) in Charles's written response to *The Secret Garden*. Can you see the areas in which he has become a self-directed reader? What new purposes is Mrs. O'Brien considering for James?

BECOMING LEARNER-CENTERED: EFFECTING CHANGE IN THE CLASSROOM

Raylene has been working on her writing, but cannot seem to get any further for the time being. She looks up from her paper and glances around her fifth grade classroom. About a third of the students are intently reading a variety of books—some are lying on the floor, some are at their desks. A group of five students is clustered around a table discussing a book they have all been reading. They are preparing a short skit of one scene in the book to present to the class. A few students are out of the room at the library. Mrs. O'Brien is reading with a student who has recently returned to the room from his Chapter 1 program, in which he receives special help. One student is working at the computer. The rest of the students are at various stages in their writing. Joe is working on a cover for his finished story and is reaching for some crayons when Raylene arrives at his desk to see if he can help her. He seems hesitant at first, but when Raylene simply starts to read her story, he stops what he is doing and listens. When she finishes, she says, "So what should I say next? Is my beginning all right? Is it a proper beginning or should it go in the middle?" The following conversation ensues:

JOE: You should tell what Razor-Fang is like.

RAYLENE: He's going to die. They're rats like this big. [She indicates the size with her hands about 2 feet apart.]

JOE: I didn't know. You should introduce more. I didn't know anything about what Razor-Fang was like until you told me. You didn't say it in the story.

RAYLENE: So I should make the beginning better?

JOE: Yes.

After this conversation, Raylene returned to her seat and started adding to her story while Joe continued coloring the cover of his finished piece.

What Learner-Centered Classrooms Look Like

Learner-centered classrooms may be bare or colorful, messy or neat, but they have in common a concern with the individual children in the class. Raylene knows that her teacher is concerned about each of them, even though she is working with Philip right now; 18 other people in the class can help her. She focuses on Joe particularly; she knows that Joe writes stories that are attention-grabbers because Mrs. O'Brien has the students frequently share their stories.

A visitor entering Mrs. O'Brien's, Mrs. Mabry's, or any other learner-centered classroom would find it difficult at first to locate the teacher. She might be working with a student on his reading, as Mrs. O'Brien was; in a corner reading or writing by herself; or working with a small group of students on a reader's theater piece. She might be sitting on a stool by a student desk, talking with the student about his writing, as Mrs. Mabry so often did with her first-graders.

During one conference period, Mrs. Mabry sat with Ben, who had been trying for a few minutes to get her to stop and listen to his story.

BEN: [Reads his story and then points to his picture.] This is a space vehicle and they won't get hurt.

MRS. MABRY: The boys went in a space ship and they traveled through space, and what happened?

BEN: They saw whatever they could.

MRS. MABRY: What do you think they saw?

BEN: Animals.

MRS. MABRY: In outer space?

BEN: Stars . . . guess what else.

MRS. MABRY: [Makes a few incorrect guesses.] You tell me. [Ben responds.] Are you going to go on with your story map or are you going to finish up?

BEN: Go on with the story map.

Since Mrs. Mabry was satisfied that Ben knew what he was going to do, she left to help another student.

Although Ben is only six years old, Mrs. Mabry treats him as a peer: It is his writing, he is in charge of the conference, and he knows his story. She is interested in what he has to say about his piece and follows his lead. She spends only one or two minutes with him because she trusts him to do what he needs to do. Mrs. Mabry does not use the conference as a time for teaching, although she notices that Ben has left no spaces between his words, making it difficult for others to read his piece. If no other child in class were making this error and she felt Ben was ready to learn about word spaces, she might take a minute or two to show Ben how to separate words in order to make his writing easier to understand. She waits, however, and gives Ben and a few others with the same problem a short lesson on this later in the day. During the lesson, Mrs. Mabry has Marie share her writing because she has just started to use word spaces correctly. Mrs. Mabry knows that Marie will be able to share how she came to her understanding in ways that the other children will be likely to grasp since her zone of proximal development or emerging potential for understanding this convention of print is close to theirs.

The use of *peer teachers* is another very important aspect of a learner-centered classroom, but all students are teachers, not just the highest-achieving or most gifted child in the class. Emily and Donald, the most prolific first grade writers in Mrs. Mabry's class, began writing their stories at the beginning of the school year with appropriate spaces between their words, and would have been good candidates to help teach the lesson on word spaces to Ben and the others. However, Mrs. Mabry knows that this would not be appropriate for Emily and Donald, because their development in this area has far exceeded Ben's and having them teach the lesson would not be beneficial to their own learning. In Marie's case, however, teaching the lesson is reinforcing to her learning. Since Marie has just recently learned how to use word spaces, she is very close to this *learning curve* or emerging potential for understanding this particular print convention.

Pause and Reflect

Can you see some connections between the idea of a learner-centered classroom and matching purpose to strategy in the mediation model? How does this approach guide teachers' decisions on grouping patterns?

How to Establish the Appropriate Environment

Determining the learning curve and developmental level of each child is essential for establishing an appropriate learning environment, because these curves and levels vary from child to child. For this reason, we cannot make cooperative groupings hard and fast. Marie may have been able to teach Ben something important about word spacing, but Ben needed Sally to help him with some other aspect of his development. In her active encouragement of children working together, Mrs. Mabry grouped them at the tables for various reasons. As she explained, "I try to mix all the abilities at the tables, like I'll use Sally, because Sally will be very good with another child, who's ready, almost there; she got Ben going . . . and sometimes it's just two quiet ones and a noisy one, for behavior reasons." She also remarked that when they bring a paper up, she asks them, "Did somebody help you today?"

As we have seen, Mrs. O'Brien also encouraged her fifth grade students to help each other and work together because she understands, as does Mrs. Mabry, that the children's developmental levels and histories are different and require different responses.

Children are also deserving of respect as equals, as other human beings. In Mrs. Mabry's conversation with Ben, she did not act as the questioning teacher, but as another person in conversation with him. Mrs. O'Brien encouraged her students to work on whatever they felt was most important at the time and in whatever place was most comfortable to them. They could work with whichever partner they felt would help them the most, as well.

In these and other learner-centered classrooms, students are not only allowed, but also encouraged, to *make choices,* to make decisions about many alternatives that affect their learning. The students can choose the books they want to read and the time and place to read those books. They can often choose how to respond to those books, using a variety of ways such as discussion groups, response journals, drawing and other art media, or dramatic or musical productions. Each student chooses the topic for her writing, the length and genre of her piece, the partners with whom she will gather ideas and revise it, the audience, and the venue for publication of her writing.

If children and their work are valued in the classroom, they will have extended time periods to do their reading, writing, and other work in class and will have flexible time frames in which to complete their various tasks. They will have timely and appropriate responses to their work that encourage them to extend their learning to the next curve of development. Children will perceive that the type of work they do is validated when they observe that adults are engaged in the same kinds of tasks and that they share their work in similar ways.

Writing as an Integral Part of a Learner-Centered Approach

Adults involved in the teaching of writing will write and share their writing, if they are teaching it *authentically*. Adults who teach writing authentically must write to express themselves and to learn how the teaching/learning is progressing. When we view writing as a process, as an important end in itself (a way for people to express themselves), and as a way to learn what and how we think, we understand how it must be an integral part of the school setting. Without writing or some kind of discussion, how can we know what the children already understand or have learned about a particular subject?

UNDERSTANDING THE PROCESS OF WRITING

> But it was not until I began to write, . . . that I found the world out there revealing, because . . . memory had become attached to seeing, love had added itself to discovery, . . . the need I carried inside myself to know— the apprehension, first, and then the passion, to *connect* myself to it. (Welty 1984, 76)

Here, Eudora Welty describes what happened to her as she began to write. The same is probably true of most, if not all, writers: They become more *observant* of the world and begin to attach meaning to it, or what Welty describes as "memory" and "love." When we allow children to write from their own hearts and minds, they will also make those *connections,* observing the world more closely and understanding their places in it. They, too, will develop the need to know more and the passion to continue making the connections Welty describes. Their histories (memory and seeing) are connected to their continued development (love and discovery, love of discovery).

An Introduction to What "Real" Writers Do

Murray (1968) cogently describes what writers do when they write. He emphasizes that writing is above all exploration, both the discovery of meaning and the discovery of form, and that no hard-and-fast rules apply. Murray claims that the writer sees, finding the "ordinary extraordinary and old truths new" (12); the writer writes, having "the courage or the compulsion to reveal himself" (13) and making a commitment; and the writer rewrites, using craft to turn "inspiration into creation" (13). He describes writing as a process, "not a rigid procedure" (7). Most writers, including child writers, follow certain steps as they work through the process of writing. These steps (though not always so straightforward) are as follows:

1. prewriting activities
2. drafting
3. conferring with others
4. revision
5. editing
6. publishing

As Vygotsky intimated, we cannot teach children how to write using traditional methods or what he called "artificial training." He claimed that such training requires so much effort on the part of both teacher and student that the actual written language is relegated to the background. "Instead of being founded on the needs of children as they naturally develop and on their own activity, writing is given to them from without, from the teacher's hands" (Vygotsky 1978, 105). The strong words that Welty uses to describe her writing—*memory, passion, love, discovery*—are not words we would ordinarily use to describe student writing that emanates from the "teacher's hands." Students must be allowed to write as "real" writers do, from the heart, using *authentic methods,* the methods that writers use, and in so doing, budding writers will become involved in the essence of writing itself.

Helping Children Begin to Write

The children in Mrs. Mabry's classroom are writing in their journals, as they do almost every day, while one student is trying to decide, with the help of his two classmates, what to write.

ERIC: I don't know what to write in my journal. I've already written about the Simpsons. I want to write about Ninja Turtles, but I don't know what to write.

ALICE: Write about their weapons.

ERIC: I already know about them.

DONALD: Write about Splinter.

ERIC: I don't know how to draw him.

DONALD: You don't have to draw him. Just write words. [Eric starts drawing in his journal. Donald and Alice have both been drawing during the conversation and continue with their drawings.]

These students were able to help each other because each knew what the other was interested in and could give good suggestions for writing. After the conversation, Eric was able to write and draw extensively in his journal.

In order to help students write, writing must be *expected* and time for writing must be *allowed*. Mrs. Mabry expected her students to write daily in their journals and gave them plenty of time to do so, often 30 minutes or more. If they didn't complete what they wanted to say during the time allowed, her students knew that they could have additional time throughout the day, or could write again the next day. As a result, her students wrote (and drew) often, and about a variety of things that were important to them. They selected topics such as holiday events, their families, weekend or after-school activities, letters to friends, Teenage Mutant Ninja Turtles, school activities, things they liked, or their feelings.

Kathy wrote about her feelings to one of her best friends:

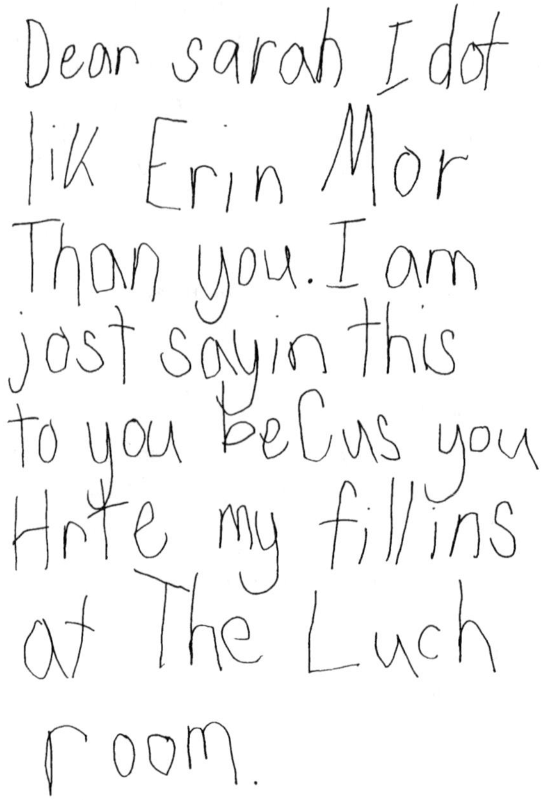

Dear sarah I dot
liK Erin Mor
Than you. I am
jost sayin this
to you beCus you
Hrte my fillins
at The Luch
room.

FIGURE 6.3 Sally's note to her friend
Dear Sarah, I don't like Erin more than you. I am just saying this to you because you hurt my feelings at the lunch room.

Sally wrote about what she did over the weekend after it snowed:

I WiT Slidinge at Ram.
The Sacint toLost was
The Bast tim Goin
Done. But The Lost
Thim Was The WosT!
I Wit Ovr The ToP and
the Sled Wit one Way
and I Wit The eirb.
and I Did a fliP in
the ere and Landid
on my BuT and
That hrt!

FIGURE 6.4 Sally's writing about her weekend
I went sliding at Ram. The second to last was the best time going down. But the
last time was the worst! I went over the top and the sled went one way and I
went the other. And I did a flip in the air and landed on my butt and that hurt!

Both of these pieces are powerful because they come from the heart and from
the students' own interests; they have developed naturally in response to their activities and their needs, especially their need to be heard and understood. Students
who are allowed to write what they wish and to make their own choices will tell
their stories so that they can be heard and understood.

Journals and notebooks are a good way for children to begin developing ideas
for their writing, as well as showing their understandings about the things that hap-

pen in their daily lives, including their school lives. A journal reveals the writer's interests and can be used to help the writer develop longer pieces. Perhaps Sally will want to combine several of her pieces about her activities in the snow to make a book about winter fun; Kathy may take the piece she wrote to Sarah and develop it into an actual letter to give her.

Meaningful writing, such as Kathy's note to Sarah, will not happen with any regularity for all students if the appropriate environment is not provided in the classroom—an environment that not only allows but also encourages *risk taking*. Students in the upper grades will not take risks that involve exposing their inner selves and their passions if such risk taking is not modeled by their teachers. Teachers, too, must write from the heart and share that writing with their students. This encourages students to begin writing and to make their writing better. A teacher who had been involved in the writing project we conducted told me that her students were enthusiastic about writing, but she was extremely tired of reading the same type of voiceless stories over and over again. Because she herself was an outstanding writer, I asked if she had shared her writing with her students. She said no, but then promised to try it. Later, she reported to me that almost immediately after this experience, her students' writing improved considerably.

Sharing/Responding to the Writing

In Mrs. Mabry's room, as we have seen, the students often shared as they began to write, but they also shared after they had written. In the following whole-class sharing session, called "The Author's Chair," Sam has just read a story he wrote about a burglar.

CARL: That was a good story.

MRS. MABRY: What was something special? What did you like about it?

CHRIS: The numchucks.

KATHY: I liked the part when the burglars came in.

SAM: There was only one burglar.

DONALD: I liked the part where he bought the numchucks.

SAM: He didn't buy them, he had them.

MRS. MABRY: Would you like him to read that part, so that you'll remember what happened?

When the students answered yes, Sam read the part again.

In this session, the students showed an interest in the story, discussing what they liked about its content. The teacher encouraged them to be more specific about what they liked. Sam, the writer, knew his story and was the expert to whom they addressed their questions. Although he had some help from Mrs. Mabry, he was in control of the situation and his story.

In a sharing/responding situation, Mrs. Mabry models how the students can respond in authentic ways to the other children's writing, and they take their cues from her. Once they have internalized appropriate ways to respond, she leaves them on their own, and the students feel confident and in control of their own processes. They give each other appropriate help, but when they feel they are not getting the help they need, they know they can go to others, as Kathy does in the following situation.

In a journal-writing session, Kathy, sitting at a table of boys, does not know what to write about—she thinks the boys write about too much "boy stuff."

KATHY: I wish girls were at this table. [She asks me] Can I go ask Sally?

SAM: How about you write about Barbie?

BEN: Space.

KATHY: [Not having heard Ben] I'm not into that stuff. [At my nod, she goes over to Sally's table but comes back.] Sally wasn't much help.

BEN: Or ask Danielle? She's your friend.

KATHY: [Goes over to talk to Danielle and comes back.] She gave me some clues.

SAM: So, what are you going to write about?

KATHY: [With a scrunched-up face and voice] None of your business!

BEN: So, what are you going to write about?

SAM: [Mimicking Kathy, turns to Ben] She said "None of your business." She probably is writing about the Texas chain massacre.

BEN: What are you writing about? Barbies? I bet you money it's Barbies.

KATHY: If you guys don't leave me alone . . . [Her words trail off, but the implication is that she won't be able to get anything done if they do not leave her alone.]

Kathy demonstrated control over her writing process in the previous situation (Newman 1985). She listened to suggestions from the boys but did not take them, preferring to go to others for ideas. She continued searching until she found someone who could spark an idea in her and then returned to begin her work, discouraging any conversation that might distract her from writing about her ideas. Students who are confident in their writing and in control of their learning will not be distracted from they want to do. Most students want to do work that is meaningful, and writing becomes even more meaningful when there is a purpose for it.

Pause and Reflect

It is important to reflect on the ultimate purpose for writing: to share ideas (meaning) with another person. With this purpose in mind, can you see the importance of learning print conventions such as punctuation, syntax, and spelling? When is learning these "skills" a meaningful task for children?

The Revision and Editing Process

Writing becomes purposeful when it has an audience and is published. "Publishing" in the classroom can take place through a variety of means, such as letters, newsletters, newspapers, literary anthologies or journals, and books—bound or unbound, class- or single-authored, formal or informal. To publish the children's writing, revision and editing are necessary so that their work can be read and understood by their intended audience. At this point, writing and editing skills must be taught.

Mrs. Mabry and Mrs. O'Brien both taught skills to their students after they saw what the students needed to learn. Often, Mrs. Mabry would ask her students if they needed some of their words put in "adult writing" so that others could read it. She taught Ben and other students how to put spaces between words and taught Emily how to make sentences, all at the appropriate points in their learning curves. Mrs. O'Brien gave a lesson to a small group of students on how to divide words at the syllables when she saw that they were dividing one-syllable words, and multisyllable words in the wrong places. Thus, it is at the end of the process, rather than at the beginning, that formal and traditional methods of teaching writing are used, and students' written work becomes the foreground, rather than the background, of the classroom environment. Once students become aware of the role writing plays in their lives, they naturally want their work to be read and are ready to learn the skills that will make their writing legible to any number of others—that all-important audience.

CONCLUSION: WRITING AND AUTHENTIC WORK

Children can see the importance that writing has in their lives not only in the area of language arts—writing for its own sake and in response to literature—but also in all other subject areas, if they are allowed to write in those areas. When we are exploring new areas of learning, writing can help us learn what we know. Writing serves the same purpose as small children's egocentric speech: "It serves [as] mental orientation, [brings] conscious understanding; it helps in overcoming difficulties; it is . . . intimately and usefully connected with . . . thinking" (Vygotsky 1986, 228). As Welty (1984) claims, writing helps reveal the world and helps us develop the need to know and to make connections to the world. Fulwiler (1987) cites research concluding that "human beings find meaning in the world by exploring it through language" (1). He explains that it is important for us to write, for strong pedagogical reasons generally based on the following assumptions about the connections between thought and language:

1. When people articulate connections between new information and what they already know, they learn and understand that new information better (Bruner 1966).
2. When people think and figure things out, they do so in symbol systems commonly called languages, most often verbal, but also mathematical, musical, visual, and so on (Vygotsky 1986).

3. When people learn things, they use all the language modes to do so—reading, writing, speaking, and listening; each mode helps people learn in a unique way (Emig 1977).
4. When people write about new information and ideas—in addition to reading, talking, and listening—they learn and understand them better (Britton 1970).
5. When people care about what they write and see connections between their writing and their own lives, they both learn and write better (Moffett 1968). (5–6)

Writing has inestimable value in helping us learn about what we know, consolidating our knowledge in a way that makes what we know clear both to us and to others. It also helps us make connections to the world and to others. As Britton (1970) states, "We cannot afford to underestimate the value of language as a means of organizing and consolidating our accumulated experience, or its value as a means of interacting with people and objects to create experience" (278).

Using Writing to Learn about Children

Writing is also a means to learn what we can about those we teach. Through our students' writing we learn where they are developmentally and what they are ready for in their curve of development—their zone of proximal development. We also learn much about their histories and the hidden factors that may be affecting those zones. For example, one bright and engaging third-grader, who was constantly in trouble in school, wrote a violent story about a mouse and his mother. In the story the little mouse comes home late because of his experiences with a cat. The mother mouse does not listen to her son's reasons for being late and hits him. The little mouse then gets a gun and shoots and kills his mother. This story was the impetus for an exploration into the child's background, in which it was found that he was an abused child.

Students want and need to tell their stories, the stories that we, as educators, need to know in order to best meet both their intellectual and their affective needs. They will not tell their stories easily if the environment is not appropriate. The appropriate environment is one that allows and encourages them to take risks and reveal themselves. Real writers must reveal themselves in order to write powerfully; the same is true of student writers. We must teach students to write as real writers do; we must teach them to write authentically.

What Is Meant by Authentic Work

Authentic work is meaningful work done for real purposes. All too often, schoolwork has been "make work" because teachers have felt that children are not ready for the work of the real world—for example, that they cannot write until they can read, and they cannot read until they know their letters and the sounds of those letters and can put them together. Vygotsky's (1986) statement about words and word meanings, "Just as the sense of a word is connected with the whole word, and not with its single sounds, the sense of a sentence is connected with the whole sentence, and not with its individual words" (245–246), points out that this idea of literacy is wrong. We must instead see literacy as a process, a continuum of understanding and development. As he wrote, "Semantically, the child starts from the whole, from a meaningful complex, and only later begins to master the separate semantic units" (219). Therefore, we must start and continue with meaningful, whole, and authentic work for students to do.

Bruner (1977) also disagrees with the idea that students are not ready for authentic work until they are taught literacy, or any other subject, in some artificial manner.

> . . . intellectual activity anywhere is the same, whether at the frontier of knowledge or in a third-grade classroom. What a scientist does at his desk or in his laboratory, what a literary critic does in reading a poem, are of the same order as what anybody else does when he is engaged in like activities—if he is to achieve understanding. The difference is in degree, not in kind. (14)

CONCLUSION

Students can and should be writers, writing as real writers do in different ways for different purposes. In this chapter, I have shown how that can happen in classrooms and how teachers can understand and apply the meaning of what Vygotsky (1978) had to say:

> . . . teaching should be organized in such a way that reading and writing are necessary for something . . . [a] purely mechanical [exercise will] soon bore the child; his activity will not be manifest in his writing and his budding personality will not grow. Reading and writing must be something the child needs . . . writing must be "relevant to life" . . . [and it must] be taught naturally . . . children should be taught written language, not just the writing of letters. (117–119)

RELATED READINGS

Spandel, V., and R. J. Stiggins. (1990). *Creating writers: Linking assessment and writing instruction.* White Plains, NY: Longman.

Tompkins, G. E. (1993). *Teaching writing: Balancing process and product.* New York: Merrill.

Welty, E. (1984). *One writer's beginnings.* Cambridge, MA: Harvard University Press.

Zebroski, J. T. (1994). *Thinking through theory: Vygotskian perspectives on the teaching of writing.* Portsmouth, NH: Boynton/Cook.

chapter **7**

The Concept of Activity

Patricia Ashton

SCENARIO

On a warm Monday morning in June, Juana Gonzales is walking across the university campus toward the library. After three years as a classroom teacher, she had decided to take some graduate courses. She began the fall semester with a classroom reading instruction course in which she was introduced to the work of Lev Vygotsky. She is especially interested in his ideas on how children's thinking develops out of instruction that provides opportunities for them to use both printed and verbal language to interact socially. With this idea in mind, Juana had decided to concentrate during the past year on designing her classroom literacy program to increase her children's opportunities to express themselves both in writing and in talking.

Last Friday when Juana was completing her end-of-the-year progress reports, she opened her file of Andrew's writing samples that she had collected over the school year. When Andrew entered first grade, he knew only how to write the letters in his name, and so he "wrote" his thoughts in squiggles and pictures. As she reviewed Andrew's writing samples, Juana noted how his concept of printed words had developed as his squiggles were replaced by both invented and correct spellings of words. His knowledge of sentence structure, punctuation, and other print conventions was also beginning to take shape. She reflected on how Andrew's comprehension of stories had also developed and how the social context of her classroom had affected that development. In November, the other children in his literature study group often had to lead or prompt Andrew to discuss their story or to participate at all. During the past week, however, Andrew became a major participant in his group's rewriting of one of the story episodes.

Juana can see Andrew's literacy development unfolding, but she wants to learn more. How does this process occur? And how can she further analyze the development of her children's thinking to guide her in giving them more effective instruction? Today she is going to the library to find more information on Vygotsky's theory of development to begin preparing for a paper she will write for her human development and learning course this semester.

In chapter 1 Dixon-Krauss introduced the major concepts of Vygotsky's theory. Vygotsky integrated those concepts into a unified theory of development with the central, organizing concept of *activity*. In this chapter, I describe Vygotsky's conception of activity as the basic unit of analysis for understanding human development, the assumptions underlying the concept of activity, and its application in literacy instruction.

HISTORICAL BACKGROUND

In 1925 the study of human mental processes was in a state of crisis in the Soviet Union. Behaviorists had abandoned the study of consciousness completely in their attempt to explain all psychological functioning through behavioral reflexes. In contrast, Vygotsky believed that "the task of psychology is to investigate those mechanisms that distinguish human conduct from animal behavior rather than to look for those that might be similar" (Kozulin 1986, 265). Introspectionists were continuing to investigate states of consciousness, but their explanation that consciousness is the product of reflection was circular. Vygotsky (1978) proposed that consciousness is created through socially mediated activity: "The internalization of socially rooted and historically developed activities is the distinguishing feature of human psychology" (57). Since Vygotsky introduced the concept of activity as the major explanatory concept in the study of the development of human thought, activity has become the chief category in psychological research in the former Soviet Union (Kozulin 1986).

Vygotsky developed his conception of the role of human activity in human thought from the work of French psychologist Pierre Janet, the philosophy of Hegel, and Marx's economic theory. Integrating Janet's conception of the social origins of individual psychology, Hegel's historical perspective on the stages of development, and Marx's concept of human praxis, Vygotsky explained how concrete, social historical activity generates human consciousness:

> . . . human behavior and mind must be considered in terms of purposive and culturally meaningful actions rather than as biological, adaptive reactions. . . . Activity then takes the place of the hyphen in the formula S-R, turning it into a formula, object–activity–subject, where both object and subject are historically and culturally specific. (Kozulin 1986, 266)

Since Vygotsky's death, other psychologists in the former Soviet Union have worked to elaborate his theory of activity as the origin of human thought and action. Leontiev (1981) has been the foremost proponent of activity theory:

> In studying development of the child psyche, we must therefore start by analyzing the development of the child's activity, as this activity is built up in the concrete conditions of its life. . . . Life or activity as a whole is not built up mechanistically, however, from separate types of activity. Some types of activity are the leading ones at a given stage and are of greatest significance for the individual's subsequent development, and others are less important. Some play the main role in development and others a subsidiary one. We can say, accordingly, that each stage of psychic development is characterized by a definite relation of the child to reality that is the leading one at that stage by a definite, leading type of activity. (As cited in Griffin and Cole 1984, 49–50)

According to Leontiev, play is the leading activity of young children and learning is the leading activity of elementary school children.

THE SOCIAL ORIGINS OF HUMAN THOUGHT

The social construction of mind is often understood to mean that social interaction is the stimulus for the development of *universal* structures of the mind (Axel 1992). For Vygotsky, by contrast, the sociocultural origin of human thought means that the organization and structure of the social interaction in *particular* activities in a *particular* sociohistorical setting determine the structure and organization of consciousness. Consequently, thinking develops differently depending on the particular setting or context in which it occurs.

> Humans' activity *assimilates the experience of humankind*. This means that humans' mental processes (their "higher psychological functions") acquire a structure necessarily tied to the sociohistorically formed means and methods transmitted to them by others in the process of cooperative [activity] and social interaction. (Leontiev 1981, 56)

In Vygotsky's words, "All higher mental functions are internalized social relationships" (1981, 164).

For the student of human development the task is to identify how different concepts and functions in consciousness develop out of specific social activities (Axel 1992). Axel explains that in Vygotsky's theory, human thought is constructed during activities based upon a dialectic between instruction and development, with instruction defined as any directive that elicits activity and development as the reorganization of consciousness through that activity. Thus, development can be thought of as "the continuous unfolding of more and more complex activities, covering still greater fields of activity" (Axel 1992, 10). In summary, "activity determines the genesis, structure, and contents of the human mind" (Davydov and Radzikhovskii 1985, 57). Axel refers to Vygotsky's description of learning to write to illustrate this principle. Vygotsky pointed out that instructions to write elicit a new activity that, depending on the type of instruction and the child's stage of development, creates new abstractions and a more complex reorganization of consciousness. Specifically, the activity of writing requires children to become conscious of and control their own thinking.

Pause and Reflect

Can you relate how inventing spellings of words "reorganizes the child's consciousness?" Think about how the child has to become conscious of and control his own thinking about printed words as he manipulates sounds and letters (symbols).

MEDIATION

The concept of mediation is central to Vygotsky's activity theory. The higher mental processes (voluntary attention, voluntary memory, and thinking) develop on the foundation of the lower mental processes (eidetic memory, involuntary attention) through mediation by psychological tools or *signs*. "For Vygotsky, a *sign* is a symbol with a definite meaning that has evolved in the history of a culture" (Davydov and Radzikhouskii 1985, 54). While engaging in activities with adults and more competent peers, children learn to use signs (e.g., language, numbers) to mediate or, in other words, to shape and define their thinking.

Vygotsky's view of mediation is grounded in the notion of **sociocultural situatedness;** that is, human thought emerges in the context of activities that are embedded in specific social and cultural settings. Thus, classroom **discourse,** both written and oral conversations, will be shaped by the styles of discourse that are preferred in the particular cultural setting in which the classroom is located, and the child's thinking will be shaped as that preferred discourse dominates classroom interaction.

> The forms of mediation (e.g., discourse, forms, pictures, and graphs) used by humans to carry out conversation, group and individual problem solving, and so forth are fundamentally shaped by the sociocultural setting in which activities are carried out. . . . As a result we are empowered as well as constrained in specific ways by the mediational means of a sociocultural setting. (Wertsch and Bivens 1992, 41–42)

For Vygotsky (1987), language is the most important mediator:

> The speech structures mastered by the child become the basic structures of his [or her] thinking. . . . Thought development is determined by language, i.e., by the linguistic tools of thought and by the sociocultural experience of the child. . . . The child's intellectual growth is contingent on . . . mastering the social means of thought, that is, language. (94)

Language gives children a powerful tool that helps them solve difficult tasks, inhibit impulsive actions, plan solutions to problems before executing them, and ultimately, control their own behavior (Vygotsky 1978).

Pause and Reflect

Let's consider Vygotsky's idea that language is the most important mediator of the child's thinking as it relates to literacy development. Review the mediation model of literacy instruction in chapter 1, and note the goal of the model: for the learner to develop her own self-directed mediating system.

ASSUMPTIONS OF ACTIVITY THEORY

Rogoff (1990) explains that using activity as the unit of analysis in the study of human development requires seven major changes in the way we think about development:

1. Development is defined as a *dynamic process* rather than a static product. The focus is on the changes that take place in the participants during an activity, rather than on the individual capacities of the participants.
2. Human activity is *goal-directed.* Consequently, activities must be understood in terms of the goals that direct them. Participants engage in activities to achieve goals. For example, children will be motivated to read and write when they feel that "reading and writing are necessary for something" (Vygotsky 1978, 117).
3. *Meaning* and *purpose* are integral to all aspects of activities and cannot be understood in terms of individual features of the individual or the context.
4. Mental activities (e.g., remembering, planning, attending) cannot be considered separately from the goal they are intended to accomplish and the *interpersonal interactions* involved.
5. Thinking is determined by the *actions,* the *context,* and the *goal.* Knowing the characteristics of the particular context is necessary for understanding how an individual will act. For example, a young child may be unable to

remember simple mathematical calculations when asked to memorize them by an adult, but may readily recall the same information when it is required in playing a game (Zaporozhets 1979–1980).

6. Human activity is a function of *culture* and *biological inheritance.*
7. Variations in cultural practices and biological conditions produce variation in human activity. Therefore, *development varies* in directions and outcomes. Development has no single universal goal.

Given these assumptions, children's cognitive development, in general, and literacy development, in particular, must be studied in context—in terms of activities. As Resnick (1991) points out, "Every cognitive act must be viewed as a specific set of circumstances. Only by understanding the circumstances and the participants' construal of the situation can a valid interpretation of the cognitive activity be made" (4).

ACTIVITY THEORY AND THE ZONE OF PROXIMAL DEVELOPMENT

In proposing activity as the unit of analysis in human development, Vygotsky believed that analysis must focus on the activity as a whole, in all its complexity, not on isolated elements (Moll 1990). Consequently, the focus is no longer on the individual acting in isolation but rather on the interactions of the individuals engaged in the activity as a whole. Wertsch identified three concepts essential for understanding the activity of teacher and students engaged in activity: situation definition, intersubjectivity, and semiotic mediation.

Situation definition refers to the way the participants represent the activity, including the setting, objects, events, and action patterns involved in the activity. Initially, the teacher's representation of the situation typically differs from that of the learner. As Wertsch explains, "Even though the [teacher] and child are functioning in the same spatiotemporal context, they often understand this context in such different ways that they are not really doing the same [activity]" (9). For example, Perret-Clermont, Perret, and Bell (1991) found that the problems students encountered in trying to solve problems were often not difficulties in their understanding of the logical and symbolic aspects of the activity but rather misconceptions in the students' interpretation of the definition of the situation. The students failed to understand what the teacher was asking them to do. (For an example, see chapter 4 by McMahon.) According to Wertsch, a major transformation that occurs in the zone of proximal development is that learners relinquish their definition of the situation in favor of a qualitatively new definition. This transition consists of an abrupt change in basic understanding of the activity—a sudden insight.

Intersubjectivity occurs when the participants in an activity share the same definition of the situation and are aware that they agree on the situation definition. In the zone of proximal development, the degree of intersubjectivity between the teacher and the learner varies. If intersubjectivity were complete, the learner would not need the teacher's assistance. In the zone, the teacher and the student negotiate an intersubjectivity in which the teacher operates with a situation definition that enables them to communicate, but the definition differs from the one the teacher would hold independently.

Semiotic mediation refers to the use of psychological **sign systems** (e.g., speech, literacy, numbers) developed by the culture to foster communication and thinking. Semiotic mediation shapes the development of higher-order thinking. To understand human activity, one must understand the psychological signs that mediate the activity (Wertsch 1984). In classrooms, semiotic mediation is the mechanism that makes communication possible. Intersubjectivity is established when the student on some level understands the teacher's comments.

Although Vygotsky emphasized the role of socially mediated activity in creating cognitive development, social interaction does not always produce cognitive growth (Resnick 1991). For example, Perret-Clermont, Perret, and Bell (1991) found that students must have the cognitive skills necessary to engage successfully in the particular activity, and the distance between the situation definition of the teacher and the learner must not be too wide. To have the strongest possible impact on a child's cognitive development, educators must create activities that fall within the zone of proximal development (Laboratory of Comparative Human Cognition 1983). As Vygotsky concluded,

> Instruction is good only when it proceeds ahead of development, when it awakens and rouses to life those functions which are in the process of maturing or in the zone of proximal development. It is in this way that instruction plays an extremely important role in development. (Cited in Wertsch and Stone 1985)

Pause and Reflect

Again consider the mediation model. Can you relate the ideas of situation definition, intersubjectivity, and semiotic mediation to the teacher's role in analyzing (purpose) and adjusting (reflection) instruction in our model?

SCHOOL ACTIVITIES AND TEXT-BASED REALITIES

The discourse in school activities has particular qualities that students must come to understand if they are to succeed in school. Wertsch (1991) describes these qualities as **text-based realities,** because they are created and maintained through language or other symbolic means. He identified four characteristics of text-based realities that children must internalize: depersonalization, boundedness, conscious reflection, and systematicity. According to Wertsch, all text-based realities are depersonalized and bounded, and much of school discourse involves conscious reflection and systematicity.

Depersonalization refers to discourse that is objective rather than subjective. As an illustration of the depersonalization of school discourse, Wertsch (1991) cites research by Michaels (1983, 1985) in which she describes how teachers shape students' speech in preparing them for literacy. Michaels pointed out that during sharing time in a first grade classroom, the teacher expected students' contributions to be "topic-centered" and criticized a working-class African-American student's "topic-associating" style for being "long and rambling, moving from one thing to the next." From the perspective of text-based realities, this student's discourse failed to meet the criterion of depersonalization. The subjectivity of the discourse made it unacceptable by classroom standards. In contrast, Michaels (1983) reports that several adult African-American participants in her research considered the topic-associating style to be superior to the middle-class, white students' topic-centered texts.

Wertsch (1991) points out that text-based realities are valued over other forms of discourse in the classroom, even when other approaches may be equally or better suited for achieving some instructional goals. For example, Au (1980) demonstrated that a topic-associating approach to teaching reading to Hawaiian children was more effective than the traditional topic-centered approach.

The second characteristic of text-based realities is their **boundedness.** According to this criterion, information that is not included in the text or is not easily inferred from the text may not be introduced into the discourse. Wertsch (1984) illustrates boundedness with an excerpt from an interaction in a first grade classroom in which the teacher was attempting to develop her students' listening skills. The teacher read the students a poem called "Surprises" and then asked the students to tell her "one thing in that poem about surprises." When students offered answers that were not included in the poem, she made it clear that their answers were not included in the text.

Conscious reflection, the third characteristic of text-based realities, is a major focus of school activity and a characteristic of all advanced higher mental functioning (Wertsch 1991). It refers to the practice of thinking about the form and content of semiotic systems (e.g., language, mathematics)—in other words, thinking about thinking. Wertsch describes two types of reflection: reflection on sign tokens and reflections on sign types. *Reflection on sign tokens* refers to speaking and thinking about concrete, contextualized signs, whereas *reflection on sign types* refers to reflection on abstract, decontexualized signs. Wertsch also distinguishes between the form and meaning of signs. He then points out that when the first grade teacher asked her students to identify the words in the poem, she was asking her students to reflect on the forms of sign tokens. He goes on to explain that observations in classrooms quickly reveal that students are required to shift frequently among the different kinds of reflection during classroom activities, suggesting that "one of the goals of formal instruction may be a kind of facility in dealing with text-based realities of several different kinds" (79).

Systematicity, the fourth characteristic of text-based realities, refers to the system of relationships embedded in texts. Wertsch (1991) cites the relationship between addition and subtraction as an illustration of systematicity. Children are expected to recognize and search for such relationships in developing their understanding of school activities.

Vygotsky (1987) believed that the systematicity inherent in text-based realities contributes to the conscious reflection he considered integral to students' development.

> School instruction induces the generalizing kind of perception and thus plays a decisive role in making the child conscious of his own mental processes. [Schooled][1] concepts with their hierarchical system of interrelation, seem to be the medium within which awareness and mastery first develop, to be transferred later to other concepts, and other areas of thought. Reflective consciousness comes to the child through the portals of [schooled] concepts. (171)

(For a more thorough discussion of schooled and unschooled concepts, see chapters 1 and 3 by Dixon-Krauss.)

In spite of Vygotsky's high expectations for the impact of schooled concepts on children's development, children experience great difficulty in recognizing the systematicity embedded in text-based realities. Perret-Clermont, Perret, and Bell (1991) conclude that

> already *within* the school pupils did not necessarily perceive the relationship among the different tasks. They did not develop . . . the expected metareflection about underlying rules, concepts, and structures or about the teacher's "background" thoughts and intentions. Each task seemed to be an end in itself. (57)

Scribner and Cole's (1981) study of the cognitive consequences of literacy sheds light on how teachers can develop students' conscious reflection. They conclude that classroom discourse fosters cognitive development when questions such as "Why do you think that?", "How did you get that answer?", and "Explain your answer." are routine.

Teachers need to be aware that because of differences in children's histories, they will differ in their readiness to respond appropriately to the text-based realities of schooling. Children who lack prior experience with text-based realities will need more support than children who have had many opportunities to adapt to the depersonalization, boundedness, conscious reflection, and systematicity that text-based realities require.

> Different cultural communities arrange different types of activities for their young, and encourage them in different ways and to different extents to participate in them. It is in the course of these everyday routine activities that children come to make sense of their socio-cultural worlds, and learn ways of thinking and behaving that are considered appropriate in their communities. (Tudge, Putnam, and Sidden 1993, 81)

A major function of the zone may be to enable children to respond appropriately to the text-based realities of school activities. Teachers, however, may need to accept other definitions of the situation that have adaptive value for their students.

Pause and Reflect

Think about school-based realities in terms of reading comprehension. Can you expand on the types of teacher questions that mediate students' reflections on their own thinking versus questions that simply check for right/wrong answers?

THE ACTIVITY OF LITERACY

The assumptions of activity theory have important implications for the development of literacy.

> Literacy is an activity, a way of thinking not a set of skills. And it is a purposeful activity—people read, write, talk, and think about real ideas and information in order to ponder and extend what they know, to communicate with others, to present their points of view, and to understand and be understood. (Langer 1987, 4)

When literacy is considered in the context of activity theory, it must be thought of as a dynamic process, shaped by the social context, and only understandable in relation to the context. In instruction, the focus must be on the purpose of the literacy activity—on its meaning for the participants.

Vygotsky's belief in the need to consider activity as a whole rather than in its isolated parts has important implications for literacy instruction. Cole and Griffin (1986) caution that

> we should be trying to instantiate a basic *activity* when teaching reading and not get blinded by the basic *skills*. Skills are always part of activities and settings, but they only take on meaning in terms of how they are organized. So, instead of basic skills, a socio-historical approach talks about *basic activities* and instantiates those that are necessary and sufficient to carry out the whole process of reading. (73)

Moll (1990) similarly argues for a focus on reading and writing as "whole activities" and rejects the idea of the zone as teaching or assessing "discrete, separable, skills and subskills" (7).

Landsmann (1991), in her study of the development of children's writing, describes the power of literacy activity to induce cognitive development. She concludes that to a preschooler the request to write provokes a kind of "mindstorm" (106). Landsmann explains that how literacy is acquired has a crucial impact on the development of consciousness. She emphasizes that "written language can be used for increasing consciousness or for developing submission, depending on the way it is transmitted, on the context of the texts, and on the role of the pupil in the process of learning" (108).

Unfortunately, Vygotsky provided no guidance on how to design instruction that would assist students in the zone of proximal development beyond proposing that "we can offer leading questions or show how the problem is to be solved and the child then solves it, or . . . the teacher initiates the solution and the child completes it or solves it in collaboration with other children" (85). Wertsch and Bivens (1992) suggest that two interpretations of Vygotsky's description of the zone of proximal development are possible: a modeling view or a text-mediational view. These two interpretations lead to important differences in instruction.

The Modeling Interpretation
of the Zone of Proximal Development

In the **modeling interpretation of the zone of proximal development,** the teacher or expert peer assumes a regulative role that the learner gradually internalizes, a transition that can be perceived as a move from other-regulation to self-regulation. Not every instance of modeling, however, is consistent with Vygotsky's theory. Semiotic mediation must be involved. Palinscar and Brown's (1984) method of reciprocal teaching is an example of a modeling interpretation of Vygotsky's theory that has been successful in increasing children's literacy (Wertsch and Bivens 1992). In reciprocal teaching, students are involved in active participation in dialogue—"a prerequisite for the transition to the intermental plane" (Wertsch and Bivens 1992, 39). They learn how to lead a discussion that involves questioning, summarizing, clarifying, and predicting. These strategies enable the students to represent "language in the form of tool (Vygotsky 1978) to be used, in a public manner, to solve the problems of understanding these texts and their inherent themes" (Palinscar, Brown, and Campione 1993, 53). Evaluation of the impact of training in reciprocal teaching suggests that the students internalize these behaviors on the intrapsychological plane.

A danger in the modeling interpretation of the zone of proximal development, however, is that it can result in excessive use of guided learning, with parents, teachers, and peers always assuming responsibility for initiating the student's learning. Such an interpretation assumes a passive view of the learner (Hatano 1993). If children are encouraged to assume responsibility for their learning, they can extend their own zone of proximal development by using the higher-order thought processes they have internalized through social interactions (Brown and Reeve 1987).

The Text-Mediational Interpretation
of the Zone of Proximal Development

The **text-mediational interpretation of the zone of proximal development** is more constructive than the modeling interpretation (Wertsch and Bivens 1992). From this perspective, texts can be considered "thinking devices" that one can engage in dialogue—and thereby construct new meanings (Wertsch and Bivens 1992, 40). Itakura's Hypothesis-Experiment-Instruction method of science teaching is an example of a program that develops the intrapsychological plane by using "texts" as a thinking device (Wertsch and Bivens 1992). In this approach, students predict the outcome of an experiment and then debate their answers with students who disagree. This approach could be adapted for use in literacy instruction.

A number of teaching strategies have been identified that are consistent with a text-mediational approach. For example, Sigel, Stinson, and Flaugher (1991) recommend the use of distancing to develop representational abilities. Distancing behaviors, by posing questions about the past or the future or requests to consider alternative views, require the child to represent events mentally. Sigel, Stinson, and Flaugher have identified three levels of distancing strategies:

1. *Level 1* distancing requires attention to the present activity (e.g., labeling, describing, observing).
2. *Level 2* requires the student to classify or relate events (e.g., sequencing, describing, and inferring similarities and differences).
3. *Level 3* distancing requires the student to make causal inferences, predictions, and generate hypotheses (e.g., evaluating, generalizing, planning, concluding).

Sigel, Stinson, and Flaugher have shown that fathers' use of Level 3 distancing strategies with their young children is significantly and positively related to the children's school achievement and intellectual ability. Posing questions that help students learn how to answer questions in general, and not simply answer specific questions correctly, is another useful strategy for developing literacy.

> If, for example, when a child cannot read the word *bus* on a word card, the teacher prompts the answer with the question, "What do you ride to school on?" the child may correctly now say, "*bus.*" But that is not a prompt that the child could give to himself the next time, because the prompt depends on the very knowledge of the word that it is supposed to cue. We are looking for assistance that at least has the possibility of helping children learn how to answer, even if we lack evidence that it in fact does. (Cazden 1981, 5)

Pause and Reflect

How can this teacher restructure the learning activity so that she can provide prompts the child can give himself later when he encounters an unknown word? Note that the key is to structure activities so that the student reads in meaningful contexts.

Moll and Whitmore (1993) have presented a compelling description of the power of a text-mediational approach to the zone of proximal development for inducing literacy. They describe a case study of a bilingual third grade classroom. The teacher mediates the children's literacy development in a "whole-language" classroom by serving as (1) guide and supporter, encouraging students to take risks; (2) participant in the children's activities, researching topics with them; (3) evaluator of their development; and (4) facilitator, planning activities that involve purposeful uses of literacy. As a consequence, these children with limited language facility

> select topics for study at the beginning of the year, choose books to read and issues to analyze, specify research questions to address, use literacy in various ways as part of classroom activities, create texts for authentic purposes, and publicly display their learning, including the development of novel products, based on their real questions about the world. The role of the adult is to provide mediated assistance, indirect help that does not displace the direction and control chidren give to the task and activities. The goal of this mediated assistance is to make children consciously aware of how they are manipulating the literacy process, achieving new means, and applying their knowledge to expand their boundaries by creating or reorganizing future experiences or activities. Our case study suggests that an apt definition of the zone . . . must include the active child appropriating and developing new mediational means for his or her own learning and development. (Moll and Whitmore 1993, 39–40)

CONCLUSION

According to Vygotsky's activity theory, literacy development occurs in the context of socially mediated activity in which children master culturally prescribed ways of speaking, reading, writing, and thinking. Literacy evolves within a complex system of motives, goals, situational definitions, values, and beliefs embedded in concrete social activities. Consequently, teachers must be sensitive to the "subtle semiotic and interpersonal dimensions" of literacy activities (Minick, Stone, and Forman 1993, 11). From the perspective of activity theory, the teacher's role in literacy development is to organize activities through which collaborative work and dialogue "awakens and rouses to life those functions that are in a stage of maturing" (Vygotsky, cited in Wertsch and Stone 1985, 165).

NOTE

1. Although the translator chose the word *scientific,* Gallimore and Tharp (1980) point out that the word *schooled* may better capture Vygotsky's meaning here than the word *scientific.*

RELATED READINGS

Davydov, V. V., and L. A. Radzikhovskii. (1985). Vygotsky's theory and the activity-oriented approach in psychology. In J. V. Wertsch (ed.), *Culture, communication, and cognition: Vygotskian perspectives,* pp. 35–65. New York: Cambridge University Press.

Kozulin, A. (1986). The concept of activity in Soviet psychology: Vygotsky, his disciples and critics. *American Psychologist* 41: 264–274.

Leontiev, A. N. (1981). The problem of activity in psychology. In J. V. Wertsch (ed.), *The concept of activity in Soviet psychology,* pp. 37–71. Armonk, NY: Sharpe.

Rogoff, B. (1990). *Apprenticeship in thinking: Cognitive development in social context.* New York: Oxford University Press.

Wertsch, J. V. (1991). Sociocultural setting and the zone of proximal development: The problem of text-based realities. In L. T. Landsmann (ed.), *Culture, schooling, and psychological development,* Vol. 4, pp. 71–86. Norwood, NJ: Ablex.

part II

Classroom Assessment

DYNAMIC ASSESSMENT AND THE
ZONE OF PROXIMAL DEVELOPMENT

Vygotsky developed the concept of the zone of proximal development in response to the educational practice of using IQ tests to measure students' potential for learning (Moll 1990; Vygotsky 1978, 1986). Kozulin presents a very straightforward translation of Vygotsky's response found in his 1934 work *Myshlenie i rech, (Thinking and Speech)*:

> Most of the psychological investigations concerned with school learning measured the level of mental development of the child by making him solve certain standardized problems. The problems he was able to solve by himself were supposed to indicate the level of his mental development at the particular time. But in this way, only the completed part of the child's development can be measured, which is far from the whole story. (Vygotsky 1986, 186–187)

Vygotsky pointed out that tests that measure the student's independent performance only measure her actual development or what she has already learned. **Static assessment** refers to measuring the student's individual performance to assess actual development or what the student has already learned. Vygotsky believed that educational assessment should also include measuring students' potential development or what they are in the process of learning. He described the zone of proximal development as encompassing the discrepancy between a student's actual level of development and the higher level she can reach when her performance is supported by assistance during collaboration with an adult or capable peers. **Dynamic assessment** refers to measuring the student's assisted performance during collaboration to assess potential development or what the student is in the process of learning.

Dynamic assessment and Vygotsky's idea of the zone focus on social interaction as the key to learning. Learning through social interaction is particularly true of literacy development. As Heap (1985) explains, social conventions such as language or reading could not be learned alone, because there could be no conventions in a world of one. He adds that the question of how one learns is actually a question of how one learns from and with others. This emphasis on the social nature of literacy has a major impact on literacy teaching and learning (Pearson 1993) and on our changing view of literacy assessment (Harp 1991).

Literacy assessment is moving from a static individual approach to a dynamic social approach. The key feature of the dynamic approach is that it links assessment with instruction because it occurs during instruction rather than after the fact. Dynamic assessment provides the teacher with different types of information than static assessment, and it requires different methods for obtaining and analyzing this information. The most important feature of dynamic assessment is that the type of information it provides can be used by teachers to address problems, issues, and concerns in classroom instruction.

Part II of this book examines some important ideas and issues related to dynamic assessment. It builds on the mediation model and the idea that the teacher continually solves instructional problems and makes instructional decisions by analyzing what she is teaching and how her students are learning. In the following chapters, the authors address some specific problems and issues that classroom teachers are facing by discussing these problems within the context of assessment. These include:

- How to use portfolios for dynamic assessment of literacy development
- How to provide instruction for underachieving students or those whose literacy development might be considered at-risk
- How to provide instruction for students from culturally diverse population

This introduction provides background information on dynamic assessment discussed within Vygotsky's idea of the zone of proximal development. Two themes of Vygotsky's zone, *time* and *inclusion,* are used to describe how researchers have expanded and applied it to dynamic assessment of literacy development.

ASSESSMENT AS A CONTINUOUS PROCESS

Time is an underlying theme in Vygotsky's explanation of the zone of proximal development for educational assessment. Vladimir Zinchenko (1994) writes that the analysis of intellectual development must merge the past, present, and future; it is impossible to single out when one act is completed and the next begins. Vygotsky used the terms *fossilized* and *ripe* to describe how static assessment using standardized individual tests tells us only what the student has learned in the past and can perform independently (Vygotsky 1986). In contrast, he uses the terms *emerging* and *ripening* to describe how dynamic assessment of the student's assisted performance during collaboration tells us what the student is learning now and anticipates what the student will be able to do in the future.

Assessment that encompasses students' past, present, and future literacy development is an important concern for classroom teachers. This idea of time helps to clarify some of the problems associated with how we measure literacy development with traditional, static forms of assessment. For example, the teacher observes her students' reading development unfolding as they work through various classroom reading activities during day-to-day classroom instruction. She forms a valid perception of what and how her students are learning as she collaborates with them and observes their performance. However, when she surveys her students' end-of-the-year standardized achievement tests in reading, she finds that their scores fall below their reading performance that she has observed in the classroom. The standardized test measures only the students' fossilized or past reading development, whereas the teacher's analysis includes the total of their past, present, and emerging future development. This example illustrates two important problems with standardized tests of reading:

1. Standardized tests do not portray an accurate picture of the student's total literacy development.
2. Standardized tests do not provide information about the student's emerging literacy development at which instruction should be aimed.

ASSESSMENT AS AN INCLUSIVE PROCESS

Another theme in Vygotsky's zone is inclusion. He explained that assessment of the student's zone must include two elements: (1) the student must engage in a highly difficult learning task, and (2) the student's performance of the task must be mediated by an adult or by collaboration with capable peers (Vygotsky 1978, 1986). In dynamic assessment, analyses of these two elements—task difficulty and the social context of the student's assisted performance—are integrated to provide information about students' literacy development and how to provide instruction to maximize this development.

Task Difficulty

The difficulty level of reading texts is an important issue in classroom literacy assessment. A popular type of reading assessment used to match students with reading texts of appropriate difficulty is the Informal Reading Inventory (IRI) introduced by Betts (1943). An advantage of the IRI compared to standardized tests of reading achievement is that the IRI measures the student's reading performance while she is actually engaged in reading a passage. The **Informal Reading Inventory** is a series of graded passages with accompanying comprehension questions used to identify the student's **instructional reading level,** or the level of text at which the student should be placed for classroom instruction. The concept of instructional reading level has traditionally been associated with basal readers, classroom textbooks, and other reading materials arranged in difficulty by grade levels.

The idea of an instructional reading level is misleading when we apply Vygotsky's zone of proximal development. Powell (1984) points out that the IRI ignores the social context of instruction because it is a static test of the student's individual reading performance. Therefore, matching students to reading texts based on their instructional reading level results in underplacement since the IRI does not actually measure the students' potential to benefit from assistance (Powell 1984). When the IRI is modified to a dynamic test of students' assisted performance, they can read and comprehend texts from two to three levels above their instructional reading levels (Brozo 1990; Dixon [Krauss] 1985; Kragler 1986; Stanley 1986).

An expansion-contraction view of reading growth helps to further clarify the issue of text difficulty. Powell (1993) suggests that students intermittently make surges into more difficult and challenging reading material. These states of expansion exceed the boundaries of their achievement and move them forward into and across their zones of proximal development. Students then "contract" back to read less challenging material that re-creates a state of relaxation. In order to maximize the students' potential, they need to be reading expansive materials approximately 65 percent of the time. With this in mind, we can see that underachieving students need to be included in, rather than isolated from, more challenging classroom reading activities beyond their current reading levels.

The expansion-contraction view of literacy development helps to clarify some of the classroom teacher's literacy problems related to task difficulty. For example, teachers often express the concern that their students need opportunities to read good literature, but the selections are beyond their students' reading levels. This problem is a particular focus of teachers who have underachieving students and students from diverse backgrounds in mainstream classroom settings. These teachers are correct in their assumption that their students need to have expansive reading experiences with more challenging, high-quality literature that moves them forward and across their zones of proximal development. But adjusting text difficulty is only half of the answer, and only the first step in solving the problem. Adjustment of text difficulty must be balanced with the social context of assistance during classroom instruction.

Social Context

The social context of the student's assisted performance is also an important issue for literacy assessment. Dynamic assessment of students' assisted performance provides a different type of information about their literacy development than static assessment of their individual performance. Static tests measure how well students do or how badly they fail on learning tasks. This type of information has traditionally been used for sorting students into groups (those who perform well, those who do average, and those who fail). In contrast, dynamic assessment provides information on the amount and type of help students need to perform the tasks (Newman, Griffin, and Cole 1989). This type of information enables the teacher to design and adjust classroom literacy instruction so that her students from diverse backgrounds are included in, rather than isolated from, challenging tasks that tap their potential.

Analysis of the social context includes both the amount and the quality of assistance provided for the student. The amount of assistance can range from direct to indirect support. For example, when reading material is extremely difficult, more direct assistance in the form of choral, echo, or reading along with a taped model can be used. Clarification of important terms or ideas in a text, allowing time for rereading, and discussion are examples of less direct assistance that may be appropriate for moderately difficult texts. The teacher determines how to adjust the amount of assistance by observing and analyzing the social interaction that unfolds while the student is performing the learning task. As the student gains competence in the task, the teacher releases responsibility to the student by decreasing the amount of assistance provided (Pearson and Gallagher 1983).

Adjustment in the quality of assistance enables the teacher to provide literacy instruction that helps students gain proficiency in the mainstream culture and is, at the same time, responsive to their ethnic culture. Au (1993) provides suggestions that teachers can use to provide culturally responsive literacy instruction. Culturally responsive literacy instruction includes maintaining high expectations and goals for diverse students while considering the social context beyond the classroom to ensure that these expectations reflect the ethnic culture's values and practices. For example, students from a culture that practices sibling caretaking would benefit from assistance provided by peer collaboration. Those raised in a culture valuing autonomy should be allowed more autonomy in self-selection of topics for writing and materials to read (Au 1993).

Culturally responsive instruction should be based on the idea that literacy learning is a continuous process of successive approximations from emerging literacy knowledge toward proficient use of the conventions of print (Au 1993). From these approximations, the teacher can determine how the student's literacy proficiency is developing, what the student needs to learn next, and what type of or how much assistance the student needs to move forward in this development.

OVERVIEW OF PART II

The chapters in Part II provide further explanations of obtaining, analyzing, and using dynamic assessment information. Each of the chapters reflects the Vygotskian perspective that assessment is a continuous process that includes the social context of learning and instruction. From this perspective, the authors address some of the issues and problems of classroom literacy instruction within the context of dynamic assessment.

In chapter 8, Nile V. Stanley reflects on issues and concerns for teachers whose classrooms contain students from both mainstream and diverse cultural backgrounds. He provides insights into how the teacher can develop positive, accepting attitudes for various ethnic cultures and provide instruction that reflects the values of these cultures.

Chapter 9 deals with problems and issues related to dynamic assessment for students who are at-risk of not developing proficient use of literacy. Sherry Kragler integrates instruction with assessment by providing examples of how teachers can adjust the quality of assistance to meet the needs of at-risk learners.

In chapter 10, Lyn Wagner and Dana Brock discuss how to use portfolio assessment to mediate literacy instruction. They explain how portfolios can become more than a container for storing students' work samples. This includes using portfolios to assess students' zones and mediate their learning, particularly in the area of metacognitive awareness.

The final chapter of the book extends Vygotsky's ideas about how using cultural signs affects learning to a view of the future when technology is a new "psychological tool" that will be used in the classroom. Joe M. Peters explains how technology can become a psychological tool that mediates children's thinking and learning. He describes the various forms of technology available (from desktop publishing to telecommunications), gives examples of how technology can be applied to classroom literacy instruction, and provides notes on technology resources.

chapter **8**

Vygotsky and Multicultural Assessment and Instruction

Nile V. Stanley

SCENARIO

Ms. Brown, age 50, white, and middle-class, teaches in a rural school in the Southwest. She received her teaching certificate long before the "authentic assessment" and "full inclusion" were issues in classroom assessment. Today she has some very important decisions to make about a new transfer student. Maria, a Mexican American of limited English language, has recently moved into the district with her migrant-worker family. There are no records from her previous school. Maria told a counselor that her family left Los Angeles in a hurry to "get away from the gangs" and to live with relatives.

Ms. Brown's principal has an educational diagnostician test Maria so they can find out her potential. The test results indicate that Maria scores within the mentally handicapped range of intellectual functioning and is a severely disabled reader. The diagnostician recommends that Maria receive bilingual and/or English as a Second Language (ESL) services. The school does not have these services, so Maria is placed into special education as a learning-disabled student because it is felt that this is where she can get the best help.

Ms. Brown places Maria in the lowest reading group with other children like her. Now Maria cries almost everyday because her mother told her that the school thinks she is a slow learner. After a month working with Maria, Ms. Brown begins to question the label "slow learner": Not only is Maria good at art, but she can also sing many Spanish songs from memory, and she is learning English words in print faster than many of the other children in the class.

Ms. Brown's concerns about Maria's assessment illustrate the dilemma faced by teachers working with an increasingly culturally diverse population. Correcting the mismatch between testing and actual classroom performance is one of the greatest promises of the Vygotskian perspective. "Diagnosis should relate test patterns to observations" (Manzo and Manzo 1993, 48). In other words, testing results should always be questioned and "reality tested." Test results should be validated and reconciled through observation and trial teaching.

Research (Rodriquez 1982) indicates that minority group children, particularly Hispanic children, are disproportionately placed in special education compared to Anglo children. The "Triumph of Guadalupe Quintanilla" (Blank 1984) is a *Reader's Digest* true account of a Mexican-American girl considered mentally retarded who overcomes this devastating label and goes on to earn a doctorate and to become a high-level university administrator. Also, because her own children were labeled "slow" and she knew they were bright, she fought the educational system to ensure they would get the same quality education as Anglo children. Dr. Quintanilla, now assistant provost for the University of Houston, still occasionally hears, "You like being a secretary there?" She delivers motivational talks on racial discrimination in education.

This chapter lays the foundation for understanding the dynamic perspective, advocated by Vygotsky, on assessment and instruction of multicultural students. It examines the need to address the "crisis in equity" between mainstream and culturally diverse students' literacy achievement, and the inadequacy of current assessment procedures for addressing multicultural issues. The rationale and procedures for using dynamic assessment are explained as an alternative that merges instruction and assessment and promotes advocacy for culturally diverse students. Finally, ten specific guidelines are provided to help teachers use the dynamic assessment procedures in their classroom literacy instruction.

CULTURAL DIVERSITY

In assessing the role of teachers as we approach the year 2000, Stanley (1994) has emphasized the need for teachers to know how to provide reading instruction for students of diverse backgrounds. Five renowned reading educators (Aaron et al. 1990) agree that the greatest challenge facing literacy educators in the next 20 years will be helping the underclass of poor students, soon to be the majority in classrooms.

Smith (1990) raises an interesting paradox: More than half of teachers in American schools are over 50, white, female, and middle-class, yet their students tend to be increasingly poor and minorities. Au (1993) cites population trends predicting that by 2020, only one of two young people will be Euroamerican and one of four will be Hispanic. Furthermore, by 2020 the schools will be expected to meet the needs of 20 million children living in poverty (37 percent more than the 14.7 million of 1984). Similarly, Schwartz (1990) notes that "the population is growing fastest in those segments with which American education has traditionally been least success-ful: Blacks and Hispanics" (5). More than 50 percent of the K-12 population in Texas is Hispanic. Alverman and Guthrie (1993), co-directors of the National Read-ing Research Center (NRRC), state that a major mission of their consortium will be to address the problem of "the crisis in equity; . . . to acknowledge and confront the persistent disparity in the reading achievement of mainstream and non-mainstream students in the United States" (1). Furthermore, the NRRC's approach will be to move away from decontextualized, "laboratory" research toward encouraging stud-ies that examine the *social contexts* of literacy instruction.

Goodman (1985), a whole language advocate, believes that the goal of attain-ing universal literacy is the manifestation of a basic human characteristic and that it must be socially rooted.

> It [literacy development] must take into account the values, cultural experi-ences, life opportunities, and access to functions requiring literacy. So lit-eracy programs must be rooted in the realities of the communities they serve, and they must relate to real opportunities to use literacy in improve-ment of the quality of life. (391)

Powell (1989) also argues that literacy programs of the future should use in-struction embedded in social reality. An advocate of incorporating Vygotsky's (1962) sociohistorical theory as the cognitive framework for reading instruction, Powell (1989) contends:

> Each program will have a form and function which is distinctive. It will have the shape and operations peculiar to the total context in which each teacher has to work. Other than using natural reading materials for teach-ing reading, teachers may not have a common set of factors. Each situ-ation is unique. (2)

In other words, today, but even more so in the future, educators must personalize assessment and instruction within the confines of socio/cultural reality and political policy. Teachers will have to provide nurturing learning environments for an in-creasingly diverse population in which all students are encouraged to become liter-ate for a variety of purposes dictated by the sociocultural context.

Cultural Bias in Assessment

A review of the literature on cultural bias in tests reveals that standardized intelli-gence and achievement test scores often make a major difference in where children are placed in school programs, colleges, and eventually jobs (Stanley 1992). These tests supposedly yield accurate measures of intelligence or academic achievement. Critics of standardized tests charge that the tests are **culturally biased** against ra-cial, ethnic, and economic minorities. That is, for racial minorities, ethnic groups, and low socioeconomic classes, the tests usually yield significantly lower results than for white, middle-class students. The overrepresentation of minority group children in special education has been well documented (Rodriquez 1982).

During the first part of the twentieth century, the testing movement in the United States was tainted by racist implications. Differences in intelligence scores were assumed to be hereditary. These attitudes are still being fought today. Current demographics (Edmonds 1994) indicate that schools are more racially segregated than ever before; almost two-thirds of black and three-fourths of Hispanic students attend schools where fewer than half the students are white.

Some of the roots of Public Law 94–142 lie in the abolition of racism. Congress passed this law in 1975 to guarantee that all handicapped students have a free, appropriate education. A court case that preceded and influenced the law concerned culturally biased tests being used to assign black children to low-ability groups or tracks. Judge Skelly Wright ruled that the standardized aptitude tests were inappropriate for use with a large segment of the student body (cited in Salvia and Ysseldyke 1991). Because the tests were standardized on a white middle-class group of students, the scores were not valid for culturally diverse groups.

Test results may lack validity if certain behaviors are absent during testing (Salvia and Ysseldyke 1991). For example, tests given in English require English-speaking subjects to be valid. Unfortunately, testing of non-English-speaking children was so common that a group of parents sued a school district in *Diana v. State Board of Education* in 1970 (Salvia and Ysseldyke 1991). Today, inappropriate diagnostic instruments and procedures are still widely used with multicultural populations.

Sociocultural factors that may cause bias in test results include language or dialect difference, test content, motivation, and attitudes toward the testing situation. When the test results are used for placements or to allot resources, the potential exists for discrimination against those of lower socioeconomic classes or minorities. Mercer (cited in Rodriquez 1982) states that

> schools are the primary social institution assigning persons to roles in American society . . . the amount and kind of education a person obtains determines whether he/she will participate in the mainstream of American life. As a result, educational decisions which systematically favor one group over others predetermine which group will occupy the seats of favor and which group(s) will remain powerless . . . society has an efficient way of pushing aside problems by assigning individuals a status which carries specified role expectations. These roles are established so as to exclude individuals from certain social activities. (7)

Cultural Identity Shaped by Social Interaction

Bayer (1990), who has developed a "collaborative, apprenticeship curriculum" based on Vygotsky's work, describes the teacher or a more capable peer as a mentor, and the learner as the protégé. The Vygotskian perspective, interpreted in this way as resembling a mentoring relationship, has useful implications for the formation and nurturing of cultural identity. Taylor (1992) has elaborated on the theory of the dialogical in describing the socially derived cultural identity. Taylor suggested that our cultural identity is not learned in isolation but is negotiated through social dialogue, partly overt, partly internal, with others. Taylor (1992) states:

> The thesis is that our identity is partly shaped by recognition or its absence, often by the misrecognition of others, and so a person or group of people can suffer real damage, real distortion, if the people or society around them mirror back to them a confining or demeaning or contemptible picture of themselves. (25)

The labeling of minority children as inferior, deficient, or slow should be considered a major problem for education. Intentional as well as unintentional racial oppression is well documented. For example, Toni Morrison's (1970) novel *The Bluest Eye* poignantly shows the grievous wounds a society can inflict, saddling its victims with a crippling self-hatred. The protagonist of that book, Pecola, an African-American adolescent, actually goes insane because she does not have the blue eyes of the "prettier, blond white girl" who is idolized by the media. As Taylor (1992) states, "Due recognition is not just a courtesy we owe people. It is a vital human concern" (26). Culturally different children have not fared well under the "melting pot" theory of education, which emphasizes deficits rather than recognizing differences.

ASSESSMENT FOR CULTURALLY DIVERSE STUDENTS

The Status Quo: Current Assessment Procedures

Collier (1988) stresses that the assessment of culturally diverse students involves five sociocultural areas:

1. culture and linguistic background
2. experential background
3. stage and pattern of acculturation
4. patterns of sociolinguistic development and language transfer
5. cognitive learning styles

The major questions typically addressed within those five areas include: What is the child's dominant language? Fluency? How congruent is the child's culture with the school's? What is the child's level and frequency of education? Socioeconomic status? Mental expectancy? Achievement levels? Social adjustment? Learning style? What classroom modifications have been successful?

Collier (1988) advocates an assessment process for minority students that is representative of the status quo. Current assessment procedures include the three major elements of referral, staffing, and placement.

1. In the initial **referral,** the teacher requests assistance because the child is unable to succeed in the regular classroom. Gathering preliminary information on the child typically includes review of records, observation, parent and child interviews, work samples, testing, and analytic or trial teaching. If available, a professional should conduct a language proficiency and language dominance evaluation to determine which language the child should optimally be tested in.
2. **Staffing** includes further screening and comprehensive assessment conducted by a multidisciplinary group made up of a school psychologist, a diagnostician, a nurse, an audiologist, an occupational therapist, a language specialist, a bilingual or ESL teacher, or other professionals.
3. The final phase of the assessment process involves **placement,** determining which programs (i.e., special or regular education, Chapter 1 reading, bilingual program, speech therapy, etc.) will best meet the needs of the child in the least restrictive environment. The process of evaluating culturally diverse students is usually funded and highly regulated by federal, state, and local legislative regulations and standards.

Although the goal of the assessment process should be to provide the best educational intervention for the child, the dismal reality is that diagnosis is often nothing more than a labeling or classification process for obtaining needed funding. The bottom line of diagnosis frequently is: What program does the child qualify for? Seldom is the diagnosis a blueprint for instruction. Often the classroom teacher is left with tautological conclusions such as "The child cannot read because he has a reading problem." Also, as previously stated, minority children are more likely than Anglo children to be labeled "learning-disabled." Many schools do not have adequate funding resources for properly trained diagnosticians, bilingual, and ESL programs. Many non-English-speaking children are invalidly tested in English anyway because of the school's lack of bilingual examiners.

The Status Quo, the current assessment paradigm of assessing students of diverse backgrounds, is characterized by Cummin (cited in Au 1993) as **legitimization-oriented assessment.** That is, traditional assessment locates the cause of the student's academic difficulties within the student. The standardized tests, then, are not used to find ways to help the student but simply to legitimize such deficit labels as "mentally handicapped," "learning-disabled," and "language-impaired."

In contrast, the new direction in diagnosis has been to use **advocacy-oriented assessment.** An underlying premise of this movement of empowerment is that not only should diagnosis be a blueprint for instruction based on looking for strengths; it should also involve a shift toward looking for the cause of the problem in the social and educational context, not within the student. In other words, examiners are not just asking what is wrong with the child, but also what is wrong with the child's instruction.

Pause and Reflect

What are some implications for teachers in designing and implementing instruction if diagnosis includes looking at the educational contexts? Can you draw connections between this idea and instruction that focuses on the social and functional use of literacy?

A Dynamic Perspective of Assessment

According to Vygotsky (1978), the formation of higher mental functions has its origins in social interaction. Vygotsky believed that the verbal dialogues between adult and child were pivotal in the development of the child's thinking. Adult language restructures the child's mental processes through a process of **internalization.** This means that the child develops intellectually because adult **mediation,** or guided social interaction, moves the child from "other-regulated" to "self-regulated" functioning. The notion is that what the child can do with assistance today, he or she can do alone tomorrow. Vygotsky addressed the issues of diagnosis and placement for instruction (1962, 1978) with the formation of his concept of the **zone of proximal development** (ZPD). Vygotsky (1978) defined the ZPD as

> the difference between the actual development level as determined by independent problem solving and the higher level of potential development as determined through problem solving under adult guidance or in collaboration with more capable peers. (86)

The basic assumptions underlying Vygotsky's (1978) perspective on diagnosis are as follows:

1. A true measure of a learner's potential must involve measuring both unassisted and assisted performance.
2. Traditional or static tests that measure only independent performance underestimate the learner's potential.
3. Emerging learning processes are observed when the learner is engaged in highly difficult learning tasks under adult guidance or with capable peers.
4. Instruction leads development and should be aimed at the "ripening" or maturing, not the "ripe" or mature, mental functions of the student.

The Dynamic Assessment Procedure (DAP)

Many researchers (Lidz 1987; Rogoff and Wertsch 1984; Stanley 1993) have advocated the use of the Dynamic Assessment Procedure (DAP) in a wide variety of areas (e.g., math, reading, memory, problem solving, etc.) for children from infancy to adolescence. Exceptional populations such as the gifted, the learning-disabled, the mentally handicapped, and the deaf, as well as diverse cultural groups, have been studied.

The DAP, summarized here as gleaned from the literature (Budoff 1987; Campione and Brown 1985; Feuerstein et al. 1987), involves the following components of a test-train-retest procedure (Minick 1987; Kletzien and Bednar 1990):

1. Test the learner working alone (static mode) to provide a *baseline* measure (the highest level obtained without assistance) of skills on a task.
2. Provide a controlled protocol of assistance and instruction (dynamic mode) while the child works on a comparable task.
3. Posttest with an alternate form of original measure while the learner works alone (static mode) on the task.
4. Compare test and retest measures to establish the learner's *zone of proximal development* (ZPD) (the range from the baseline to the highest level obtained with assistance).
5. Analyze the learner's performance both *quantitatively* and *qualitatively* on both product and process.

   a. Identify the upper limit of the ZPD as expressed by mental age, grade equivalent, or reading level (quantitative).
   b. Investigate processing strengths and weaknesses and learning style to determine the specific kind of assistance required to obtain optimal performance (qualitative).

The DAP for Reading Assessment

Several researchers using the DAP have investigated using the DAP to determine its validity in predicting **reading placement,** or matching students with appropriate reading materials (Dixon [Krauss] 1985; Kragler [Newman] 1986; Stanley 1986, 1988). The major intent of their studies was to determine which method of placement, a traditional static method (the administration of an Informal Reading Inventory [IRI]) or the DAP (a mediated IRI), better predicted a grade-level placement that would maximize benefit for reading instruction. In the traditional method, subjects were tested without instruction. In the DAP, subjects received mediation (i.e., an interactive dialogue focusing on building background and defining unfamiliar vocabulary) prior to testing. Differences between the grade-level placements were significant. The DAP was found to place subjects two to three grade levels higher than the traditional method. Follow-up analyses indicated that the students were capable of sustaining much higher reading levels (i.e., some as high as four levels upward) than the classroom teacher had previously judged. Data from the studies suggest that current testing practices that do not incorporate trial intervention are likely to underplace children for reading instruction.

Teachers are encouraged to use the DAP in placing their own culturally diverse students for instruction. Also, the DAP can be used to validate the predicted instructional placements indicated from standardized tests. Manzo and Manzo (1993) describe the use of the DAP in this way as **improvisational observing,** the use of nonstandard procedures with standardized test formats or protocols.

The examiner exercises a clinical option to probe beyond conventional test protocols to induce a student's peak performance, or to uncover how the student operates under different levels of challenge. . . . This often can provide a more realistic assessment of a student's actual instructional need. It is, in effect, a way to reach a more qualitative type of "instructional reading level." (183)

The DAP is essentially just good, sound diagnostic teaching or "trial teaching." Teachers can optimize their students' placements for reading by using trial lessons. The **trial lesson** is a valuable tool that can verify the highest book-level placement a reader can sustain with teacher guidance better than an informal reading inventory or standardized tests. It can provide information about the "fit" of the learner to the book's difficulty, the teacher's style, the quantity and quality of instruction, and the student reader's group interactions. It can also address many questions left unanswered by standardized tests: Is the book too hard or easy? What type of instruction produces the most gain? Are the children efficient collaborators in constructing meaning? Do the children respect and tolerate each other's cultural and learning style differences?

The DAP for Diverse Gifted Students

The practical applications of the dynamic assessment procedure for the identification of culturally different gifted populations have been investigated. (For a thorough review of the literature see Stanley [1993].) For example, Skuy, Kaniel, and Tzuriel (1988) studied the use of dynamic assessment techniques with academically superior children in an Israeli community of low socioeconomic economic status (SES). Findings suggested that when dynamic measures were used in place of conventional measures, more low-SES children would qualify for inclusion in a gifted program.

The feasibility of the DAP for identification of gifted Hispanic students has also been researched (Stanley et al., in press) with measures of receptive vocabulary often used to estimate mental ability. By using context mediation, students were tested under the conditions of instruction, and results revealed that the DAP showed promise for optimizing the number of gifted candidates from underrepresented minority populations. When the Hispanic students were given minimal instruction upon approaching the vocabulary task, their test scores dramatically increased; with mediation, about 50 percent of the Hispanic students scored within the gifted range (i.e., standard score = 130).

Trial teaching can be useful in the determination of marginally qualified students for gifted programs, because the focus of assessment shifts from an almost exclusive examination of the products of learning to the processes of learning. *Diagnosis should be a blueprint for instruction, not an end in itself.* It is necessary to understand the nature of the teaching processes that foster and maintain giftedness. Teachers working with the culturally diverse should determine which students can benefit from gifted instruction, rather than trying to find who qualified as gifted before instruction.

Pause and Reflect

When is diagnosis an end in itself? How can it be used as a blueprint for instruction?

MERGING ASSESSMENT AND INSTRUCTION

Table 8.1 highlights the distinguishing characteristics of static versus dynamic assessment procedures, as well as clarifying the advantages of the latter. Static tests, with their emphasis on finite scores, measure only the child's independent problem-solving capability. Traditional achievement tests and intelligence tests do not tap, as do dynamic measures, the child's modifiability due to instruction. As Tannenbaum (1988) explains:

> The idea of mediating the child's entering behavior in a test situation is novel in that it revises the role of examiner from that of objective observer to a participant observer who orients the child to the cognitive principles involved in the test experience. (35)

In the DAP, the examiner assumes the role of teacher and trial interventions are used. The goal of the DAP is not to legitimize a deficit label such as "learning-disabled," but rather to advocate for the child by discovering her strengths. The test

TABLE 8.1 Comparison of static versus dynamic assessment

Static	Dynamic
*Legitimization-Oriented**	*Advocacy-Oriented**
exclusionary	collaborative
examiner is observer	examiner is participant
examinee is unassisted	examinee receives mediation
*Transmission-Oriented**	*Reciprocal, Interaction-Oriented**
diagnosis/instruction	diagnosis = instruction
separate	linked and ongoing
product	process
retrospective: "the ripe"	prospective: "the ripening"
decontextualized	real context
low transfer	high transfer
test/task	test = talk

*These characteristics are described in Au (1993).

environment is a social one. The focus or the assessment (Meyers 1987) is not on the characteristics of the person, but on the *social interaction* between the examiner and the child in solving a given task.

The instructional methods used during assessment are described as "active, constructivist-interactional" as opposed to "passive, behaviorist, transmission." The processes as well as the products of learning are examined. For example, in diagnosing a child's processing strategies for reading, the examiner might determine whether the reader uses active rehearsal or paraphrasing. In most traditional tests, children work independently on tasks often far removed from the actual tasks they will be asked to complete in their classroom reading programs. The DAP allows the examiner to observe the student's cognitive processes, perseverance, and ability to cooperate with another in a social setting. For example, in diagnosing a child's cognitive processing strategies for reading, the examiner might determine whether the reader uses active rehearsal or paraphrasing.

Campione and Brown (1985) demonstrate how the DAP can be used within the context of a specific task that is important for school achievement. They focused on the improvement of reading comprehension, and diagnosed children's individual approaches to constructing meaning so that practical interventions for remediation could be implemented. Another example of linking diagnosis within the context of instruction is *trial mentoring*. The DAP could help determine the match between the learning style of the protégé and the teaching style of the mentor.

Implementing Dynamic Assessment

Several recommendations for teachers are suggested by the Vygotskian perspective on assessment. Application of this perspective offers guidelines to teachers for optimizing their culturally diverse students' progress.

1. Be a decision-maker, not an assistant to test scores.   There is nothing magical about standardized testing; it is no more than a structured sampling of the students' performance in a given domain such as reading or math. Classroom teachers observe their students daily. Teachers should seek a broader knowledge of assessment principles and techniques. Lunsford and Pauls (1992) highlight the key elements indicative of the trends in diagnosis. Assessment is:

- *ongoing,* an indispensable part of reflective teaching.
- based on a range of *authentic literacy tasks.*
- based on *multiple indicators* of learner progress, such as formal, informal, and constructed response measures; portfolio-based; anecdotal records; and journals.
- aligned with the *context* of teaching and learning.

2. Question the instructional placements derived from standardized tests.
Traditional standardized tests are likely to underestimate students' instructional placements because they ignore the instructional dimension. Vygotsky's concept of

the zone of proximal development emphasizes that a true measure of a learner's potential must involve measuring both unassisted and assisted performance.

Traditional or static tests that measure only independent performance underestimate the learner's potential. While a standardized test may indicate that a child has a 4.2 instructional level in reading, in reality, reading level cannot be measured that precisely. Furthermore, a child's reading level is more fluid and may range from a zone of third through sixth, depending on such factors as motivation, interest level, background experience, methods used to assign readability levels to a text, and quantity and quality of teacher instruction.

3. Use trial teaching to optimize students' instructional placements. In the trial lesson, teachers are encouraged to question their pupils' current placements for instruction in the various content areas. Teachers verify the validity of designated placements by trial-teaching pupils upward on successive levels of content difficulty and assessing their performance. For example, if an individual or group were thought to have a third grade instructional reading level, then the teacher would trial-teach them at that level with a selection from a third grade content-area textbook using the directed reading activity (i.e., building background, vocabulary, setting purposes, etc.). Comprehension is evaluated through questioning and/or summarizing the selection. The procedure should be repeated at the next book level and continued until frustration is reached. **Frustration reading level** is the level reached when the students comprehend less than 76 percent of what they read. This can be done with each new content unit or children's literature selection.

4. Question the labels assigned to children generated by standardized testing. Culturally diverse groups of children, because they are often assessed using inappropriate tests and techniques, are more likely to be labeled "mentally handicapped," "mentally retarded," or "learning-disabled." These labels have derogatory connotations and can lead teachers to have low expectations of these learners. The self-fulfilling prophecy comes into play when these minority students are tracked into "slower" classes and hence receive inferior instruction. Teachers should never dismiss children as incapable of learning. Instead, they must seek to find and nurture the unique gifts and talents in every child by actively instructing them.

5. Be proactive in promoting curricular renewal. When the school fails to meet the needs of the diverse learner because of inadequate methods of diagnosis and/or instruction, curricular change and innovation should be initiated. For example, one school in New Mexico was dissatisfied with the existing process of identifying minority gifted students. Because the school was relying solely on culturally biased standardized IQ tests, no minority students were qualifying for the gifted program. The teachers decided to implement a new gifted referral process. Instead of testing the children, the teachers are now identifying giftedness through a diagnostic teaching model in the Vygotskian approach. The question now is not, are the children gifted, but how do the children respond to gifted instruction? The children were observed under the conditions of instruction. Teachers can also seek out new information on assessment and instruction of the culturally diverse in the professional literature of learned societies such as Bilingual Education, the Council for Exceptional Children, and the International Reading Association.

6. Establish a social environment that is culturally congruent with the students.   Teachers should be intentionally inviting, but not violate the traditions, customs, and mores of the group. For example, Hispanic children often respond negatively when placed in situations involving individual competition. The Hispanic child is frequently accused of cheating when in fact her culture dictates that she be cooperative. Similarly, Native American children feel threatened by boisterous, large-group discussions. Teachers can confer individually with students to discover their comfort zones and learning styles.

7. Support bilingualism.   The issue of multicultural education revolves around the question, What is the best approach to teaching nonnative speakers of English? Should we allow instruction only in standard English, teach ESL, or use bilingual programs? Au (1993) states, "Studies of academic achievement suggest that students who participate in bilingual programs probably achieve at higher levels than comparable students who have not had the benefit of these programs" (147). Forbidding children to speak their native language in school may contribute to a negative self-image. The argument for allowing children to use their native language to learn is straightforward. As Bayer (1990) contends, learning has a social origin; "students have to make connections between new ideas discussed in class and their prior knowledge . . . and they use language to help make these connections" (7). But if language is the tool for learning, how can a nonnative speaker work at understanding if the mediator (teacher) speaks only English? English-only instruction for nonnative speakers is out of their zone of proximal development. In order for instruction to be effective, it must begin at the students' present levels of *actual development* (native language) and expand to include *potential development* (English) through collaboration. Furthermore, to delay a child's learning of concepts until he has mastered English unnecessarily puts the student behind his contemporaries.

8. Provide instruction that is socially mediated within the students' zones of proximal development.   Minority children are overrepresented in special education. Unfortunately, in special programs, students often get less instruction, less teacher attention, and less social interaction. Vygotsky stressed that all learning occurs first on the social plane. Many children in special education receive less social interaction than do children in regular education, especially when individualized, self-paced seatwork is the main method of instruction. Opportunities for cooperative learning, choral reading, and games with more capable peers are often lacking. Furthermore, students are seldom intellectually challenged because the emphasis is on basic skills. Failure to challenge and engage students in materials that stimulate their minds will lead to apathy and boredom. Teachers are encouraged to provide enrichment opportunities aimed at students' ZPDs. It is essential for the teacher to remember that children have two levels of functioning: an **independent reading**

level (what the student can accomplish alone because students can comprehend 90–100 percent of the text) and a **mediated level** (redefined here as instruction within the student's ZPD, up to the highest level of accomplishment with teacher or peer guidance).

9. Emphasize increased collaboration with others.   Bayer (1990) advocates collaborative-apprenticeship learning, and Vygotskian theory provides the foundation for the social interactivist perspective. Vygotsky (1978) argued that every function of the child's cultural development appears first on the social level and later on the individual level. Unfortunately, peer collaboration is not yet prevalent in classrooms (Bayer 1990). Rather, the teacher in the front of the room as information-dispenser and assignment-checker of individual seatwork seems to be the preferred teaching style. Bayer (1990, 20) has developed a curriculum model, *collaborative-apprenticeship learning* (CAL), based on the Vygotskian perspective. The CAL K–12 teaching model involves:

- Starting with what students know
- Sharing that prior knowledge
- Building on that knowledge collaboratively
- Embedding language as a tool for learning throughout the process
- Increasingly supporting student initiative

Inherent in the CAL model is the belief that students must assume more responsibility for learning and that students learn language best by using language through collaborating, listening, reading, and expressive talking and writing.

10. Improve cross-cultural relationships.   The teacher's role needs to shift from that of "information-dispenser" to "social mediator." Because U.S. society has experienced much disintegration (e.g., divorce, unemployment, and racial strife), teachers will be expected to promote social harmony (Stanley 1994). Teaching for diversity and racial tolerance has become a major concern for the profession, as evidenced by the plethora of "cultural diversity" mandates, conferences, workshops, and packaged curricula. Although "cultural diversity" has become a bandwagon, the racial oppression that many minority groups feel is real. Teachers should therefore educate themselves about multiculturalism. Above all, however, teachers need to teach children communication skills so that they can get along with various cultural groups. Chenet (1994), who believes that the primary objective of promoting cultural diversity is building healthy relationships, has developed guidelines for promoting multicultural communities. Summarized below are elements of his "mutuality model," which he contends is the heart of multiculturalism:

1. At the heart of cultural diversity is the idea that each cultural group has values and knowledge that the others need. No one person or culture is whole without the others.
2. No one culture should be dominant to the exclusion of the others. When dominance occurs, we lose the balance that is essential to wholeness.

3. Our goal should be to appreciate differences as difference—nonjudgmentally.
4. We *must* take the time to listen to our differences.

Au (1993) recommends using multiethnic literature for helping students of diverse backgrounds feel pride in their own identity and heritage. For example, by using African-American literature, students learn about diversity, gain a more balanced view of history, and can explore issues of social justice.

Conflicts to Be Resolved

A number of conflicts must be resolved before the Vygotskian perspective will be accepted broadly by practitioners working with culturally diverse students:

- *Resistance to training.* Examiners will be reluctant to adopt a procedure that is more complicated, time-consuming, and lacks the convenience and the "precision" of machine-scored, computer-interpreted, standardized tests.
- *Lack of standardization, reliability, and validity.* At present, the DAP is more a philosophical orientation about assessment, an alternative way to administer and interpret existing tests, than it is a streamlined instrument or procedure.
- *Complexity of the learning climate.* The multitude of cognitive processes to be assessed is both overwhelming and extremely complex because observable behaviors, effective mediations, and instructional interventions are not clearly operationalized. Furthermore, in order for the DAP to be truly empowering, it is necessary that teachers provide and sustain quality instruction after conducting assessment.
- *Paradigm shift.* The theoretical underpinnings of the DAP are based on Vygotskian sociohistorical and social constructivist theories, and the dominant paradigm in the schools is still very much Piagetian (Smith, Goodman, and Meredith 1976). Some would argue pessimistically that the purpose of the school—the "hidden curriculum"—is to maintain the status quo, the social inequality that permeates society. After all, the idea that all peoples, regardless of sex, creed, or color, have the right to be educated equally is somewhat threatening to the privileged.

Pause and Reflect

Which of these four conflicts will be the most difficult for educators to overcome?

CONCLUSION

The Vygotskian perspective and dynamic assessment have profound implications for diagnosis and instruction. However, some educators will find Vygotskian theory and such terms as *zone of proximal development* and *mediated functioning* esoteric or, perhaps, too theoretical. Others will consider the notion that some culturally diverse people are oppressed and not treated equitably by the educational system as threatening, or even as leftist propaganda. However, most teachers already sense that the traditional standardized testing approaches are inadequate in meeting the needs of an ever-increasing multicultural population. Furthermore, most teachers believe all children should be encouraged to reach their fullest potentials.

America was founded on a democratic imperative (Jefferson 1776): "that all men are created equal, that they are endowed by their Creator with certain unalienable Rights, that among these are Life, Liberty and the Pursuit of Happiness." Unfortunately, for many African Americans, Hispanics, and other disenfranchised minorities, our nation's founding promises of justice and equality have been hollow and unfulfilled. It has been argued in this chapter that the use of inappropriate diagnostic tests has contributed to the exclusion of minorities from the benefits of mainstream education. Minority children are overrepresented in special education classes and underrepresented in gifted programs.

The Vygotskian perspective offers much promise in helping educators become advocates for the equal and fair education of the culturally diverse. In the past, the aim of education appeared to be molding the child to fit the "norm." Traditional assessment has served only to legitimize deficits, to find weaknesses. Dynamic assessment, in contrast, seeks to unlock the unique gifts within every child. The purpose of this chapter has been to argue that the child should be not so much "molded" as "unfolded."

RELATED READINGS

Au, K. H. (1993). *Literacy instruction in multicultural settings.* Ft. Worth, TX: Harcourt Brace Jovanovich College Publishers.

Bayer, A. S. (1990). *Collaborative-apprenticeship learning: Language and thinking across the curriculum, K–12.* Mountain View, CA: Mayfield.

Collier, C. (1988). *Assessing minority students with learning and behavior problems.* Lindale, TX: Hamilton Publications.

Manzo, A. V., and U. C. Manzo. (1993). *Literacy disorders: Holistic diagnosis and remediation.* New York: Harcourt Brace Jovanovich College Publishers.

Rodriquez, R. F. (1982). *The Mexican American child in special education.* (ERIC Document Reproduction Service No. ED 212 437).

Salvia, J., and J. E. Ysseldyke. (1991). *Assessment.* Boston: Houghton Mifflin.

Taylor, C. (1992). The politics of recognition. In A. Gutman (ed.), *Multiculturalism,* pp. 25–73. Princeton, NJ: Princeton University Press.

chapter 9

Vygotsky and At-Risk Readers: Assessment and Instructional Implications

Sherry Kragler

SCENARIO

Ms. Simpson, the guidance counselor, and two teachers at Swann Elementary School, Mr. Anthony and Ms. Ryan, are seated around a table in the school media center. They are explaining the at-risk program they designed for their school to Mr. Hobbs, the principal of another school in their district. The program began last year when the faculty decided they wanted an alternative to using standardized tests to identify and help students they thought needed a special program to support their literacy growth. Ms. Simpson, Ms. Ryan, and the other fourth grade teachers worked as a team to select 25 students based on classroom observations (students who were not working to their potential, who seemed disinterested or frustrated, etc.) and other social or home factors that could hamper their progress (students from transient families, with divorced parents, or living in poverty, etc.).

Mr. Anthony explains how he designed his classroom program to support the students' literacy development by providing a variety of opportunities for them to use printed and spoken language. These included: allowing students at least 15 minutes daily to read self-selected books and meeting weekly in groups to share their books; composing on two classroom computers and on computers in the school lab; integrating subjects into thematic units and allowing students to select the topics the class would study; process writing; and writing in literature logs, learning logs, and dialogue journals. He describes a partner tutoring project his class began three weeks ago with a third grade class. Each of his fifth-graders selected a book to read to a third grade partner, practiced rereading the book, and designed the tutoring session. During Mr. Anthony's daily read-aloud sessions, he explained and modeled various strategies (questioning, prediction, vocabulary, etc.) that his students could try with their younger partners. After each tutoring session, the students again collaborated with their own classmates, sharing what had happened and deciding what they would do for the next tutoring session. Mr. Anthony further explains that these types of activities not only provided his students with more opportunities for social dialogue, but also allowed many of the students to assume control of their learning situations rather than being silent observers or nonparticipants in their classroom literacy activities.

Providing appropriate assessment and instructional programs for at-risk readers is still a problem in many cases. In contrast to the program described in the scenario, many students are being placed in reading programs based on the results of standardized achievement tests or other standardized reading placement tests. Once these students are placed in a remedial reading program, many receive a program that is fragmented and steeped in a skills view of reading (Allington 1990). Problems for these students arise both in the type of assessments they encounter and in the types of instructional programs they are involved with in their special programs and their regular classroom reading program. The reading growth that at-risk students will achieve depends on the following two factors:

1. The assessment model that guides decision making regarding their reading placement levels
2. The types of instructional programs at-risk students will face

This chapter concerns the implications of using Vygotsky's theory, specifically the zone of proximal development, on decisions regarding reading assessment placement and the types of reading instructional strategies to use with at-risk readers. First, reading assessment models will be discussed, distinguishing between static and dynamic assessment types. Then, reading instructional implications of Vygotsky's zone of proximal development will be presented, including classroom context, apprenticeship learning, teacher modeling, questioning, and discussion.

READING ASSESSMENT MODELS

Traditional Assessment

Currently, students are placed in reading programs based on information from a variety of sources, such as level of last book read, scores on standardized reading tests, or performance on an informal reading inventory. Many tests of reading are based on outdated concepts regarding reading and measure reading in a different manner than what reading theory tells us reading is.

Reading is an interaction between the reader, text, and context (Valencia and Pearson 1987). According to this theory, comprehension is facilitated when there is an overlap among the reader, the text, and the context. Many factors related to each of these can facilitate or hamper comprehension. For example, if readers do not have the appropriate background knowledge needed for the text, they will not be able to adequately understand it. Or, if the teacher misdirects the students by setting an inappropriate purpose for reading, the students' attention will be focused on unimportant parts of the text. However, this reader-text-context interaction is missing in traditional standardized achievement and reading achievement tests (Harker 1990).

Tests that lack interaction are called **static.** In the static model of assessment, the students are tested without any support. They are then taught based on the test scores and possibly retested. The tests used in the static model have established procedures for their administration and interpretation. Although these procedures are necessary for reliability and other quantitative information, they place children in an "artificial environment" during the testing session (Barr 1990; Wozniak 1975).

The static model assumes that the children and the tester view the testing context identically. This assumption places a constraint on the children because their understanding of the task may be different from the tester's. In one test, for example, the students were asked to "mark the picture of the person at work." A child whose parents were both teachers marked the picture of a person reading. According to the test developers, the correct choice was the picture of a person digging a hole. Because of the testing procedures, the child's answer was wrong; for him, however, it made sense because both parents did a great deal of reading for their jobs, or "work."

Another problem related to the static test model concerns the use of tests. Many of these tests are used to classify students by a variety of criteria. Consequently, students are placed in special programs based primarily on their performance on these tests. Or, students' instructional programs are adapted based on their test results (Haywood 1990). Because students scored low on their reading tests, they receive an instructional program that has lowered expectations for them (Stanovich 1986).

Students' lack of ability to function on a standardized reading test can be due to a variety of reasons, such as lack of background knowledge, an inability to read the test, inadequate test-taking behavior, and other behaviors. Because of the nature of these tests, we cannot determine what factors were problematic to the students. Nor do we know how these scores relate to the students' reading during their actual classroom instruction (Royer and Cunningham 1981).

Pause and Reflect

Why do you think the teachers at Swann Elementary School decided to use classroom observations and social factors to select students for their special program? What role would the guidance counselor play in this selection process?

Rationale for New Assessment

Vygotsky's (1978) theory of cognitive development provides a basis for the reformulation of many current reading placement and teaching strategies for at-risk students. Vygotsky's general concept of cognitive development is that it occurs first between the adults and the children, and then within the children (Wertsch 1984). Vygotsky claimed that the very structure of children's mental functioning is derived from these social interactions. He also asserted that any problem solving children can do now with adult mediation, they can do alone "tomorrow." Language and mediation provide the social context for the development and internalization of these processes.

Vygotsky's zone of proximal development entails the role of language, mediation, and social context in the development of children. He defined the **zone of proximal development** as the distance between the actual developmental level, as determined by independent problem solving, and the level of potential development, as determined through problem solving under adult guidance or in collaboration with more capable peers (1978). For Vygotsky, children's ability to benefit from instruction is more indicative of their potential than are test scores based on independent problem solving. A focus on independent problem solving in testing (and instruction) highlights students' past achievement, which does not help teachers in planning appropriate programs. Vygotsky's zone of proximal development provides one rationale for a shift in assessment and instructional practices of at-risk readers.

Another rationale for the need to change assessment and instructional practices for at-risk readers is information about the interactive nature of the reading process as well as research into reading behaviors of good readers. As our knowledge regarding the reading process becomes more refined, assessment instruments and instructional strategies that are used with at-risk readers need to parallel this body of knowledge (Bednar and Kletzien 1990; Glazer and Searfoss 1988; Valencia and Pearson 1987).

Dynamic Assessment

Dynamic assessment flows from Vygotsky's zone of proximal development. At the heart of this concept is the dialogue between the students and the adult. The **dynamic assessment** model looks at both what the students can do individually and their potential growth as indicated by the interaction between the examiner and students. During the dynamic assessment, students are given cues and other support by the examiner. Because of the cues and support given during the test, teachers can identify types of student responses that facilitate learning as well as responses that inhibit learning. Because of the interactive nature of assessment and instruction in this model, dynamic assessment should lead the way to a change in the students' reading behavior (Coiffi and Carney 1983; Lidz 1987).

The impact of the zone of proximal development on testing can be seen in the dynamic assessment models of Feuerstein (1980) and Budoff (1972). These approaches take a process-oriented approach to testing the intelligence of learning-disabled and mentally retarded students. Feuerstein's model involves:

1. testing with interaction
2. training in deficient areas
3. retesting without interaction

The goals of Feuerstein's model are: (1) to assess modifiability of the student when she is confronted with conditions that may produce change and (2) to determine the amount of teacher intervention necessary to bring about a given amount of change.

In studies of learning-disabled and mentally retarded students dealing with general reasoning tasks, both Feuerstein and Budoff show higher IQ scores with the dynamic mode than with the traditional mode. The dynamic model is a qualitative model emphasizing the amount and type of instruction and teacher support needed to bring about learning, not just the number of trials needed to learn an activity (Brown and Ferrara 1985; Campione and Brown 1985; Elliot and Piersel 1982; Hilliard 1982). For example, during testing, a student may need to ask questions of the examiner to clarify or direct her performance on the learning problem. If the student cannot do so, the examiner will model appropriate questions. Then the examiner will give a prompt to see if the student can ask a question. If the student still cannot generate any questions, the teacher will continue prompting until she can. During this time, the teacher can monitor not only the types of prompts needed to get the student to ask questions, but also the types of prompts the student needs to accomplish the learning problem.

Pause and Reflect

Can you think of some examples of how dynamic assessment could be used in reading? Think about how difficult the text must be in order for the student to need assistance or prompts.

Dynamic Assessment and Reading

Although there is limited amount of reading research dealing with the zone of proximal development, evidence suggests that we may be underestimating children's potential to process prose in reading (Kragler 1991). This is especially true of at-risk readers (Gamblin and Bountrogianni 1985).

The dynamic assessment model can give a better picture of the students' reading placement levels than the traditional model, as well as instructional information for the teacher. Two studies investigating reading placement of at-risk students have supported the concept of a mediated reading level (Powell 1984). These **mediated reading levels** would be the highest level students could achieve given adult support. These levels are higher than the students' instructional reading levels and are more analogous to Vygotsky's concept of *emerging development.* Kragler (1991) compared the effects of the dynamic and traditional testing models on reading placement levels of Chapter I students. The students tested using the dynamic model had higher reading placement levels than the students tested with the traditional model. In a similar study using sixth grade Chapter I students, Homan, Hines, and Kromrey (1993) found support for mediated reading levels as evidenced by the success of the students placed in the frustration group. Both studies conclude that the key to the effectiveness of the mediated reading levels is the amount of support of the teacher and the active engagement of the student in the reading activity. Without the appropriate support, students will not be able to maintain their mediated reading levels.

By using the dynamic paradigm for reading assessment, feedback is provided to the teacher on what the next instructional steps should be (Duffy and Fedner 1978; McClelland 1973; Walker 1986). For example, Vygotsky, in studies of reading comprehension abilities of underachievers, found that underachievers could recall stories as well as normal readers but were unable to answer questions of causality of the characters' actions (Wozniak 1975). Given this information gained with the dynamic paradigm, the teacher can then plan a more appropriate instructional program than would be possible with the static paradigm. Bednar and Kletzien (1990), in a study of at-risk high school students, found the dynamic procedure effective because the teachers were able to use information gained in the study to plan which reading strategies to use with their students.

Because of this interaction, a more complete picture of students' reading ability emerges than a traditional assessment allows. With dynamic assessment we gain knowledge of:

1. the current level of reading
2. the reader's use, misuse, or lack of strategy use
3. the reader's capacity for change—his mediated reading level (Brozo 1990; Kletzien and Bednar 1990; Powell 1984)

However, the effectiveness of the dynamic model for reading placement is dependent upon the abilities and knowledge of the examiner. The examiner needs to be able to accurately interpret the students' reading performance as well as overall behavior. Consequently, students could have different zones or mediated reading levels depending on the ability of the examiner (Braun, Rennie, and Gordon 1987).

INSTRUCTIONAL PROGRAMS

Traditional Instructional Programs

Traditional reading programs have relied heavily on the use of basal reading programs and phonic programs to teach students to read. Although basal programs are comprehensive, they present some problems regarding reading practices. Basal systems represent a skills approach to reading. The philosophy of such systems is that reading is separated into discrete skills, and if we teach them individually and independently, students will apply them while reading whole texts. Consequently, students spend a great deal of time doing workbook pages, learning new vocabulary words, and eventually reading. In many cases, the students spend so much time during reading lessons on these activities that little time is left for the students to read. In a 30-minute reading period, students may spend only 2 or 3 minutes actually reading (Gambrell 1986).

At-risk readers face a "double jeopardy" in their instructional programs: (1) difficulties presented with their regular classroom reading programs, which are based on a skills philosophy; and (2) difficulties with their remedial programs. Research has shown that only 10 to 30 percent of their remedial reading time is spent in contextual reading (Allington 1983; Allington et al. 1986; Gambrell, Wilson, and Gantt, 1981; Quirk et al. 1975). Most of the time allocated to remedial reading is spent on behavior management, word-recognition activities, round-robin reading, worksheets, and other nonreading tasks (Allington 1983; Cornbleth and Korth 1980; Gambrell, Wilson, and Gantt 1981; Gelzheiser and Meyers 1991; Quirk et al. 1975). In general, such reading programs are fragmented, heavily emphasize skills, and do not lead to positive reading experiences or achievement (Allington 1990; Garcia and Pearson 1990).

Vygotskian Principles of Learning

At the base of Vygotsky's zone theory is the concept of mediation. It is through social dialogue with adults and/or more capable peers that language concepts are learned. Therefore, the role of adult language is critical in bringing about the expansion and development of children's language and thought processes. Instruction plays a decisive role in this process (John-Steiner and Tatter 1983). Teachers need to allow students time to engage in dialogue with teachers and other students in the classroom. Without social mediation, growth within the zone of proximal development would be negligible (Vygotsky 1978; Wertsch 1983).

Within the zone are varying degrees of adult support. At first, adults may do most of the thinking, reading, or problem solving. As children begin to process and learn the strategies needed to complete the task, the adult support gradually fades. The children begin to be more self-directed and assume more responsibility for the task. Eventually, the transition from other-directed to self-directed behavior is complete, and the students can perform the task without mediation. For example, in reading a new story, at first the adult may need to read most of the text. However, as children start learning the words, they read more of the text until they can read it all without adult support or intervention.

Teaching at-risk students in their zone of proximal development means that the teacher needs to anticipate and plan instruction that is slightly ahead of their current reading levels. Vygotsky (1978) suggested that good instruction is just ahead of development and leads development. He advocated the use of demonstrations, modeling and asking leading questions as ways that teachers can lead development. He believed at-risk students needed extra encouragement by the teacher to learn more abstract skills as well as the types of questions to ask.

In conclusion, the following implications emerge from Vygotsky's work:

1. Allowing children to talk in school is important.
2. Children need apprenticeshiplike learning experiences in school. They need time to practice reading "real" books.
3. Learning precedes development, so the teacher needs to provide experiences as well as model strategies that will support students' reading growth. The teacher becomes a facilitator guiding the students' reading experiences.

RECOMMENDATIONS FOR INSTRUCTION

Vygotsky's work has implications in three areas of classroom instruction: classroom context, apprenticeship learning, and teacher modeling/questioning/discussion. The following specific recommendations for instruction are derived from these three areas.

Classroom Context

Because of the role that mediation plays in thought and language as well as in reading development, the functions of the teacher and the school are vital. It is crucial for the learning context to provide an atmosphere conducive to the students' development through social dialogue (Cazden 1980; Clark 1975; DeStafano, Pepinsky, and Sanders 1982; Hymes 1972; Tough 1983; Wilkinson and Spinnelli 1982; Wozniak 1980).

Allowing dialogue not only develops at-risk students' language and reading, it also establishes an atmosphere conducive to learning. Teachers and students come to school with their own agenda of prior expectations, intentions, and understandings of the environment. It is only through dialogue that a social context is established to guide the learning environment. The dialogue also minimizes the discrepancy between the activities of the children and the expectations of the environment. It is the teacher's responsibility to determine and provide experiences that build common shared knowledge on which to base learning activities (DeStafano, Pepinsky, and Sanders 1982). Therefore, the teacher needs to establish the level at which children are functioning as well as to accept their language, background experiences, and cultures (Hymes 1972).

Recommendations from Classroom Context. Teachers also need to learn as much as possible about their students' language, background, and cultural experiences. This can be accomplished by having a sharing time with the students as well as by reading books about the various groups of children in the classroom. Students can bring artifacts from home that are part of their cultural heritage. Stocking the room with appropriate multicultural literature is also a must.

Students should be allowed to work cooperatively together during the school day. This helps foster the idea that all children can contribute and learn something from one another.

A variety of grouping patterns should be used so that children are working with all members of their class, not just students at their ability level. This not only allows for students to learn from one another, but also offers teachers opportunities to plan appropriate activities based on students' needs as determined by the dynamic assessment.

Apprenticeship Learning

The essence of the zone theory is that students learn while in apprenticeship with adults or more capable peers. The whole language movement has parallel themes in this regard. Whole language philosophy is based on children learning language while they are immersed in a culture that uses language. They also learn by using language in authentic situations and for authentic purposes, because that is what is being modeled for them by more advanced language users.

Recommendations from Apprenticeship Learning.   If teachers of at-risk students were to shift to a curriculum that embodies more of a whole language philosophy and subsequent use of literature these students would learn about reading in a way that supports and extends their literacy development within their zone of proximal development (Cole and Griffin 1986; Goodman and Goodman 1990; Indrisano and Paratore 1992; Marlow and Reese 1992; Roser, Hoffman, and Farest 1990). To become good readers, readers need time to read (Putnam 1994). This is especially true of at-risk readers.

Using an integrated approach that allows for connections to be made between reading and writing (plus other subjects) helps at-risk students approach these areas through a meaning base. It also provides opportunities for at-risk learners to engage in more genuine learning activities (Walmsley and Walp 1990).

However, if some at-risk students have difficulty learning needed reading strategies incidentally, it is the teacher's responsibility to teach the necessary strategies that will help the students maintain reading progress. This does not mean that the teacher needs to focus in on isolated skills, but the strategies should still be taught in meaningful contexts (Brophy 1990; Delpit 1986). Since students are learning the strategies with "real" books—authentic children's literature—students encounter fewer problems applying the strategies to new texts than when students are taught a strategy using a worksheet.

Teacher Modeling/Questioning/Discussion

Vocabulary.   There is a strong, positive correlation between vocabulary and comprehension, which is supported by years of research (Anderson and Freebody 1981). In the many years I taught at-risk readers, vocabulary development was crucial for my students. It was also important for them to gain a broad understanding of words, rather than just being able to parrot a dictionary definition (Athey 1983; Stahl 1983). Conceptual knowledge of a word builds associations and relationships between words that cannot be developed with a definition approach, and it provides a broader understanding of the words, thereby enhancing comprehension (Anderson and Kulhavy 1972; Beck, Perfetti, and McKeown 1982; Perfetti 1983).

Although it is impossible to teach all the words students need to learn in order to maintain growth in reading, some instruction may be needed for the words the students do not know, especially those that are necessary to the theme of a story.

Pause and Reflect

How are most sight vocabulary word lists established? Are the words on these lists important "meaning" words that are crucial to the topics or themes of stories?

Recommendations for Vocabulary. Wide reading enhances students' vocabulary development. Reading literature exposes them to all sorts of words and helps them learn basic sight words. Listening to stories being read also exposes students to new words (Jennings 1990).

Webbing and semantic maps are meaningful ways to teach vocabulary to at-risk students. While the teacher and students build the map together, there is time for discussion of the words and of how they relate to the other words on the map. Having the students categorize the words and then label the categories encourages them to use reasoning skills to discern similarities and differences among the words. While the discussion is taking place, the students get a visual representation of the words and related concepts (Nagy 1988; Stahl and Vancil 1986).

Teacher modeling the use of context clues is another strategy for helping at-risk readers. As students develop the ability to use context to determine the meanings of unknown words, they build independent word-learning strategies. As the teacher models, he "thinks aloud" the processes he goes through in determining an approximate meaning of the word (Duffy, Roehler, and Herrmann 1988).

Finally, another method of vocabulary development that parallels Vygotsky's theories is using direct (and/or contrived) experiences to teach vocabulary. These experiences can be very potent for the students (Dale 1969). For example, one teacher brought in boxes of sand with artifacts buried in them. The students used certain tools to dig for the artifacts plus graph paper to draw where artifacts were buried in the box. In this way, the teacher provided a contrived experience of an anthropologist for the students.

Comprehension Comprehension is viewed as a process in which readers construct meaning as they read whole texts. Good readers use a variety of strategies to help them gain meaning from the text, such as background knowledge, context clues, and teachers. At-risk students, in particular, need to be exposed to a variety of strategies they can use to help them build meaning as they read.

Recommendations for Comprehension. The *reciprocal teaching* strategy is one that has been effective in helping students learn how to develop appropriate reading behaviors. In this strategy, the teacher models how to do four tasks:

1. Summarize the information read.
2. Clarify difficult parts.
3. Ask questions.
4. Make predictions regarding the next segment of text.

The reciprocal teaching strategy is especially helpful because the students eventually peer-teach these strategies to others (Palinscar and Brown 1984).

Manzo's (1969) *request procedure* is another example of teacher-modeling effective reading behavior. The basic assumption of this method is that the effective learner engages in a systematic self-questioning and -monitoring behavior. To help teach this skill, the teacher models effective questioning. The students then ask the teacher questions. As the teacher continues to model good questions, the students begin to initiate similar questions. For example, many at-risk students are asked fairly low-level comprehension questions, such as "What is the name of the main character?" or "Who felt happy in the story?" However, if teachers were to ask higher-level comprehension questions, such as "What was the relationship between the two main characters?" or "Would you like the main character to be your friend? Why/Why not?", the students would begin to ask these questions themselves and more dialogue would result.

Think-aloud strategies help at-risk readers learn how to use comprehension strategies. The teacher verbally "walks through" the strategy and provides guided application of the strategy. Peer collaboration in the use of the strategy can also indicate how well the students understand and use the comprehension strategy (Baumann, Jones, and Seifert-Kessell 1993).

A strategy that uses teacher dialogue effectively is Au's (1979) *Experience-Text-Relationship* (ETR) strategy. Teacher responsiveness during the teacher/student dialogue is the key in this strategy. This means that what the teacher says or does at any point is based on the students' comments. In the ETR, the teacher guides the students through developing background knowledge necessary for comprehending the text. Then the students make predictions about and read the story. The last phase of the ETR is discussion of the story, which connects the students' experiences with the text.

Finally, the *Reading Recovery Program,* which places great emphasis on adult mediation, can be viewed as sharing similar features with Vygotsky's theories. In the Reading Recovery Program, students are engaged in constructing meaning from texts while they receive prompts, cues, and other support from a teacher. As the students become familiar with a text, the level of support for that text diminishes. However, students are continually given books that are slightly more difficult than the previous book. The students therefore receive instruction in their zone of proximal development (Clay and Cazden 1990).

CONCLUSION

Vygotsky's theories have several implications for the assessment of and instructional practices for at-risk readers. However, implementing his theories will only be effective if teachers use them consistently and interactively. It would not be beneficial to combine different theories and methodologies. If students receive a fairly traditional reading program of isolated skills, limited engaged time in reading connected text and limited strategy modeling by the teacher, then at-risk readers will be given a lower reading placement than other readers. In this type of instructional program, students should be placed and monitored using the traditional assessment methodology paradigm. However, as research has shown, at-risk students placed in these programs may make limited progress in reading.

Students can be placed at their mediated reading levels as determined by the dynamic assessment model. Placement at these levels requires that the students be involved in an apprenticeship reading program in which they actively construct the meaning of extended texts. The support of more capable peers and adults, as well as teacher modeling of reading strategies, will be necessary if they are to be successful at their mediated reading level and achieve more reading growth.

RELATED READINGS

Allington, R. (1990). Effective literacy instruction for at-risk readers. In M. Knapp and P. Shields (eds.), *Better schooling for the children of poverty*, pp. 9–30. Berkeley, CA: McCutchan Publishing.

Brown, A., and R. Ferrara. (1985). Diagnosing zones of proximal develoment. In J. V. Wertsch (ed.), *Culture, communication, and cognition: Vygotskian perspectives*, pp. 273–305. Cambridge, MA: Cambridge University Press.

Cole, M., and P. Griffin. (1986). A sociohistorical approach to remediation. In S. Castell, A. Lube, and K. Egan (eds.), *Literacy society and schooling: A reader*, pp. 111–131. New York: Cambridge University Press.

Garcia, G., and P. Pearson. (1990). Modifying reading instruction to maximize its effectiveness for all students. In M. Knapp and P. Shields (eds.), *Better schooling for the children of poverty*, pp. 31–59. Berkeley, CA: McCutchan Publishing.

Lidz, C. (1987). *Dynamic assessment: An interactional approach to evaluating learning potential*. New York: Guilford Press.

Newman, D., P. Griffin, and M. Cole. (1989). *The construction zone: Working for cognitive change in school*. New York: Cambridge University Press.

chapter **10**

Using Portfolios to Mediate Literacy Instruction and Assessment

Lyn Rothwell Wagner and Dana Brock

SCENARIO

It is a brisk autumn morning as Mr. Speer's first-graders, with bright-eyed, rosy-cheeked and smiling faces, file into the classroom. Each of the children proudly hands Mr. Speer his or her portfolio as he greets them. Trailing at the end of the smiling faces is John. He pauses, casts his eyes down at his shoes, and as he hands Mr. Speer his portfolio, mumbles, "My mom wrote a note. It's inside."

As the children are getting settled, Mr. Speer reads the note:

> Dear Mr. Speer,
> John's father and I were concerned about what will become of his portfolio at the end of the year. We know that John is very advanced for his age, and he can read several of his books to us at home. We are concerned that if his portfolio is sent to his teacher next year, she may think he is behind because of the misspelled words on his papers. Will he be graded down because of the poor spelling?

At the first opportunity that morning, Mr. Speer calls John back to a table to discuss his portfolio. After talking about what John sees as his strengths, Mr. Speer writes what John wants to say:

> I see that I write longer and can say more. I write more stuff now. We can't read what this old stuff says—but I can read most of my new stuff. If I can't spell words, I guess. But I can spell more words in the new stuff.

When the children leave for art class, Mr. Speer calls John's mother. He explains that the portfolio is used to help John develop awareness of his own learning, see his progress, and set his own reading and writing goals. Mr. Speer further explains that the portfolio helps John's teachers look at how his knowledge of print and letter patterns is growing as he moves through first grade. He then copies John's dictated thoughts to send home with the portfolio, so John's parents can look at his work again.

Terry (first-grader):

This year I'v lrd how t rit detter. I wot to do math a lot. and rit a lot. and read hordr book. I wot a good tethr. goals fur Terry.

("This year I've learned how to write better. I want to do math alot and write alot and read harder book. I want a good teacher. *Goals for Terry.*")

Steven (preservice teacher):

I plan to have my students develop their own literacy portfolios so that *they can see their literacy development.* Perhaps, this will be a key method which will interest the parents. While using this (portfolio development) in the classroom, I will continue to contribute artifacts to my own literacy portfolio.

Adrian (preservice teacher):

I have learned through this portfolio that I definitely do not do enough personal writing and reading. I need to do more in order to *help me improve my own literacy.* I plan to do more reading during my school break by checking out some religious books from the library, so I can better see where I stand with my views and why.

Marie (first-grader, dictated to teacher):

I like to make my portfolio because it was fun. I'll keep my portfolio till I die.

The preceding excerpts are authentic examples from students' literacy portfolios. Today many school districts require teachers to use various forms of performance assessment, including portfolios. In many instances, though, use of portfolios has been mandated without teachers receiving adequate information and training.

Teachers frequently ask us, as university professors, for assistance when implementing portfolios in their own classrooms. Generally, our first response has been, "What is the purpose?" Teachers new to portfolio assessment may be unaware of the purposes that portfolios can serve. Thus, they tend to use portfolios mainly as storage containers for student work samples and test results (Wagner, Brock, and Agnew 1994). This approach does not make use of the invaluable source of information and learning that portfolio development by students can provide.

A *portfolio* has been described as a container for evidence of an individual's knowledge and skills. Artists, for example, have traditionally used portfolios to document their achievements and range of abilities. However, limiting the description of a portfolio to a "storage device" fails to recognize that the use of portfolios implies a dynamic view of assessment, embodying the belief that learning is more richly and accurately portrayed by *multiple sources of evidence collected over time in relevant settings* (Paulsen, Paulsen, and Meyer 1991; Valencia 1990; Wolf 1991). Kieffer and Morrison (1994), recognizing this more dynamic view, write, "a portfolio can represent a possible container for the kind of assessment information that really matters" (411).

We have found that the use of portfolios also implies a dynamic view of teaching and learning—not just assessment. As students collect artifacts, reflect on them in writing, and discuss artifacts and reflections with peers and teachers, students, teachers, and parents are rewarded with windows onto students' next likely area of accomplishment. This fits in exactly with Vygotsky's idea of the zone of proximal development. Additionally, as students involve themselves in the process of portfolio development, their current abilities seem to actually become what previously were only potential abilities in their zones of proximal development. The zone for each student changes continually, as students achieve metacognitive awareness of their own strengths, needs, and modes of learning and achieving. Through regular involvement in conferences with students and through reading of students' ongoing portfolios, teachers always obtain up-to-date information about students' strengths and needs—continual, authentic assessment that can inform instruction for individuals and for the whole class. This is called **portfolio assessment.**

We instituted literacy portfolios in multiple sections of a language-arts methods course for preservice teachers. Our students developed their own literacy portfolios and also helped elementary school students create their portfolios. We included these experiences in the belief that students need to develop familiarity with forms of performance assessment that they might be expected to use in their own classrooms. To develop familiarity, they should participate in portfolio assessment as a means for documenting their own learning and the learning of children.

Another reason for including portfolio assessment in the preservice curriculum is to support the theme of their teacher education program: the teacher as an empowered professional. As students proceed through the program, we want them to participate in experiences that mark the empowered professional as one who engages in reflective thinking, learns from social interaction with professional peers, becomes an informed decision maker, and sets personal learning goals. Participation in portfolio assessment to document one's own learning provides numerous opportunities to engage in such empowering experiences (Wagner, Brock, and Agnew 1994). Additionally, the inclusion of literacy portfolios in our classes supports the mediation model for literacy instruction presented in chapter 1 of this book.

In this chapter, we present a framework for using portfolios to mediate instruction and assessment. This framework is based on our own experiences in developing and using portfolios with preservice teachers and elementary students. First, we will review the mediation model and describe it in relation to portfolio development. Next, we will describe our initial experiences while using portfolios with our preservice teachers using the three components of the mediation model: purpose, strategy, and reflection. Examples taken from the portfolios of students at various levels—elementary school through college—will be integrated throughout the discussion. Finally, we will summarize and restate major points.

A MEDIATION MODEL FOR PORTFOLIO DEVELOPMENT

The mediation model for literacy instruction presented in chapter 1 by Dixon-Krauss can be adapted specifically for portfolio development. In the model previously discussed, the teacher's goal was to mediate shared meanings between reader and text and to help the learner develop her own self-directed mediation system. An example was given of a teacher providing strategic support to a child as she encountered an unknown word while reading. The teacher analyzed characteristics of the reader and the text, chose a mediation strategy to meet the needs of the child, adjusted her support to the child while using the strategy, then reflected on whether the child had indeed comprehended the text and whether she could now apply the mediation strategy on her own. The teacher considered the child's zone of proximal development for this particular skill, provided support in an "other-regulated" learning activity, and then helped the child move toward self-regulation of that activity by adjusting the support provided over repeated attempts. This example typifies the mediation model for literacy instruction, incorporating the three components, *purpose–strategy–reflection.*

Use of a similar model can help a teacher mediate shared meanings between authors and readers of portfolios, or between authors of the portfolios and the text they are composing. This can help the teacher facilitate the development of scientific concepts by the authors and by the readers of the portfolios. (See chapter 1 for a discussion of Vygotsky's classification of concepts as spontaneous or scientific.) The learners also develop their own self-directed mediation systems relative to portfolio development and use, incorporating many literacy skills with much broader application than just portfolio development.

Kieffer and Morrison (1994) describe an exchange between two second-graders in which one told the other why she had chosen a particular piece of writing for her portfolio. This helped the second child begin to formulate his own criteria (mediation system) for choosing pieces for his portfolio.

We observed similar peer social learning and support at the college level. One criterion for our language arts portfolios was to document various ways students used listening in their lives. At first, many students were at a loss to portray the role of listening with artifacts in their portfolios. However, in interim peer conferences, students questioned each other and shared many ideas, which stimulated other ideas for some who had difficulty defining how and why they listened. Eventually, everyone documented multiple ways they listened, with evidence ranging broadly from cassette tapes and written notes from college classes, to long-distance phone bills, private journal entries about conversations with their children and spouses at home, to following oral directions to get somewhere or to make something, to church bulletins, jokes, poetry, music—the list goes on. By discussing what they

TABLE 10.1   A mediation model for portfolio development

	Reflection	
Reviews portfolio.	(On reflection, did outcomes match present purposes?)	Reflects on whether the learner successfully comprehended, composed, conferenced, etc.
Reviews strategies used.		Assists learner in building self-knowledge through reflection on both the portfolio product and the process used to create the product.
Projects goals.		

saw as the role of listening in their own lives, some of the students served as models for other students, who did not simply copy the models' ideas, but also discovered and applied the strategies employed by their peers to their own situations. That is, they were guided through the use of strategies by peers, then were able to modify or create their own strategies to solve problems.

Table 10.1 summarizes three components of the mediation model for literacy instruction as they pertain to portfolio development. The teacher's goal is both to mediate shared meaning between author and reader or between author and his own artifacts and reflections, and to help the learner develop his own self-directed mediation systems.

USING THE THREE COMPONENTS OF THE MEDIATION MODEL FOR PORTFOLIO DEVELOPMENT

Purpose

The purpose of the portfolio needs to be articulated in the beginning, since purpose affects all other decisions that the learner and the teacher make about the portfolio (Arter and Spandel 1992). First, the teacher analyzes the characteristics of the learner and the proposed portfolio to see what the learner needs to do to comprehend/create that text. Next, the teacher guides the learner in analyzing the purposes for the portfolio so that strategies for selecting artifacts and writing reflections can be determined. In the beginning, the role of the teacher is to provide guidance and support and to make adjustments when needed so that the learner may move from an other-regulated learning activity toward self-regulation of that activity.

In our classes, a course goal was used to determine the purposes to be served by the portfolios: Each student was to develop further understanding of himself or herself as a language user. Students were asked to document their understanding of themselves through literacy portfolios by providing evidence of their literacy functioning in the following areas:

- Earliest memories about learning to read and write
- Reading for different purposes
- Writing for different purposes
- Using all stages of the writing process
- Mastery of a word processing system
- Oral interpretation of children's literature
- Significant literacy role models in their own or others' experiences
- Talking and listening for different purposes
- Interpreting data in the preceding areas to: (1) show awareness of the dimensions of their own literacy, (2) describe their roles as teachers of literacy, and (3) project their own further literacy goals

Although we prescribed the areas to be addressed, student choice was evident in the selection of artifacts for inclusion in the portfolios. Some students used the same artifacts to address multiple areas, such as various drafts of an original poem to document use of the writing process, writing for different purposes, and mastery of a word processing system.

Other students chose several artifacts to document a single area. For example, to document her earliest memories of learning to read and write, one student provided a copy of a favorite childhood book, scribbles saved from when she first experimented with making marks on paper as a young child, and a photograph of herself with her sisters playing "school." Other items students chose to use in the portfolios were assignments from this and other courses.

Strategy

Julia (first-grader, reflection on a photograph of herself and another child doing math problems at the chalkboard—dictated to teacher):

> We were playing baseball math. I was doing a math problem. The girls are playing against the boys. I like math.

At the second stage of the mediation model, the teacher guides the learner in applying chosen strategies, which may include the following:

1. Steps for preparing the portfolio
2. The process approach to writing
3. Skill building through mini-lessons (direct teaching)
4. Conferencing with teacher and peers

We modeled the portfolio process by sharing our own portfolios with our preservice students. This established a positive climate for the duration of the semester. Students were able to observe us as participant learners rather than as expert surveyors of information and assigners of tasks. We showed them artifacts we had collected, spoke a little about each and why it had been chosen, and read first drafts of reflections we had written about selected artifacts. Likewise, our preservice students shared their portfolios-in-progress with the elementary school children they were helping to create portfolios.

Later, we engaged our students in Jane Hansen's (1992) steps for preparing portfolios:

1. collecting
2. selecting
3. reflecting
4. projecting

First, students collected artifacts that they felt represented significant elements of their own literacy development. They brought these to class and shared them in small peer groups, discussing them informally. Artifacts included books they had read as children, diplomas, photographs, papers written for previous classes, and so forth.

Next, the students selected some of these artifacts to reflect on in writing. At another class meeting, they brought drafts of their written reflections and the accompanying artifacts to share with small groups of peers in a writing-conference format. This cycle of collecting, selecting, and reflecting continued over the course of the semester, as students discarded some of their earlier choices of artifacts and added new ones.

When working with elementary children to create their portfolios, our preservice students used strategies similar to those we used in class. But we encouraged them to adapt these and develop other strategies that were appropriate to the specific situations and children. In our class meetings, we regularly discussed what worked for these children so our students could adopt and refine methods that were effective for others. This sharing of ideas proved to be very useful in getting reluctant or confused children started or involved in their portfolios.

Almost all the children, like the adult students, were motivated by seeing others' portfolios and having a chance to discuss the content with the portfolios' authors. The preservice students found that sharing what they had already done was a good beginning—and that working alongside the children, each on his or her own portfolios, was very helpful to the children. In this way they modeled and shared not only the product but also the process by which the product was created. For example, one preservice teacher found that writing notes to a fifth-grader was helpful. The child wrote notes back, sometimes outlining plans for his portfolio as illustrated by the following excerpts.

Mr. Harris (preservice teacher):
Dear Jerry,
I have really enjoyed working with you so far this semester. If you can think of anything that you would like to do with your portfolio let me

know. Did your mom like the portfolio? I think it is a good idea for you and me to put this together, however, we need some more documents for it. Hopefully, over the weekend, you can find some old report cards, your best papers, or some other information that you would like for someone to see. Keep up the great work.
Mr. Harris

Jerry (fifth-grader):
Mr. Harris,
I've enjoyed working with you too and I have a great plan for the portfolio and it is that if me and you can do this then it will work. Make a diagram (concept map) of ourselves and take a real close picture and put it in the portfolio. My mom did like the portfolio a lot and I would like to do a report on how we can guess each of ourselves when I growup and when you were little in the fifth grade and I will help you too. I will try to get a picture of my shotgun. Okay!
Sincerely, Jerry

The correspondence itself, along with letters from others about the portfolios, was finally included in the portfolios of both participants to document the processes they used.

Another strategy that helped some children get involved in portfolios was to take photographs of the children during various parts of the school day. Later, the children were encouraged to talk about the photographs with peers, family, and teachers (the rehearsal stage of the writing process). Finally, they wrote or dictated reflections about the photographs. For many children, this spurred additional collection of artifacts from home (e.g., favorite toys, books, drawings).

For some children, calling the collection a "scrapbook" instead of a "portfolio" helped break down resistance to or fear of the project. For others, calling it a "portfolio" added to the interest and excitement of the project, making it seem more important and "grown-up." It was critical to take cues from the children about what words to use and what elements to emphasize.

Even for older children, allowing some of the entries to be dictated instead of written by themselves encouraged longer, more thoughtful reflections. Some children were intrigued by composing on a word processor instead of with paper and pencil. Some children found multiple drafts liberating; others were reluctant to revise unless the revisions could be done through dictation. Again, considering the specific situation and child was the key, and what was successful with a given child on a given day might not be effective with the same child on another day.

The processes of collecting, selecting, and reflecting stimulated thought about areas of personal and professional development that many students had never before considered. They began to identify areas of strength and limitation in their own literacy development and current functioning. Personal strengths identified by preservice students included, for example, keeping personal journals and a deep love of reading. Areas they identified for further development were lack of ability to write organized essays, never choosing to write, reading only when it was assigned, and reading only magazines or romance novels. Children identified strengths such as being good readers, being good athletes, and liking math. They named areas to develop such as writing longer stories, reading bigger books, and moving to the next level in karate.

Portfolio development with teacher and peer guidance, especially in conjunction with the writing process—rehearsing, drafting, conferencing, revising, editing, and sharing—and with goal setting, directly and precisely taps into the author's zone of proximal development. A definite progression from "other-regulated" to "self-regulated" performance takes place as the author essentially becomes an expert about himself through the processes of collecting, selecting, reflecting, conferencing, and sharing his own and others' artifacts and reflections.

Social dialogue with teacher and peers at regular intervals provides guidance and support during portfolio development. This custom-tailored strategic support guides the author in her own understanding of the task and figuring out how to solve the problem at hand (Wertsch 1984).

As the process continues and the author gains more control, the teacher's and peers' responses begin to shift from specific questions and comments about content, writing style, or choices to more subtle questions and suggestions on how to create the portfolio, choose the artifacts, write the reflections, or respond to others' portfolios.

Portfolio development encompasses several levels of writing and thinking at once, especially through conferencing and the writing process. Students are concerned with both the *content* and the *form* of their reflections and their whole portfolios. They move away from being socially dependent on what their products "should" look like and how they should get that way. At the beginning of the process, students ask a multitude of questions about how we want each fact of the portfolio done, how long it should be, what it should look like, and so on. By the end of a semester of portfolio development, they have become very independent and individual in their choices, even to the point of asking us how we can grade their portfolios, since there is no "right" or "wrong" about them; they in essence define for themselves what their own portfolios should be like.

Creating portfolios in the way we have described actually is instrumental to this "higher mental functioning"—students develop new "scientific" or "genuine" concepts about themselves as parents, as teachers, and as literate beings, and also about how various events, objects, and processes in their daily lives affect their own learning and teaching. Through the portfolio process, the authors of the portfolios can develop both spontaneous and scientific concepts. The act of actually choosing and then reflecting on artifacts may enhance the development of scientific concepts in the same way as using a concept web enhances concept development, as described in chapter 1 by Dixon-Krauss:

The systematized body of knowledge, represented in the concept web [replace *web* with *portfolio*] restructures the spontaneous concept by detaching it from the child's practical everyday experience, representing it with a written symbol, and placing it within a position in a system of relation-

TABLE 10.2   Comparison of portfolio development and concept development

| | Steps in Concept Development |
Steps in Portfolio Development	*Spontaneous Concept Development*
Collecting.	Categorizing objects into heaps or randomly.
Ordering artifacts and reflections.	Thinking in complexes.
	Relationships established.
	Scientific Concept Development
Refining the ordering.	Stage of potential concepts.
Conferencing, redrafting, and refining reflections and goals.	Developing abstract and logical bonds and relationships of "genuine" concepts.
This development is mediated through: the author's own words, both oral and written. talking and sharing with peers and teacher in conferences.	Development of these genuine scientific concepts is mediated through words and social interaction.

ships, within a scientific concept. . . . the child must use a concept before she has deliberate control over it and knows it as a fully developed scientific concept.

In portfolio development, authors similarly "detach" artifacts from their everyday experiences, and "use" the words representing those artifacts in their reflections (written symbols). Through this use, what was previously perhaps only a "spontaneous concept" in some ways becomes more fully understood and more deliberately under the control of the author. Table 10.2 compares the steps for preparing portfolios to Vygotsky's stages of concept development.

Reflection

At the reflection stage of the mediation model for portfolio development and at the reflection stage of the portfolio process, several areas of concern are addressed. The author/learner reviews the artifacts and reflections contained in his portfolio, along with input received from peers, family, friends, and the teacher. At this point, the author is asked to:

1. Make judgments about what he may consider to be his areas of *strength* as revealed by the portfolio.
2. Identify his areas of particular *interest.*
3. Set *goals* for further investigation, skill building, practice, experimentation, or achievement.

At times, the author may have trouble identifying particular areas of strength just by viewing the products included in the portfolio, but by considering the process, strengths may be revealed. The following transcription includes Jawanda's strengths, interests, and goals:

Jawanda (first-grader, dictated to teacher):

I am a good reader. I am also good at adding and doing math. I'm good at writing stories. I like poems. I like to memorize poems and songs. My goal is to have a good memory so I can memorize more things. I would like to write longer stories.

This child was helped to realize her strengths when a sensitive adult sat with her as she showed and talked about the items in her portfolio. An important discovery she made was that liking certain things (e.g., poetry) is a strength. This reflection was accomplished by listening to and conversing with the child and writing down verbatim what the child said during the conversation.

Conferences with peers or with a teacher can help the author recognize her strengths and formulate goals for further development. Participating in these activities (conferences, identifying strengths and goals) engages the author in metacognitive thinking about *what* she does, and *how* it is done. This can lead to development of self-directed mediation systems for the learner. For example, if a learner has discovered, through the process of selecting artifacts and writing reflections about them, that he reads only a very narrow selection of books, he may decide to set a goal to read more widely. However, he may also have discovered that he has no clue how to find other types of books that might interest him. Through talking with peers about this discovery during portfolio conferences, the peers may informally suggest books they have enjoyed. He may, then—especially after reflection about the whole process and setting a goal to read more widely—decide that he will talk to others regularly about what they enjoy reading in order to discover possible reading materials for himself. The learner will have developed his own self-directed system for choosing books of other types to read. The following examples show how students are beginning to realize their strengths and formulate their goals.

Adam (first-grader, dictated to teacher):

I see that I used to write shorter, now I write longer. I write more stuff because it is fun to do it. I can't read what this old stuff says—it's hard to read the words. I can read my new stuff. The words are spelled good.

David (fourth-grader, dictated to teacher):

I can draw real good and I have good reports in class. I can write stories better. I can read better. You said I got better. I can spell some words I didn't know how to spell. That's all. I can't think of anything else. I can fish and hunt, but that's not in my portfolio. I want to be able to draw as good as you. I guess I can work on using my imagination more and not using "and" so much. I want to write better like Stephen. Stephen writes good stories. He's better than me.

Jerry (fifth grader):
I am good at football, baseball, karate, running, driving a go-cart, shopping, swimming, skating, jogging, drawing, skateboarding, racing, reports, and Nintendo, English, spelling, math, staying on task, writing. And not do drugs at all! That's what I can do!

Casandra (preservice teacher):
. . . from learning about myself in this portfolio, I now know that my literacy experiences are going to bleed into my literacy program. How I feel about this subject will affect my program, my efforts, and my students' outcomes. I know that in order to excite them, I have to be excited myself. I know that I want to do this and I am trying to change the attitude within myself that I developed as I was growing up.

At the reflection stage of the mediation model for portfolio development, the teacher helps engage the learner in his personal review, reflection, and goal-setting activities. In our classes, we accomplished this by setting aside class time for students to share their portfolios with peers and to receive both oral and written feedback from their peers. We also required that the portfolios be turned in to us periodically so that we could respond in writing to what the authors were doing. Additionally, we discussed and modeled the formulation of personal summations of strengths and goal setting, and made that step a required part of the portfolio process.

The teacher, however, is also involved in reflection on another level as part of the mediation model. Besides assisting the learner in his own reflection process, the teacher investigates whether the learner has been successfully engaged in the development of his own portfolio. She assesses whether he has participated successfully in conferences with peers and with the teacher, discovered his own strengths, learned particular skills through the process (perhaps something as specific as use of capital letters for proper nouns through writing his reflections on specific people and places), set realistic and important goals for the future, and moved toward development of self-directed mediation systems for solving problems he encountered during the development of the portfolios. The teacher compares outcomes of the portfolio process for that particular learner or group of learners with the preset purposes developed at the beginning of the mediation cycle. Using that knowledge, the teacher sets new purposes and reenters the cycle. This cycle of purpose setting, applying strategies, reflection, and adjusting by both the learner and the teacher evolves naturally during this type of portfolio development. Portfolios are never truly "finished," since they are growing and continually evolving as the learner projects new goals.

Roosevelt (first-grader, dictated to teacher):
I can read train books. I like books about trains. I also like train whistles. I like to get football cards. I got them at Christmas. I can write longer sen-

tences now. I make the writing on the page longer. I can tell you what happened in the stories. I don't have to look at the book anymore. I can draw with those stencils. I could read other books: dinosaur books, art books, fox books, whistle books. I want to read more books. I want to read 30 books a week. I guess I need to write more. I whine when I write. I need to not do that.

Rasheed (third-grader):

I have a goal that I learn to do math. I have a goal to do that I can write good. I have a goal that I can read more books.

Charlie (preservice teacher):

. . . another goal for me is to be able to write better. I tend to write in circles just like I speak. My mom sent a journal book, so I plan to write in it over the summer. If I write and then go back a day or so later and read it, maybe I'll see what I am missing to make it more clear.

CONCLUSION

In this chapter, we have presented a framework for using portfolios to mediate instruction and assessment using the three components of the mediation model for literacy instruction: purpose–strategy–reflection. Adapting this model specifically for portfolio development, the teacher's goal is to mediate shared meaning between author and reader or between author and his own artifacts and reflections, and to help the learner develop his own self-directed mediation systems. Since this is the teacher's goal, it follows that during the first stage of the mediation model, the teacher's role is to provide guidance and support, and make adjustments when needed so that the learner may move from an other-regulated learning activity toward self-regulation of that activity.

During the second stage, the teacher guides the learner in using a variety of strategies in developing the portfolio. For example, the teacher may engage the learner in the steps for preparing the portfolio, the process approach to writing, skill building through mini-lessons (direct teaching), and conferencing with teacher and peers. Multiple strategies provide the learner with numerous opportunities for peer social interaction and support. At the reflection stage, the teacher guides the learner in his own reflection process and reflects on the learner's involvement/success in the portfolio process. Using that knowledge, the teacher sets new purposes and reenters the cycle.

Furthermore, the process of creating portfolios can assist students in developing scientific concepts. The steps for portfolio development presented in this chapter facilitate the learner's movement from spontaneous concepts to scientific concepts through words and social interaction.

RELATED READINGS

Farr, R., and B. Tone. (1994). *Portfolio and performance assessment: Helping students evaluate their progress as readers and writers.* New York: Harcourt Brace.

Glazer, S. M., and C. S. Brown. (1993). *Portfolios and beyond: Collaborative assessment in reading and writing.* Norwood, MA: Christopher-Gordon Publishers.

Harp, B. (ed.). (1991). *Assessment and evaluation in whole language programs.* Norwood, MA: Christopher-Gordon Publishers.

Tierney, R. J., M. A. Carter, and L. E. Desai. (1991). *Portfolio assessment in reading/writing classrooms.* Norwood, MA: Christopher-Gordon Publishers.

Valencia, S. W., A. H. Hiebert, and P. P. Afflerbach. (eds.). (1994). *Authentic reading assessment: Practices and possibilities.* Newark, DE: International Reading Association.

chapter **11**

Vygotsky in the Future: Technology as a Mediation Tool for Literacy Instruction

Joe M. Peters

SCENARIO

It is 9:00 in the morning, and Ms. Adams stands back to survey her fourth grade classroom.

Joey, Patrick, and Xavier are at one classroom computer reviewing the daily space shuttle news from NASA after watching a live view of the space shuttle liftoff through the Internet yesterday. They are very excited because the astronauts are going to send them an e-mail about a collaborative project in space science they worked on with a team from 15 schools throughout the country.

Maria, Shannon, and Crystal are spell-checking and attaching classroom movie clips to the poetry documentary they developed as part of a language arts assignment. They took video camera spots of students reading poetry and still shots of the subject matter related to the poems. Now they are using multimedia tools to integrate the poetry and video into an "electronic book" that will be available globally for other classes to share through the Internet.

Brenda is enthusiastically writing a letter to a pen pal student who lives in South America, with whom she has been corresponding since she left Brazil in first grade.

Steven and Evan are checking out the World Wide Web of Internet servers using Mosaic. They are looking for the answer to a mathematics challenge problem that was found on the new classroom on-line server developed at the local university.

The rest of the class is viewing the data projector display as their student teacher, Ms. Montello, reviews various student concept maps of the plot of a story they have been reading.

Pause and Reflect
Would you like to be a student in this class? Would you like to be the teacher?

The three basic themes of Vygotsky's theory, presented in chapter 1 of this text, are reliance on the developmental method, the association between higher mental processes and their origin in social processes, and the idea that mental processes can be understood if we understand the tools and signs that mediate them. Each of these interdependent themes is applicable to a discussion of the role of technology in literacy education, as the following viewpoints based on Wertsch (1985) indicate:

- Today's technological devices and associated media are designed to facilitate instruction that is developmentally slightly ahead of the learner's development. This makes the new tools of education pertinent to the mediation periods associated with internalization. *Learning is continuous.*
- Social processes, necessary in development, can be either facilitated through or imitated by the computer and associated media devices. In other words, computers can act as the "more competent peer" in some situations, enhancing the zone of proximal development and artificially providing a sociocultural means of mediation. *Learning is inclusive.*
- Computers and other technologies have their own symbol systems, created by society throughout time. Internalization of these symbols acts to mediate change on their own accord, but, more importantly, the use of technology can create the internal tools (much like language) that facilitate learning of other signs and symbols during the traversal between stages of cognitive development. *Learning is aimed at potential for development.*

Eisenhart and Cutts-Dougherty (1991) point out that access to knowledge, including literacy, is socially constructed, and what is learned is constrained by social arrangements. When information is not learned, it is probably because social barriers or cultural norms limit the learning. Included in their suggestions for what can be done to improve literacy education are placing reading and writing in familiar contexts, building scaffolds, reorganizing teacher-student relationships, accommodating peer cultures, and broadening school knowledge. In reality, the textbook—the backbone of the curriculum in most schools—is socially isolating because the children generally read on their own. Additionally, the texts cannot present the richness associated with the sights and sounds of everyday life, nor can the text be reorganized in different ways for each reader. This is a major obstacle for the previously stated ideals of literacy education. One answer to this problem, however, is the use of technology.

The viewpoint of the U.S. Congress Office of Technology Assessment (OTA) (1993) parallels that of Eisenhart and Cutts-Dougherty and suggests how technology can be used in literacy education. The OTA states that "today's technology offers enormous potential for substantially changing the field of adult literacy" (14). In regard to multimedia, they propose that "computer-assisted instruction could enable learners to proceed at their own speed with materials relevant to their lives, tailored to their personal interests, and compatible to their individual learning styles" (14). Interactive telecommunications networks, they postulate, "could bring the best teachers from around the country to the most remote learners" (15). Crook (1991) suggests that computers can act much like a human partner or classroom teacher within the zone of proximal development.

This chapter will discuss ways in which technology can act as a knowledgeable other and accomplish these goals. It begins with a look at the recent chronology of technology, discusses current technological applications for literacy instruction from a social psychology perspective, and finally presents a rationale for using technology in the classroom.

EARLY USE OF COMPUTERS IN EDUCATION

"The microchip, in effect, has fertilized education with a host of electronic genes— and done so with mesmerizing speed" (Davies and Shane 1986, 1). This quote sums up the advancement in computer usage in today's classrooms. Computer availability has changed drastically from a ratio of 125 students for each computer in 1984 to a ratio of 14 students per computer in 1994 (Schurman 1994). Computers were not always the primary technological tool at work in classrooms. Technology changes throughout time, and each time there is a technological change, there is an associated reform in education.

From Teaching Machines to Computers

Teaching machines, the precursors to computers, were used by educators during the behaviorism era from 1914 to 1948. The theory behind the teaching machine was to present more individualized instruction in which students could not progress without correct answers. Pressley was one of the first researchers to concentrate on the use of teaching machines (Gotkin and Sweeney 1967). In the early years of the behaviorism era, teaching machines were mostly supplemental to classroom instruction, and a Skinner or Pressley machine functioned primarily as a reinforcement tool. As the technology became more sophisticated, so, too, did teaching machines. Older machines were replaced with more reliable and less restrictive ones that could better serve the student (Gotkin and Sweeney 1967). There continued to be drawbacks in programming the machines, however, and with the dawning of the cognitive science era, these issues were never fully resolved.

Spurred by the development of the computer and the need for a new associated research agenda, a group of distinguished scientists met at the Hixon Symposium in 1948. This conference on the "Cerebral Mechanisms of Behavior" led researchers to a new task of comparing the new logical device (computer) to the nervous system (mind) (Gardner 1985). The cognitive scientists began to challenge the behaviorist theories of Pavlov, Skinner, Thorndike, and Watson, and new names such as George Miller, Herb Simon, Alan Newell, Noam Chomsky, Jerome Bruner, Jean Piaget, George Kelly, and Lev Vygotsky began to gain attention. The focus of learning theory shifted from the public methods of observing behavior based on the environment and exclusive of the mind, society, or thought processes, to the new study of cognitive science.

The Cognitive Science Paradigm Shift

This emerging paradigm of cognitive science involved neuroscience, anthropology, psychology, philosophy, linguistics, and artificial intelligence. The focus, again, was on the individual as a complex organism, and research proceeded on the representation of information in the mind, at first from a serial computer-processing viewpoint and then later from a parallel-processing viewpoint. *Stimulus-response theory,* characterized by observations of overt behavior, was replaced by neural networks (McCulloch and Pitts 1943), Shannon and Weaver's information theory (Wiener 1961), and *cognitive theories,* such as Kelly's personal construct theory, Piaget's stages of development, and Vygotsky's notions of social interaction and mediation in internalization.

The development of the microcomputer in the 1970s brought with it associated word and number recognition programs, drill-and-practice routines, tutorial activities, games, computerized simulations, and word-identification software. The lack of prepackaged programs for teaching machines appeared to be coming to an end, and there were high hopes for the computer as an educational tool. By 1985, 92 percent of secondary schools and 82 percent of elementary schools had at least one instructional computer, with an average of 13 and 5, respectively (Cuban 1986). Computers continued to have disadvantages, however. Programming of the software was still a problem, as it had been with teaching machines (Ravitch 1987). There were a few examples of student control of the computer through programming with Logo (Emihovich 1989; Harel and Papert 1990; Papert 1980), but the early modes of individual children facing a "remediation machine" still existed. It was not until the development of multimedia that student interaction with computers began to flourish.

THE ADVENT OF MULTIMEDIA

Multimedia

Multimedia, or "hypermedia," as it is sometimes called, gathers any combination of heading text, word-processed text, clip art, freehand graphics, animation, movie clips, sounds, and control buttons into a format that is interactive with the user. This interaction takes place when the user points a mouse-driven, on-screen arrow at a predefined area of the screen and presses *(clicks)* the input button on the mouse. This activates a multimedia hidden command *(button)* and either causes a change

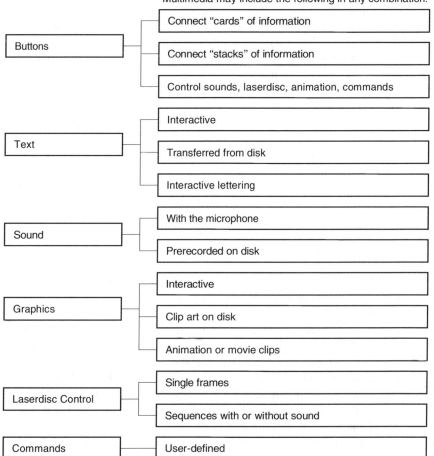

FIGURE 11.1 The components of multimedia

in the screen image (*cards* in a *stack*), plays a sound, plays a movie clip, or controls another software program or hardware device, such as a laserdisc. Figure 11.1 illustrates the components of multimedia.

The value of multimedia is that each user can choose her own path to take through the visual and audio collection. Multimedia makes it possible for the student to search for information based on her individual preferences and prior knowledge (Bolter 1990). Some educators contend that this allows the student user to have more control of the learning process. She can immediately progress or regress to control her own nonlinear instructional sequence, matching it to her capabilities. Multimedia becomes, in a Vygotskian sense, a *tool* for students. It acts as a "step en route to their growing independence of intellectual functioning" (Salomon 1993, 184). It allows them to function at a higher level on their own, as well as on a higher level in partnership with the tool (Salomon 1993). In other words, it acts as a **scaffold** between superordinate and subordinate concepts, linking the learner's prior knowledge to new knowledge. Using the computer in this way gives children active control of their environment, as with Piagetian philosophy, and goes one step further to provides an adultlike "knowledgeable other" interaction as well (Scott, Cole, and Engel 1992).

When multimedia is used with the computer, the hardware and software become an interactive device that provides the mediation tool necessary to attain the concept. From a Vygotskian standpoint, the interaction aspect is important, since the environment (computer) is no longer providing the path for the student to take, as the teaching machines and early literacy computer software did. With multimedia, control shifts to the individual. In Vygotsky's developmental theory, this is viewed as an important component in distinguishing between elementary and higher mental functions (Vygotsky 1978). From a literacy development standpoint, the better we are at effectively extending the zone of proximal development through interactive literacy events, the better the child will learn to read and write (Teale 1986). Research in the use of multimedia supports this idea.

Lehrer (1993) discusses HyperComposition as a form of electronic composition. In his study of two groups of eighth grade students (five "successful" and five less successful), he found that there was a high degree of involvement in designing a Civil War presentation for both groups. Both groups went beyond the scheduled class time and spent time after school, during study halls, and eventually on weekends in support of the project. One interesting aspect of the study was that one group self-selected a top-down approach to organizing the material, whereas the other group used a bottom-up approach. This helped organize the information appropriately for each group, as was evidenced in a successful long-term follow-up study. The computer, acting as a knowledgeable other, provided the mediation necessary for students in both groups to recall key information on the Civil War, despite differences in how the information was arranged.

Spiro and Jehng (1990) report on the use of the *Exploring Thematic Structure in Citizen Kane* hypertext to provide an advanced understanding of the film. The program provided mini-cases that allowed Kane to be examined from different viewpoints as students developed their own conceptual links between information. The individualized application of knowledge by students allowed development of various points of view on a content sequence. The learners, in this case, could go beyond what an individual teacher or text could provide and see interrelationships between the multiple perspectives. Again, the mediation provided by the computer allows the learner to achieve *internalization*. Investigations by Spoehr (1993), Lehrer (1993), and Harel (1991) further illustrate various uses of multimedia.

Finally, investigation by Carver and her colleagues (1992) indicates that when properly coached, students using the integrated technology of hypermedia can successfully create multiple representations of an idea or concept.

Pause and Reflect

Can you relate students' development of their own conceptual links between information with the Vygotskian idea of movement from spontaneous to scientific concepts?

Multimedia and Programming

Papert (1980) feels that a child learning to program changes the learning into an active and self-directed process. In particular, he believes that the knowledge students obtain when programming is for a recognizable personal purpose. This is "learning" as opposed to "teaching." His visionary use of Logo as reported in his book *Mindstorms* (1980) represents children programming the computer as opposed to computers programming the children. Multimedia takes this vision one step further, since it is more diverse and can be used across the curriculum. The use of multimedia develops an understanding not only of content but of how students learn as well (Wisnudel and Spitulnik 1994). Because students incorporate personal experience and popular culture into their multiple representations of the content, they are using the computer to scaffold or bridge between their prior knowledge and new meaningful concepts.

In a similar investigation (Peters 1991; Peters et al. 1994), it was established that preservice teachers develop a deeper understanding of the science concepts while developing multimedia stacks for children's use. This ongoing study involves students in the elementary science-methods courses of the undergraduate teacher education program. Each student is required to develop a small (10–20 card) stack for use with elementary students. The stack must be based on a scientific concept, such as the life cycle of a frog, volcanoes, magnetic attraction, or the seasons. Students are generally inexperienced with multimedia software and initially experience frustration with learning the system. They find that the language of the program is different from what they are used to. After a few hours, however, they become comfortable with the terminology and can then focus on the content. Soon they find that the power of multimedia allows them the flexibility to include various representations of the concept in a way that their elementary school students can learn. This study has led to a sizable collection of disks, each containing a few programs for classroom use. Participants can then use the programs during student teaching and later in their own classroom. Because the presentation software component, *Hyperstudio* and *Hypercard*,[1] of the software packages is usually available or reproducible free of charge, the teachers have continued to use the collection in their classrooms.

Multimedia Use by Students in the Classroom

Students can either create new multimedia or use existing multimedia in the classroom. When children construct their own programs with multimedia, they experience the same advantages as those of Logo (Papert 1980), in that they are using materials they find around them, including the models and metaphors suggested by the surrounding culture. Multimedia's capability to be programmed by the user allows the learner to internalize the signs and symbols associated with the software while creating her own lesson. This has two distinct advantages:

- Students become familiar with the language used in the program.
- Problem areas of classroom computer use are eliminated.

First, students are familiarized with the symbol system, or the language used in the program, which will be internalized so that they will be able to understand interactions within the computer environment. Salomon (1994) discusses how symbol systems, or codes, used by the media can "require skills and thus cultivate them" (126). These codes become nonlinguistic mental tools acting much like a language system, but are clearly their own internal symbol system.

Second, problematic areas of computer usage in classrooms, such as difficulty in programming student-centered software and the standardization of classrooms with preauthored software packages (Ravitch 1987), can be eliminated. Instead, software lessons can be custom-made by teachers or students for a particular classroom or individual. The fact that these lessons are authored by the students themselves means that the lessons will be original and unique. With multimedia's combinations of text, visuals, and sound, the student is not locked into a particular mode, such as reading from a book, listening to a tape, or watching a video. Each source of information is readily available and can be organized in a manner coherent to the student.

There are many uses of multimedia with children. Hypermedia can be used as a prompting tool whereby the student is provided information and then prompted to create a written response. This makes multimedia an excellent medium for interactive journals. Students can integrate text, pictures, sounds, and even movie clips into their daily journals. Taking this idea a step further, students can use hypermedia as an interactive portfolio or assessment instrument. (See chapter 10 for a discussion of portfolio assessment.)

OTHER TECHNOLOGICAL ADVANCES

School is no longer the major source of information for children. The entertainment industry, with television, videotapes, and other media, provides information as well as a common heritage, much like the print industry did in the past (White 1987). Technology can assist in student learning, whether it is defined as instructional technology for solving instructional problems, or as educational technology that is perceived as a combination of technologies used to solve educational problems (Gentry 1991). Each supporting technology can facilitate learning.

Pause and Reflect

With multiple sources of information from various sources in our society, how are the roles of school and teaching changing?

Interactive Compact Disk

The **interactive compact disk** (CD-I) is a medium that can hold computer software, 100,000 still images or pages of text, two hours of audio, or an hour of video (Heinich, Molenda, and Russell 1993). This tool requires active participation from the user, much like multimedia programs do. CD-I can be used either in a stand-alone compact disk unit or in connection with a computer and CD player where software acts as a control interface between the user and the information on the disk. Although this medium is new, disks such as *The New Grolier Electronic Encyclopedia*[2] and *The Multimedia World Fact Book*[3] by Software Tools allow users to experience information access in a new way. These types of CDs provide immediate searches of information by use of a search word. In addition, related topics are presented by clicking the mouse button to access topics. The entire encyclopedia, text and pictures, is on one compact disk. Other disks integrate text, pictures, movie clips, and sound.

Ecodisc,[4] from ESM, represents a new kind of simulation in which experiences are controlled by the user, who selects pictures, text, and movies as they proceed. This disk mimics a real nature preserve and allows the user to "walk" around the reserve, consult experts on a topic, observe and collect information about the flora and fauna, and see simulated population charts of species for up to 50 years in the future. When students use this type of media in the classroom, the information transmitted through symbolic systems can readily substitute for direct experience (Olson and Bruner 1974).

The Virtual Museum[5] from Apple Computer is an interactive museum that allows users to go from room to room looking at exhibits. Hypercard permits the student to control the "virtual navigation" through displays where they can pan, or explore in detail, any area of the museum. *QuickTime*[6] provides movie clips as students progress through each area. Understandably, this structure allows students almost real-life experiences.

Other successful interactive programs, such as the CPR video developed by David Hon of the American Heart Association, have paved the way for the CD-I market. Its small size and ability to integrate software and media make CD technology excellent for classroom use.

Desktop Publishing

The difference between *word processing* and *desktop publishing* is that **word processing** is usually an individual task limited to creating and editing text. **Desktop publishing,** however, generally involves a document produced through the collaboration of multiple authors and may contain features analogous to multimedia. Vygotsky (1978) argued that "teaching should be organized in such a way that reading and writing are necessary for something" rather than "taught as a motor skill and not a complex cultural activity" (117–18). Similarly, other researchers feel that writing is more memorable to children when they write on topics that are important to them (Routman 1988), and that writing is an intense social process (McLane 1990).

Simonson and Thompson (1994) discuss improvements in students' attitudes: a willingness to improve their writing and the sense that they are writing to a real audience. One cannot deny that desktop publishing promotes social interaction, whereas word processors can scaffold the process approach to writing (Moeller 1993). When students collaborate on school newspapers, class reports, or classroom books, they learn from each other more than what is printed in the final copy. The advantage of collaborative writing is that students use all the language arts: writing, listening, speaking, and oral reading (Heap 1989). Students are also exposed to a culturally rich environment in which they have to read, critique, edit, negotiate, and share, much like the small-group reading environment discussed by Au and Kawakami (1984).

In their studies of the writing process, Goodman and Goodman (1990) and Male (1994) discuss the need for authentic experiences in a whole language classroom. Students need to be

> engaged in purposeful and meaningful use of language, both oral and written. There is no artificial breaking down of language learning into sequences of abstract skills and no synthetic language designed to control the form of written language out of the context of its functional use. (Goodman and Goodman 1990, 247)

The classroom they describe has many features, such as a "publishing company." In this classroom, students "found many opportunities to talk, to read, and write, and to discover many conventions about how and why they used the various functions and forms of language in the ways they did" (Goodman and Goodman 1990, 247). Most important, however, is that writing in this classroom is relevant to life as it should be (Vygotsky 1978), and the written work has all the characteristics of a published book.

Pause and Reflect

Can you draw connections between the writing process (discussed in chapter 6) and using technology? Consider the print convention skills taught in editing.

Telecommunications

Perhaps the most promising development in literacy education is that of telecommunications. Although many systems can be referred to as telecommunications systems (radio, broadcast and satellite television, audio teleconference), the discussion here is limited to the most propitious: computer communications through the *Internet.* Never before has the social environment been enhanced in such a way that students can instantaneously and globally communicate with peers. Formal and informal reading and writing experiences captivate students as they explore new worlds of learning through the computer. The technology necessary to make this a reality is a classroom computer with a modem and a connection point to the Internet.

In Vygotsky's discussion of the zone of proximal development (1978), he indicated that information selected for use with students should be sufficiently within their field of experience to be meaningful, yet adequately beyond that of their field of experience to challenge them. The **Internet,** or network of networks, is composed of hundreds of individual computers linked together in smaller interconnected networks. These computers have the capability to provide information to other nodes on the Internet through a common language, or *protocol,* called TCP/IP. This tremendous amount of information, in text, pictures, video clips, software, multimedia stacks, and on-line discussions, becomes an instantaneous resource for each student who connects into the network. Information is available on almost any topic—the latest pictures from space, the works of Shakespeare and numerous other books, large data bases on the environment, current weather maps, and the latest in politics, for example. If the information is out of their range of independent ability, students can receive other related information to mediate understanding. They can also access experts in many fields, who act as knowledgeable others by making concepts clear and providing scaffolds for learning.

Telecommunications is also a powerful tool for developing technologically literate students. Any present-day discussion of literacy must include a component of technological literacy because technology has become such a large part of our culture (Fleming 1989; Wedemeyer 1991). Using the Internet contributes to this technological literacy and empowers teachers as well (Waggoner 1992). It is an established fact that the Internet will one day be as much a part of our culture as television, radio, and the telephone are today. Therefore, students need to become familiar with the tools of telecommunications.

Tools of the Internet

Electronic mail, known as **e-mail,** is generally the starting point of Internet use. E-mail programs such as *Eudora*[7] allow messages to be sent to any Internet-connected computer in the world. Messages originate with various mail software packages specific to the user's machine and then, in a matter of seconds, are transferred to the receiver's machine through *Simple Mail Transfer Protocol* (SMTP). The message received can be read, forwarded to another user, or replied to.

The use of e-mail promotes informal writing and reading. It is also an exceptional vehicle for cultural transmission. As individual students, classrooms, and even entire schools establish communication partners, they often go beyond the boundaries of their building or school district. Many classrooms have formed pen-pal associations with Latin American or European counterparts. The benefit of e-mail in such partnerships is that, once the computer is connected to the Internet (often a local telephone call through a modem), it is free to send mail anywhere in the world. The speed of transmission allows information to be exchanged concurrently with students expressing an interest in it.

File Transfer Protocol (FTP) allows the user to copy a file from another remote computer to her own machine. The user anonymously links up, with a program such as *Fetch*,[8] to the remote machine, locates, and then transfers a file. Users can receive free documents, games, pictures, computer programs, or video clips. *Telnet,* or the Macintosh equivalent, *NCSA Telnet,*[9] is a similar tool that allows the individual access to public information on remote computers. So long as the user remains logged into the remote site, she can look for and transfer files, access data bases, and even peruse the electronic card catalogs of most libraries. This readily available source of information on virtually every topic empowers students and teachers to go beyond the materials available in their location and to seek out new resources.

Listserv[10] is a resource available through the *BITNET* (Because It's Time Network) that facilitates mail exchange between groups of users based on common interests. Numerous Listservs are available; once an individual is a member of a list, he immediately receives a message each time it is sent to a central address for that list. In this way, ideas and information are shared with many people at one time, as opposed to sending out individual messages to each user.

Usenet news groups are bulletin board–type discussion groups available on many Internet networks. Its more than 2,000 topics are composed of many major categories, such as computers, news, science, social issues, current events, hobbies, and miscellaneous information. The user can read the messages and respond to what is said. Each response to an original message is added on to the end such that other users can view the responses.

Gopher[11] and *Mosaic*[12] servers are software programs that provide easy access to information. These protocols are critical for searches on the Internet. They are designed to help the user browse for information, download it on his machine, and provide related menus of information. Specific addresses for Gopher sites, Mosaic servers, Listservs, FTP, and Telnet locations change daily as new ones are added and some are supplanted. Most bookstores carry books and directories about the Internet[13] that can help the novice get started in telecommunications.

Presentation Software

Presentation software can compensate for weaknesses in content or information-processing capabilities. Salomon (1994) indicates that media in these instances are beneficial since they allow the user to do what he cannot do for himself, such as organize material. **Presentation software,** much like hypermedia software, facilitates instruction that is developmentally slightly ahead of the learner's. It allows the user to move from what is independently known to what can be learned through mediation. From a Vygotskian standpoint, the knowledgeable other (or presentation software developed by others) becomes a tool for the learner. When it is well constructed, the media act as a scaffold between superordinate and subordinate concepts, linking prior knowledge to new knowledge.

Presentation software goes beyond chalkboards, marker boards, and bulletin boards. It integrates text, full-motion video, sounds, and control buttons, acting somewhat like multimedia programs. Because it is designed to easily put information into an organized format, presentations can be made by children. One exceptional use of presentation software is for students creating active books. In this instance, they experience language to its fullest extent; they can go beyond simple written text and crayons to actual movie clips of each other reading or playing characters in a story.

FACILITATING THE USE OF
TECHNOLOGY IN THE CLASSROOM

The use of technology in literacy education provides a new role for the teacher. No longer is the teacher considered "in charge." Students are empowered to take responsibility for their learning as they interact with the computer, designing and using their own instructional materials. This places the classroom teacher in the role of a guide or facilitator, who intervenes only as necessary, allowing students time to work collaboratively to solve problems. This new role begins with an understanding of the technology by the teacher, as well as an understanding of the social environment of his own particular classroom. Teachers will generally find that students working in this new atmosphere of cooperation are more involved with the learning process and willing to take on the new responsibility.

The teacher's new role begins with modeling the technology for the students until they can internalize it enough to understand the basics and proceed on their own. In some cases, the teacher must complete in-service or self-study on the software.

One roadblock to the use of technology in classrooms appears to be lack of supportive equipment. Many classrooms have outdated computers or limited software packages. So long as technology is viewed as a remediation tool or gifted class "extra," administrators, parents, taxpayers, and others cannot justify purchasing upgraded technology. One way to overcome this is to show the technology critics how the equipment is used—that it is not a babysitter for students who finish early and need a game to occupy them, or for students who are so disadvantaged that more time spent on more "drill and kill" couldn't hurt. Computers and other technology must be presented as the mainstay of current classroom practice, just like the literature available for whole language activities, the manipulatives associated with mathematics, or the equipment provided for science experimentation. When seen in this light, purchases can be justified. Finally, as new equipment is used, it is essential to invite the critics to view the new learning environment and its potential.

CONCLUSION

The use of word processors, electronic networks, telecommunications, and multimedia technologies in the classroom can help organize student activity and scaffold the cognitive and social processes involved in students' literacy practice (Moeller 1993). Today's technology and technologies of the future are student-centered and designed to facilitate instruction through interactive mediation processes. The use of these technologies promotes social processes that are considered necessary in students' development. The computer becomes a mediation tool that acts as a more competent peer, allowing internalization of information and development of tools for future learning.

In his book *Mindstorms,* Papert (1980) makes the following statement:

> I see the classroom as an artificial and inefficient learning environment which society has been forced to invent because its informal environments fail in certain essential learning domains, such as writing or grammar or school math. I believe that the computer presence will enable us to so modify the learning environment outside of the classroom that much if not all the knowledge schools presently try to teach with such pain and expense and such limited success will be learned, as the child learns to talk, painlessly, successfully, and without organized instruction. This obviously implies that schools as we know them today will have no place in the future. But it is an open question whether they will adapt by transforming themselves into something new or wither away and be replaced. (8–9)

Literacy activities completed individually or in small groups using today's software tools could be the most promising answer to the crisis in education. Basal readers, subject-specific texts, and endless worksheets focusing on sub-skills and completed in assembly-line fashion will not promote the learning and problem-solving skills necessary for students to function in the next century. Teachers need to redefine their role as the provider of knowledge and look at how best to support the learning process in the classroom. Computer technology is the mediator, the psychological tool, that can enable them to do this.

NOTES

1. *Hyperstudio* is an Apple IIGS–compatible hypermedia program available through Roger Wagner Publishing at 1050 Pioneer Way, Suite P, El Cajon, CA 92020. *Hypercard* is available from Claris at 5201 Patrick Henry Drive, Box 58168, Santa Clara, CA 95052–8168.
2. *The New Grolier Electronic Encyclopedia* is a compact disk encyclopedia by Grolier Encyclopedia.

3. *The Multimedia World Fact Book* is a compact disk of facts from the CIA factbook and is available through Software Tools.
4. *Ecodisc* is an ecology simulation disk available through ESM.
5. *The Virtual Museum* is a compact disk museum tour available from Apple Computer at 20525 Mariani Avenue, Cupertino, CA 95014.
6. *QuickTime* is a movie-making software program available from Apple Computer at 20525 Mariani Avenue, Cupertino, CA 95014.
7. *Eudora,* created by Steve Dorner of Qualcomm, is the most popular e-mail program for the Internet. It is free of charge and available through many popular Internet server sites.
8. *Fetch* is a file transfer program written by Jim Matthews of Dartmouth College, and is considered the best Macintosh format for retrieving programs and files at remote Internet sites. It is available free through Internet servers.
9. *NCSA Telnet* was developed at the National Center for Supercomputing Applications (NCSA) and, like other NCSA software, is available through Internet servers.
10. *Listserv* is a program that causes messages sent to a list address to be delivered to everyone who subscribes to that "mail list."
11. *Gopher* is an information-retrieval software program that searches Gopher sites on the Internet for information. *TurboGopher* is the Macintosh version, which was developed at the University of Minnesota and is available free through Internet servers.
12. *Mosaic* is another NCSA program that searches the Internet for information at various sites. It is available through NCSA or other Internet sites.
13. An excellent Internet directory is *The Internet Yellow Pages* by Harley Hahn and Rick Stout (Osborne McGraw Hill Publishers 1994).
   Note: For those not familiar with the Internet, *The Internet Starter Kit: Macintosh* and *The Internet Starter Kit: Windows,* by Adam Engst (Hayden Books, 1993), are excellent resources and include software to access the Internet, plus complete information on e-mail, Telnet, FTP, Gopher, Mosaic, Listserv, and other popular topics.

RELATED READINGS

Bolter, J. D. (1990). *Writing space: The computer, hypertext, and the history of writing.* Hillsdale, NJ: Lawrence Erlbaum & Associates.

Crook, C. (1991). Computers in the zone of proximal development: Implications for evaluation. *Computers and Education* 17(1): 81–91.

Gentry, C. G. (1991). Educational technology: A question of meaning. In G. Anglin (ed.), *Instructional technology: Past, present, and future,* pp. 1–10. Englewood, CO: Libraries Unlimited.

Lajoie, S., and S. Derry. (eds.). (1993). *Computers as cognitive tools.* Hillsdale, NJ: Lawrence Erlbaum & Associates.

Glossary

abstract synthesis. The developmental transformation of school children's concrete, spontaneous concepts into abstract, scientific concepts; the mental process of abstracting certain traits, synthesizing these traits, and symbolizing them with a sign.

advocacy-oriented assessment. Assessment that includes looking for the cause of a student's academic difficulty within the social and educational context; focusing on a student's strengths and how the student learns to determine how to design and adjust instruction; contrasted with *legitimization-oriented assessment.*

assisted read-aloud. The teacher pauses intermittently during text reading to allow children to comment about the text or formulate and ask questions.

assisted reading. The teacher reads text aloud for children or assists children as they read by providing directives to help children perform at a higher level than when they read alone.

assisted shared reading. The teacher reads aloud from enlarged text, tracks the print as it is read, and encourages children to join in the reading when they are able.

book club. A small-group, student-led discussion of topics and issues related to a text.

book clusters. A collection of children's literature systematically webbed around subtopics related to a topic of study.

boundedness. Discourse used in school activities that excludes information not included in the text or not easily inferred from the text.

classification strategies. Instructional activities that enable the learner to access, elaborate, and integrate concepts by placing them within a systematic, organizational structure; see also *graphic organizers.*

collaborative group. A group of students with varying abilities working together to solve a problem or complete a learning task.

community share. A total-class, teacher-led discussion of topics and issues related to a text.

complexes. The second stage of concept development; concrete, factual bonds among diverse objects are established based on the child's analysis of the objects' traits or characteristics.

conscious awareness. The ability to intentionally regard and voluntarily manipulate concepts and their relationships.

conscious reflection. The practice of thinking about the form and content of semiotic systems such as language or mathematics; thinking about one's own thinking.

constructivist model of reading. The reader draws on text information and prior knowledge to construct text meaning during reading.

creative thinking. The mental process by which an individual creates new ideas or recombines existing ideas.

critical thought. Reflective thinking focused on what to think or believe.

cultural mental behavior. Higher mental functions found in humans. Examples: logical memory, selective attention, decision making, comprehension of language.

culturally biased. In assessment, tests that usually yield significantly lower scores for racial minorities, ethnic groups, or low socioeconomic groups than scores of the mainstream group.

depersonalization. Discourse used in school activities that is objective rather than subjective.

desktop publishing. A collaborative task of multiple authors creating a co-produced document that may contain the various features of multimedia; see also *Multimedia.*

discourse. Conversation; written or oral treatment of a particular subject.

dynamic assessment. Measuring the student's assisted performance during collaboration on a highly challenging learning task to assess what the student is in the process of learning; a measure of the student's potential or emerging development; contrasted with *static assessment.*

e-mail. Messages sent from and received on computers connected to the Internet.

egocentric speech. Young children speaking aloud to themselves without reference to an audience.

emergent literacy. A stage of literacy growth associated with preschool and kindergarten children; a continuous period of the young child's literacy development that includes his attempts to interpret or communicate using symbols.

extended texts. A completed written composition that has been drafted, revised, and edited; examples: book critique, comparison paper.

frustration reading level. The grade level of text in which students comprehend less than 75 percent of what they read and have an oral reading accuracy rate of less than 90 percent.

genuine concepts. Abstract, systematized knowledge common to a particular culture; mature concepts.

goal interdependence. Small groups of children working together to achieve a goal, with each group member held accountable for the end results of a task or project.

graphic organizers. Visual diagrams that portray the relationships among concepts. Examples: tree diagram, T-bar chart, discussion web.

guided participation. Instruction that uses modeling with verbal interactions, which provides the teacher with feedback for adjusting support during instruction and students with feedback to develop their conscious awareness of their own learning.

heaps. The first stage of concept development; objects grouped into random categories.

improvisational observing. The use of nonstandard dynamic assessment procedures with standardized testing formats and protocols to determine students' instructional reading levels.

independent reading level. The grade level of text at which students comprehend 90–100 percent of what they read and have a 99 percent accuracy rate in oral reading.

informal reading inventory (IRI). A series of graded passages with accompanying comprehension questions used to identify the student's instructional reading level.

inner speech. Soundless speech used by older children and adults to structure and control their thinking.

instructional reading level. The grade level of text at which students comprehend 75–89 percent of what they read and have a 95–99 percent accuracy rate in oral reading.

instrumental method. An experimental method in which the subject's behavior is analyzed while she is engaged in a highly difficult problem-solving task.

interactive compact disk (CD-I). A medium that can hold computer software, 100,000 still images or pages of text, two hours of audio, or an hour of video, providing the user with immediate searches of information.

internalization. The progressive transfer from external social activity among humans mediated by signs to internal control by the individual.

Internet. A network of networks of computer communications; hundreds of individual computers linked together in smaller interconnected networks.

interpsychological. External social activity that includes dialogue or communication between two or more humans.

intersubjectivity. A shared social reality that occurs when participants of an activity share the same definition of the situation; see also *situation definition*.

intrapsychological. Internal mental behavior that developed previously within a context of social dialogue during external activity.

language experience approach (LEA). A knowledgeable other records children's dictation about a topic.

learner-centered. Classroom instruction that emphasizes the child's perspective and active engagement in meaningful literacy activities.

legitimization-oriented assessment. Assessment that locates the cause of a student's academic difficulty within the student; contrasted with *advocacy-oriented assessment*.

mediated reading levels. The grade levels of texts above the student's instructional reading level at which the student can read and comprehend with assistance.

mediation. In dynamic assessment, adult-guided social interaction used to determine the child's levels of assisted problem-solving performance.

mediation model for literacy instruction. A model used to guide teachers' decisions on planning instruction and on adjusting the amount and type of support they provide students during instruction.

metalinguistic awareness. A conscious awareness of the structure and function of printed and spoken language; the ability to reflect on language.

mini-lesson. A teacher-directed instructional activity used to provide increased assistance for students by modeling or providing more explicit directives on how to perform a particular skill or use a particular strategy.

modeling interpretation of the zone of proximal development. During instruction, the teacher assumes a regulative role in a learning activity that the student gradually internalizes through active participation in dialogue; transition from other-regulated to self-regulated behavior. Example: reciprocal teaching.

modeling reading. The demonstration of reading behaviors using physical movements and verbal explanations.

monitoring strategies. Instructional activities that develop students' conscious awareness and deliberate control of their thinking. Examples: summarizing text information, prediction, Question-Answer-Relationships.

more knowledgeable other. A person who can complete a particular learning task and lead another in completing the task by providing directives through dialogue. Examples: a teacher, a parent, or capable peer.

multimedia. Any combination of heading text, word-processing text, clip art, freehand graphics, animation, movie clips, sounds, and control buttons into a format that is interactive with the user.

natural mental behavior. Lower biological forms of mental behavior found in humans and some animals. Examples: elementary perception, memory, attention.

optimum moments. The points during instruction at which a general principle needed to solve a problem or complete a learning task becomes clear to the learner; the points at which assistance is relinquished or shifts to what the learner needs to know next.

organizational patterns. Physical arrangement or groupings of students for instruction. Examples: individuals, pairs, small groups, whole class.

organizational tools. Record-keeping devices used to gather and organize information about students' learning. Examples: surveys, conference logs.

peer tutoring. A high achiever or older child tutors a lower achiever or younger child.

placement. Determining which special educational program will best meet the needs of a student who is not performing successfully in a classroom.

portfolio assessment. Multiple sources of evidence of a student's learning selected, collected, reflected on, and discussed over time in relevant settings.

potential concepts. The third stage of concept development, which lasts through the years of formal schooling; the transition period when logical bonds and relationships of abstract concepts are being formed.

prediction. Making a hypothesis about what might occur in a story or what information might be included in upcoming text.

presentation software. Computer software that allows the user to put information into an organized format for presentation using text, full-motion video, sounds, and control buttons.

psychological tools. Signs used by humans to carry out conversation, solve problems, or other mental and social activities. Examples: speech, print, numbers, forms, pictures, graphs.

reader-text analysis. Identifying and matching the informational and structural characteristics of a text with students' personal knowledge about the information and the thought processes they need to acquire the text information.

reading logs. Students' individual writings in response to texts they read, usually kept in the form of a journal.

reading placement. Matching students with appropriate reading tasks and materials; placing students for instruction in the grade-level text that coincides with their instructional reading levels.

reader response strategies. Instructional activities in which readers use various media (art, print, video, drama) to create unique individual or similar interpretations of text and share meanings.

referral. The teacher's request for assistance for a child who is unable to perform successfully in the classroom.

reflective understanding. The teacher's knowledge about students' perceptions of their own learning, usually obtained through classroom observation or questioning students about what they think, feel, or are doing during a learning task.

rehearsal of text. Talking children through a text before reading by providing language to focus attention on important text aspects, and showing readers what they need to think about as the text is read.

scaffold/scaffolding. The teacher or adult structures a learning task and provides directives and clues using dialogue to guide the learner's participation in the learning task.

scientific concepts. Abstract, systematized knowledge common to a particular culture, usually learned by children during formal schooling; also interpreted as "schooled" concepts.

semiotic flexibility. An adult's shifts in speech, during adult-child dialogue, that provide responses or directives that guide the child in creating understanding of a learning task and figuring out how to solve a problem.

semiotic mediation. The transformation of natural, lower forms of mental behavior to higher, cultural forms of behavior through the use of signs.

sign. Something that represents an object, a set of objects, or a phenomenon; a symbol with a specific meaning that has evolved in the history of a culture. Examples: a word, a picture, a number, a dollar sign.

sign system. A set of signs and a system of rules regulating how to combine these signs.

situation definition. The way participants represent an activity including the setting, objects, events, and action patterns involved in the activity; a participant's personal understanding of an activity.

socially meaningful activity. Humans using symbols such as language to interact or share meaning with one another.

sociocultural situatedness. The emergence and development of human thought in the context of activities within specific social and cultural settings.

sociohistorical theory. Vygotsky's approach to psychology; the study of human development in the social and historical context within which it occurs; the study of how the developing individual acquires advanced forms of thinking from his culture through social interaction with others.

spontaneous concepts. Unstable, concrete knowledge gained through direct everyday experiences; see also *heaps* and *complexes.*

staffing. Comprehensive assessment of a student conducted by a professional, such as a psychologist or diagnostician, for gathering information about why the student is not performing successfully in a classroom.

static assessment. Measuring the student's individual performance to assess what the student has learned; a measure of the student's actual development; contrasted with *dynamic assessment.*

systematicity. The system of relationships embedded in texts. Example: the relationship between addition and subtraction.

text-based realities. Qualities of discourse used in school activities that are created and maintained through language or other means. Examples: depersonalization, boundedness, conscious reflection, systematicity.

text-mediational interpretation of the zone of proximal development. During instruction, texts are used to encourage student thinking using dialogue. Examples: predicting outcomes, describing, generating hypotheses, making causal inferences, planning, generalizing, concluding.

think-sheet. A sheet with specific questions about a text to which students write a response.

trial lesson. Teaching a sample lesson of a text to informally analyze the match between students' reading performance and text difficulty; used to verify reading placement obtained through static testing procedures.

word processing. An individual task limited to creating and editing text.

zone of proximal development (ZPD). The gap between the child's current or actual level of development determined by independent problem solving and the child's emerging or potential level of development determined by problem solving supported by an adult or through collaboration with more capable peers.

References

INTRODUCTION TO PART I

Blanck, G. (1990). Vygotsky: The man and his cause. In L. C. Moll (ed.), *Vygotsky and education: Instructional implications and applications of sociohistorical psychology,* pp. 31–58. New York: Cambridge University Press.

Downing, J. (1988). Comparative perspectives on the development of cognitive psychology of reading in the USSR. In J. Downing (ed.), *Cognitive psychology and reading in the U.S.S.R.* Amsterdam: North-Holland.

Kozulin, A. (1986). Vygotsky in context. In L. S. Vygotsky, *Thought and language* (A. Kozulin, trans.), pp. xi-lvi. Cambridge, MA: MIT Press.

Leontiev, A. N., and A. R. Luria. (1968). The psychological ideas of L. S. Vygotskii. In B. B. Wolman (ed.), *The historical roots of contemporary psychology,* pp. 338–367. New York: Harper & Row.

Moll, L. C. (1990). Introduction. In L. C. Moll (ed.), *Vygotsky and education: Instructional implications and applications of sociohistorical psychology,* pp. 1–27. New York: Cambridge University Press.

Rosa, A., and I. Montero. (1990). The historical context of Vygotsky's work: A sociohistorical approach. In L. C. Moll (ed.), *Vygotsky and education: Instructional implications and applications of sociohistorical psychology,* pp. 59–88. New York: Cambridge University Press.

Vygotsky, L. S. (1962). *Thought and language* (E. Hanfmann and G. Vakar, eds. and trans.). Cambridge, MA: MIT Press.

Yaroshevsky, M. (1989). *Lev Vygotsky* (Sergei Syrovatkin, trans.). Moscow, Russia: Progress Publisher.

CHAPTER 1

Anderson, R. C., and P. D. Pearson. (1984). A schema-theoretic view of basic processes in reading comprehension. In P. D. Pearson, R. Barr, M. S. Kamil, and P. Mosenthal (eds.), *Handbook of reading research,* Vol. 1, pp. 225–253. White Plains, NY: Longman.

Bozhovich, L., and L. Slavina. (1972). Fifty years of Soviet psychology of upbringing. In J. Brozek and D. Slobin (eds.), *Psychology in the USSR: An historical perspective,* pp. 161–180. White Plains, NY: International Arts and Sciences Press.

Bruner, J. (1986). *Actual minds, possible worlds.* Cambridge, MA: Harvard University Press.

Clay, M. M. (1966). *Emergent reading behavior.* Unpublished doctoral dissertation, University of Auckland, Auckland, New Zealand.

Cole, M. (1990). Cognitive development and formal schooling: The evidence from cross-cultural research. In L. C. Moll (ed.), *Vygotsky and education: Instructional implications and applications of sociohistorical psychology.* New York: Cambridge University Press.

Dalgliesh, A. (1954). *The courage of Sarah Noble.* New York: Macmillan.

Dixon-Krauss, L. (1994). *A mediation model for dynamic literacy instruction.* Paper presented at the International Conference on L. S. Vygotsky and the Contemporary Human Sciences, Moscow, Russia.

Edelsky, C., B. Altwerger., and B. Flores. (1991). *Whole language: What's the difference?* Portsmouth, NH: Heinemann.

Goodman, Y. M., and K. S. Goodman. (1990). Vygotsky in a whole language perspective. In L. C. Moll (ed.), *Vygotsky and education: Instructional implications and applications of sociohistorical psychology.* New York: Cambridge University Press.

Griffin, P., and M. Cole. (1984). Current activity for the future: The zo-ped. In B. Rogoff and J. V. Wertsch (eds.), *Children's learning in the zone of proximal development,* pp. 45–64. San Francisco: Jossey-Bass.

Harste, J. (1990). Jerry Harste speaks on reading and writing. *Reading Teacher* 43: 316–318.

Leontiev, A. N. (1981). The problem of activity in psychology. In J. V. Wertsch (ed.), *The concept of activity in Soviet psychology,* pp. 37–71. Armonk, NY: Sharpe.

Luria, A. R. (1976). *Cognitive development.* Cambridge, MA: Harvard University Press.

———. (1979). *The making of mind: A personal account of Soviet psychology* (M. Cole and S. Cole, eds.). Cambridge, MA: Harvard University Press.

McCaslin, M. M. (1989). Whole language: Theory, instruction, and future implementation. *Elementary School Journal* 90: 223–229.

Minick, N. (1987). Implications of Vygotsky's theories for dynamic assessment. In C. S. Lidz (ed.), *Dynamic assessment: An interactional approach to evaluating learning potential,* pp. 116–140. New York: Guilford Press.

Moll, L. C. (1990). Introduction. In L. C. Moll (ed.), *Vygotsky and education: Instructional implications and applications of sociohistorical psychology,* pp. 1–27. New York: Cambridge University Press.

Pearson, P. D. (1993). Teaching and learning reading: A research perspective. *Language arts* 70: 502–511.

Powell, W. R. (1993). *Classroom literacy instruction and assessment from the Vygotskian perspective.* Paper presented at the 38th annual convention of the International Reading Association, San Antonio, TX.

Scribner, S., and M. Cole. (1981). *The psychology of literacy.* Cambridge, MA: Harvard University Press.

Sulzby, E., and W. H. Teale. (1991). Emergent literacy. In R. Barr, M. S. Kamil, P. Mosenthal, and P. D. Pearson (eds.), *Handbook of reading research,* Vol. 2, pp. 727–757. New York: Longman.

Teale, W. H. (1988). Developmentally appropriate assessment of reading and writing in the early childhood classroom. *Elementary School Journal* 89: 173–183.

Valsiner, J. (1988). *Developmental psychology in the Soviet Union.* Bloomington: Indiana University Press.

Vygotsky, L. S. (1962). *Thought and language* (E. Hanfmann and G. Vakar, eds. and trans.). Cambridge, MA: MIT Press.

———. (1978). *Mind in society: The development of higher psychological processes* (M. Cole, V. John-Steiner, S. Scribner, and E. Souberman, eds.). Cambridge, MA: Harvard University Press.

———. (1981). The genesis of higher mental functions. In J. V. Wertsch (ed.), *The concept of activity in Soviet psychology,* pp. 144–188. Armonk, NY: Sharpe.

———. (1986). *Thought and language* (A. Kozulin, ed.). Cambridge, MA: MIT Press.

Wertsch, J. V. (1980). The significance of dialogue in Vygotsky's account of social, egocentric, and inner speech. *Contemporary Educational Psychology* 5: 150–162.

———. (1984). The zone of proximal development: Some conceptual issues. In B. Rogoff and J. V. Wertsch (eds.), *Children's learning in the zone of proximal development,* pp. 7–18. San Francisco: Jossey-Bass.

CHAPTER 2

Clay, M. (1991). *Becoming literate: The construction of inner control.* Portsmouth, NH: Heinemann.

Combs, M. (in press). *Developing competent readers and writers in the primary grades, K–4.* Englewood Cliffs, NJ: Prentice Hall.

Dixon-Krauss, L. A. (1994, September). *A mediation model for dynamic literacy assessment.* Paper presented at the International Conference on L. S. Vygotsky and the Contemporary Human Sciences in Moscow, Russia.

Holdaway, D. (1979). *Foundations of literacy.* Portsmouth, NH: Heinemann.

Powell, W. R. (1993). *Classroom literacy instruction and assessment from the Vygotskian perspective.* Paper presented at the 38th annual convention of the International Reading Association, San Antonio, TX.

Temple, C., R. Nathan, F. Temple, and N. A. Burris. (1993). *The beginnings of writing.* Boston: Allyn & Bacon.

Vygotsky, L. S. (1981). The genesis of higher mental functions. In J. V. Wertsch (ed.), *The concept of activity in Soviet psychology,* pp.144–188. Armonk, NY: Sharpe.

———. (1986). *Thought and language* (A. Kozulin, ed.). Cambridge, MA: MIT Press.

Wertsch, J. V. (1984). The zone of proximal development: Some conceptual issues. In B. Rogoff and J. V. Wertsch (eds.), *Children's learning in the zone of proximal development,* pp. 7–18. San Francisco: Jossey-Bass.

———. (ed.). (1985). *Vygotsky and the social formation of mind.* Cambridge, MA: Harvard University Press.

Wood, A. and D. Wood. (1984). *The napping house.* San Diego, CA: Harcourt Brace Jovanovich.

CHAPTER 3

Aardema, V. (1975). *Why mosquitoes buzz in people's ears: A west African tale.* New York: Dial Press.

Alverman, D. E. (1991). The discussion web: A graphic aid for learning across the curriculum. *Reading Teacher* 45: 92–99.

Anderson, T., and B. Ambruster. (1984). Content area textbooks. In R. C. Anderson, J. Osborn, and R. J. Tierney (eds.), *Learning to read in American schools: Basal readers and content texts,* pp. 193–226. Hillsdale, NJ: Lawrence Erlbaum & Associates.

Atwell, N. (1987). *In the Middle.* Portsmouth, NH: Heinemann.

Au, K. H. (1990). Changes in a teacher's views of interactive comprehension instruction. In L. C. Moll (ed.), *Vygotsky and education: Instructional implications and applications of sociohistorical psychology,* pp. 271–286. Cambridge, MA: Cambridge University Press.

Brozo, W. G., and C. M. Tomlinson. (1986). Literature: The lively content courses. *The Reading Teacher* 40: 288–293.

Crook, P. R., and B. A. Lehman. (1991). Themes for two voices: Children's fiction and nonfiction as "whole literature." *Language Arts* 68: 34–39.

Dixon [Krauss], L., N. V. Stanley, and W. R. Powell. (1984). *Emergent reading levels in expository and narrative materials.* Paper presented at the 33d Annual National Reading Conference, Austin, TX. (ERIC Document Reproduction Service No. ED 240 541).

Gallimore, R., and R. Tharp. (1990). Teaching mind in society: Teaching, schooling, and literate discourse. In L. C. Moll (ed.), *Vygotsky and education: Instructional implications and applications of sociohistorical psychology,* pp. 175–205. Cambridge, MA: Cambridge University Press.

Kellogg, S. (1988). *Johnny Appleseed: A tall tale retold.* New York: Scholastic.

Kragler, S. (1991). Mediated reading levels of chapter I third grade students. *Reading Improvement* 28: 121–125.

Krauss, L. D. (1992). Whole language: Bridging the gap from spontaneous to scientific concepts. *Journal of Reading Education* 18: 16–26.

———. (1995). Partner reading and writing: Peer social dialogue and the zone of proximal development. *Journal of Reading Behavior* 27(2).

Levstik, L. S. (1990). Research directions mediating content through literary texts. *Language Arts* 67: 848–853.

Maclachlan, P. (1989). Through Grandpa's Eyes. In *Under the moon level 5,* pp. 57–66. Glenview, IL: Scott Foresman & Company.

Mason, J., J. Stewart, and D. Dunning. (1986). What kindergarten children know about reading. In T. Rapheal (ed.), *The context of school-based literacy,* pp. 97–114. New York: Random House.

McConaughy, S. H. (1980). Using story structure in the classroom. *Language Arts* 57(2): 157–165.

Minick, N. (1987). Implications of Vygotsky's theories for dynamic assessment. In C. S. Lidz (ed.), *Dynamic assessment: An interactional approach to evaluating learning potential,* pp. 116–140. New York: Guilford Press.

Moll, L. C. (1990). Introduction. In L. C. Moll (ed.), *Vygotsky and education: Instructional implications and applications of sociohistorical psychology,* pp. 1–27. New York: Cambridge University Press.

More, D. W., and J. E. Readence. (1984). A quantitative and qualitative review of graphic organizer research. *Journal of Educational Research* 78: 11–17.

Ogle, D. M. (1986). K-W-L: A teaching model that develops active reading of expository text. *Reading Teacher* 38: 564–570.

Rosenblatt, L. (1991). Literature—S.O.S.! *Language Arts* 68(6): 444–448.

———. (1993). The literary transaction: Evocation and response. In K. E. Holland, R. A. Hungerford, and S. B. Ernst (eds.), *Journeying: Children responding to literature,* pp. 6–23. Portsmouth, NH: Heinemann.

Sanacore, J. (1993). Supporting a literature-based approach across the curriculum. *Journal of Reading* 37: 240–244.

Spiegel, D. L. (1987). Using adolescent literature in social studies and science. *Educational Horizons* 65: 162–164.

Stanley, N. V. (1986). A concurrent validity study of the emergent reading level (doctoral dissertation, University of Florida, Gainesville, Florida). *Dissertation Abstracts International* 47: 1675A.

Sulzby, E., and W. H. Teale. (1991). Emergent literacy. In R. Barr, M. S. Kamil, P. Mosenthal, and P. D. Pearson (eds.), *Handbook of reading research,* Vol. 2, pp. 727–757. New York: Longman.

Tischler, R. W. (1992). *How to use children's literature to teach mathematics.* Reston, VA: National Council of Teachers of Mathematics.

Vygotsky, L. S. (1962). *Thought and language* (E. Hanfmann and G. Vakar, eds. and trans.). Cambridge, MA: MIT Press.

———. (1978). *Mind in society: The development of higher psychological processes* (M. Cole, V. John-Steiner, S. Scribner, and E. Souberman, eds.). Cambridge, MA: Harvard University Press.

———. (1986). *Thought and language* (A. Kozulin, ed.). Cambridge, MA: MIT Press.

White, E. B. (1952). *Charlotte's web.* New York: Harper.

Wiseman, D. L. (1992). *Learning to read with literature.* Boston: Allyn & Bacon.

CHAPTER 4

Anderson, R. C., E. H. Hiebert, J. A. Scott, and I. A. G. Wilkinson. (1985). *Becoming a nation of readers: The report of the commission on reading.* Washington, DC: U.S. Department of Education.

Babbitt, N. (1975). *Tuck everlasting.* New York: Farrar, Straus & Giroux.

Bruner, J. (1989). Vygotsky: A historical and conceptual perspective. In J. V. Wertsch (ed.), *Culture, communication, and cognition.* New York: Cambridge University Press.

Coerr, E. (1977). *Sadako and the thousand paper cranes.* South Holland, IL: Yearling Books.

Edwards, D., and N. Mercer. (1987). *Common knowledge.* New York: Methuen.

Goodman, K. S., P. Shannon, Y. Freeman, and S. Murphy. (1988). *Report card on basal readers.* Katonah, NY: Richard C. Owen Publishers.

Maruki, Toshi. (1982). *Hiroshima, no pika.* New York: Lothrop, Lee & Shepard.

McMahon, S. I., T. E. Raphael, and V. Goatley. (in press). Changing the context for classroom reading instruction: The Book Club Project (J. Brophy, ed.). Greenwich, CT: JAI Press.

Raphael, T. E., and C. S. Englert. (1990). Writing and reading: Partners in constructing meaning. *Reading Teacher* 43: 388–400.

Raphael, T. E., and S. I. McMahon. (1994). "Book Club": An alternative framework for reading instruction. *Reading Teacher* 48(2): 102–116.

Vygotsky, L. S. (1978). *Mind in society: The development of higher mental psychological processes* (M. Cole, V. John-Steiner, S. Scribner, and E. Souberman, eds.). Cambridge, MA: Harvard University Press.

Walmsley, S. A., and T. P. Walp. (1989). *Teaching literature in elementary school.* (Report Series 1.3). Albany: State University of New York, Center for the Learning and Teaching of Literature.

Wertsch, J. V., (ed.). (1985). *Vygotsky and the social formation of mind*. Cambridge, MA: Harvard University Press.

Yukio, Tsuchiya. (1988). *Faithful elephants*. Boston: Houghton Mifflin.

CHAPTER 5

Aardema, V. (1975). *Why mosquitoes buzz in people's ears: A west African tale*. New York: Dial Press.

Aronson E. (1978). *The jigsaw classroom*. Beverly Hills, CA: Sage.

Beaver, C. F. (1981). *My mom travels a lot*. New York: Frederick Warne.

Briggs, R. (1970). *Jim and the beanstalk*. New York: Coward-McCann.

Dewey, J. (1916). *Democracy and education*. New York: Macmillan.

———. (1910). *How we think*. Boston: Heath.

Duffy, G., and L. R. Roehler. (1993). *Improving classroom reading instruction: A decision-making approach* (3d ed.), p. 245. New York: McGraw-Hill.

Ellis, S. S., and F. S. Whalen. (1990). *Collaborative learning: Getting started*. New York: Scholastic.

Ennis, R., and R. H. Ennin. (1985). Goals for a critical thinking curriculum. In A. Costa (ed.), *Developing minds: A resource book for teaching*. Alexandria, VA: Association for Supervision and Curriculum Development.

Gallagher, J. J. (1985). *Teaching the gifted child*. Boston: Allyn & Bacon.

Jennings, C., J. Jennings, J. Richey, and L. Dixon-Krauss. (1992). Increasing interest and achievement in mathematics through children's literature. *Early Childhood Research Quarterly* 7(2): 263–276.

Jennings, C., and G. Terry. (1990). Children's stories: A nature path to teaching thinking. *Dimensions* 18(2): 5–9.

Johnson, D., and R. Johnson. (1984). *Circles of learning*. Alexandria, VA: Association of Supervision and Curriculum Development.

Kozulin, A. (1993). Vygotsky in context. In A. Kozulin (ed. and trans.), *Thought and language*. Cambridge, MA: MIT Press.

Leontiev, A. N. (1981). The problem of activity in psychology. In J. V. Wertsch (ed.), *The concept of activity in Soviet psychology*, pp. 37–71. Armonk, NY: Sharpe.

Miller, J. L. (1990). *Creating spaces and finding voices: Teachers collaborating for empowerment*. Albany: State University of New York Press.

Rothlein, L., and A. M. Meinbach. (1991). *The literature connection: Using children's books in the classroom*. Glenview, IL: Scott Foresman & Company.

Sharan, S. (1984). *Cooperative learning in the classroom: Research in desegregated schools*. Hillsdale, NJ: Lawrence Erlbaum & Associates.

Slavin, R. E. (1983). When does cooperative learning increase student achievement. *Psychological Bulletin* 94: 429–445. Cambridge, MA: MIT Press.

———. (1984). Students motivating students to excel: Incentives, cooperative tasks and student achievement. *The Elementary School Journal* 85: 53–62.

———. (1990). *Cooperative learning: Theory, research and practice*. Englewood Cliffs, NJ: Prentice Hall.

Smith, F. (1986). *Insult to intelligence*. New York: Arbor House.

Steig, W. (1987). *Sylvester and the magic pebble*. New York: Simon & Schuster.

Vygotsky, L. S. (1962). *Thought and language* (E. Hanfmann and G. Vakar, eds. and trans.). Cambridge, MA: MIT Press.

———. (1976). Play and its role in the mental development of the child. In J. Bruner, A. Jolly, and K. Sylvia (eds.), *Play: Its role in development and evolution*. Middlesex, Eng.: Penguin Books.

———. (1978). *Mind in society: The development of higher psychological processes* (M. Cole, V. John-Steiner, S. Scribner, and E. Souberman, eds.). Cambridge, MA: Harvard University Press.

———. (1979). Consciousness as a problem of psychology of behavior. *Soviet Psychology*, pp. 1729–1730.

———. (1981). The instrumental method in psychology. In J. Wertsch (ed.), *The concept of activity in Soviet psychology*. Armonk, NY: Sharpe.

———. (1986). *Thought and language* (A. Kozulin, ed.). Cambridge, MA: MIT Press.

CHAPTER 6

Britton, J. (1970). *Language and thought*. Harmondsworth: Penguin.

Bruner, J. S. (1966). *Towards a theory of instruction*. Cambridge, MA: Belknap Press of Harvard University.

———. (1977). *The process of education: A landmark in educational theory*. Cambridge, MA: Harvard University Press.

Burnett, F. H. (1938). *The secret garden*. New York: Scholastic.

Emig, J. (1977, May). Writing as a mode of learning. *College Composition and Communication* 28: 122–128.

Fulwiler, T. (ed.). (1987). *The journal book*. Portsmouth, NH: Boynton/Cook.

Moffett, J. (1968). *Teaching the universe of discourse*. Boston: Houghton Mifflin.

Murray, D. M. (1968). *A writer teaches writing: A practical method of teaching composition*. Boston: Houghton Mifflin.

Nelson, O. T. (1975). *The girl who owned a city*. Minneapolis: Lerner Publications.

Newman, J. M. (ed.). (1985). *Whole language: Theory in use*. Portsmouth, NH: Heinemann.

Vygotsky, L. S. (1978). *Mind in society: The development of higher psychological processes* (M. Cole, V. John-Steiner, S. Scribner, and E. Souberman, eds.). Cambridge, MA: Harvard University Press.

———. (1986). *Thought and language* (A. Kozulin, ed.). Cambridge, MA: MIT Press.

Welty, E. (1984). *One writer's beginnings*. Cambridge, MA: Harvard University Press.

CHAPTER 7

Au, K. (1980). Participation structures in a reading lesson with Hawaiian children. *Anthropology and Education Quarterly* 11: 91–115.

Axel, E. (1992). One developmental line in European activity theories. *Quarterly Newsletter of the Laboratory of Comparative Human Cognition* 14(2): 8–17.

Brown, A., and B. Reeve. (1987). Bandwidths of competence: The role of supportive contexts in learning and development. In L. S. Liben (ed.), *Development and learning: Conflict or congruence?*, pp. 173–223. Hillsdale, NJ: Lawrence Erlbaum & Associates.

Cazden, C. B. (1981). Performance before competence: Assistance to child discourse in the zone of proximal development. *Quarterly Newsletter of the Laboratory of Comparative Human Cognition* 3(1): 5–8.

Cole, M., and P. Griffin. (1986). A sociocultural approach to remediation. In S. deCastell, A. Luke, and K. Egan (eds.), *Literacy, society, and schooling*, pp. 110–131. Cambridge: Cambridge University Press.

Davydov, V. V., and L. A. Radzikhovskii. (1985). Vygotsky's theory and the activity-oriented approach in psychology. In J. V. Wertsch (ed.), *Culture, communication, and cognition: Vygotskian perspectives*, pp. 35–65. New York: Cambridge University Press.

Gallimore, R., and R. Tharp. (1990). Teaching mind in society: Teaching, schooling, and literate discourse. In L. C. Moll (ed.), *Vygotsky and education: Instructional implications of sociohistorical psychology*, pp. 175–205. New York: Cambridge University Press.

Griffin, P., and M. Cole. (1984). Current activity for the future: The Zo-ped. In B. Rogoff and J. V. Wertsch (eds.), *Children's learning in the zone of proximal development*, pp. 45-63. San Francisco: Jossey-Bass.

Hatano, G. (1993). Time to merge Vygotskian and constructivist conceptions of knowledge acquisition. In E. Forman, N. Minick, and C. A. Stone (eds.), *Contexts for learning: Sociocultural dynamics in children's development*, pp. 153–166. New York: Oxford University Press.

Kozulin, A. (1986). The concept of activity in Soviet psychology: Vygotsky, his disciples and critics. *American Psychologist* 41: 264–274.

Laboratory of Comparative Human Cognition. (1983). Culture and cognitive development. In W. Kessen (ed.), *Handbook of child psychology: History, theory, and methods*, Vol. 1, pp. 294–356. New York: John Wiley.

Landsmann, L. T. (1991). The conceptualization of writing in the confluence of interactive models of development. In L. T. Landsmann (ed.), *Culture, schooling, and psychological development: Human development*, Vol. 4, pp. 87–111. Norwood, NJ: Ablex Publishing.

Langer, J. (1987). A sociocognitive perspective on literacy. In J. Langer (ed.), *Language, literacy, and culture: Issues of society and schooling*, pp. 1–20. Norwood, NJ: Ablex Publishing.

Leontiev, A. N. (1981). The problem of activity in psychology. In J. V. Wertsch (ed.), *The concept of activity in Soviet psychology*, pp. 37–71. Armonk, NY: Sharpe.

Michaels, S. (1983). Influences on children's narratives. *The Quarterly Newsletter of the Laboratory of Comparative Human Cognition* 5: 2.

———. (1985). Hearing the connections in children's oral and written discourse. *Journal of Education* 167(1): 36–56.

Minick, N., C. A. Stone, and E. A. Forman. (1993). Introduction: Integration of individual, social, and institutional processes in accounts of children's learning and development. In E. Forman, N. Minick, and C. Stone (eds.), *Contexts for learning: Sociocultural dynamics in children's learning*, pp. 3–16. New York: Oxford University Press.

Moll, L. (1990). Introduction. In L. C. Moll (ed.), *Vygotsky and education: Instructional implications of sociohistorical psychology*, pp. 1–27. New York: Cambridge University Press.

Moll, L., and K. F. Whitmore. (1993). Vygotsky in classroom practice: Moving from individual transmission to social transaction. In E. Forman, N. Minick, and C. A. Stone (eds.), *Contexts for learning: Sociocultural dynamics in children's development*, pp. 19–42. New York: Oxford University Press.

Palinscar, A. S., and A. L. Brown. (1984). Reciprocal teaching of comprehension-fostering and comprehension-monitoring activities. *Cognition and Instruction* 1: 117–175.

Palinscar, A. S., A. L. Brown, and J. C. Campione. (1993). First-grade dialogues for knowledge acquisition and use. In E. Forman, N. Minick, and C. A. Stone (eds.), *Contexts for learning: Sociocultural dynamics in children's development*, pp. 43–57. New York: Oxford University Press.

Perret-Clermont, A-N., J-F. Perret, and N. Bell. (1991). The social construction of meaning and cognitive activity in elementary school children. In L. B. Resnick, J. M. Levine, and S. D. Teasley (eds.), *Perspectives on socially shared cognition,* pp. 41–82. Washington, DC: American Psychological Association.

Resnick, L. (1991). Shared cognition: Thinking as social practice. In L. B. Resnick, J. M. Levine, and S. D. Teasley (eds.), *Perspectives on socially shared cognition,* pp. 1–20. Washington, DC: American Psychological Association.

Rogoff, B. (1990). *Apprenticeship in thinking: Cognitive development in social context.* New York: Oxford University Press.

Scribner, S., and M. Cole. (1981). *The consequences of literacy.* Cambridge, MA: Harvard University Press.

Sigel, I., E. T. Stinson, and J. Flaugher. (1991). Socialization of representational competence in the family: The distancing paradigm. In L. Okagaki and R. Sternberg (eds.), *Directors of development,* pp. 101–120. Hillsdale, NJ: Lawrence Erlbaum & Associates.

Tudge, J., S. Putnam, and J. Sidden. (1993). Preschoolers' activities in sociocultural context. *The Quarterly Newsletter of the Laboratory of Comparative Human Cognition* 15(2): 71–84.

Vygotsky, L. S. (1978). *Mind in society: The development of higher psychological processes* (M. Cole, V. John-Steiner, S. Scribner, and E. Souberman, eds.). Cambridge, MA: Harvard University Press.

———. (1981). The genesis of higher mental functions. In J. V. Wertsch (ed.), *The concept of activity,* pp. 144–188. Armonk, NY: Sharpe.

———. (1987). *Thought and language* (A. Kozulin, ed.). Cambridge, MA: MIT Press.

Wertsch, J. V. (1984). The zone of proximal development: Some conceptual issues. In B. Rogoff and J. V. Wertsch (eds.), *Children's learning in the zone of proximal development,* pp. 7–18. San Francisco: Jossey-Bass.

———. (1991). Sociocultural setting and the zone of proximal development: The problem of text-based realities. In L. T. Landsmann (ed.), *Culture, schooling, and psychological development,* Vol. 4, pp. 71–86. Norwood, NJ: Ablex Publishing.

Wertsch, J., and J. Bivens. (1992). The social origins of individual mental functioning: Alternatives and perspectives. *The Quarterly Newsletter of the Laboratory of Comparative Human Cognition* 14(2): 35–44.

Wertsch, J. V., and C. A. Stone. (1985). The concept of internalization in Vygotsky's account of the genesis of higher mental functions. In J. V. Wertsch (ed.), *Culture, communication, and cognition: Vygotskian perspectives,* pp. 162–179. New York: Columbia University Press.

Zaporozhets, A. V. (1979–80). Thought and activity in children. *Soviet Psychology* 23(2): 9–22.

INTRODUCTION TO PART II

Au, K. H. (1993). *Literacy instruction in multicultural settings.* Ft. Worth, TX: Harcourt Brace Jovanovich College Publishers.

Betts, E. A. (1943). Discovering specific reading needs. *Visual Digest* 7(2): 13–20.

Brozo, W. G. (1990). Learning how at-risk readers learn best: A case for interactive assessment. *Journal of Reading* 33(7): 522–527.

Dixon [Krauss], L. A. (1985). An investigation of the zone of proximal development for reading placement. *Dissertation Abstracts International* 47–01A: 0136A.

Harp, B. (1991). *Assessment and evaluation in whole language programs.* Norwood, MA: Christopher-Gordon Publishers.

Heap, J. L. (1985, April). *Understanding what counts as reading.* Paper presented at the annual meeting of the American Educational Research Association, Chicago.

Kragler, S. K. (1986). Static versus dynamic assessment: The impact on reading placement of reading underachievers. *Dissertation Abstracts International* 86: 18648.

Moll, L. C. (1990). Introduction. In L. C. Moll (ed.), *Vygotsky and education: Instructional implications and applications of sociohistorical psychology,* pp. 1–27. New York: Cambridge University Press.

Newman, D., P. Griffin, and M. Cole. (1989). *The construction zone: Working for cognitive change in school.* New York: Cambridge University Press.

Pearson, P. D. (1993). Teaching and learning reading: A research perspective. *Language Arts* 70: 502–511.

Pearson, P. D., and M. C. Gallagher. (1983). The instruction of reading comprehension. *Contemporary Educational Psychology* 8: 317–344.

Powell, W. R. (1984). Emergent reading levels: A construct. In J. A. Niles (ed.), *Perspectives on research in reading/language processing and instruction,* 33d yearbook of the National Reading Conference, pp. 247–251. Rochester, NY: National Reading Conference.

———. (1993, April). Classroom literacy instruction and assessment from the Vygotskian perspective. In L. D. Krauss (chair), *Vygotsky in the Classroom.* Symposium conducted at the 38th annual convention of the International Reading Association, San Antonio, TX.

Stanley, N. V. (1986). A concurrent validity study of the emergent reading level. *Dissertation Abstracts International* 47: 1675A.

Vygotsky, L. S. (1978). *Mind in society: The development of higher psychological processes* (M. Cole, V. John-Steiner, S. Scribner, and E. Souberman, eds.). Cambridge, MA: Harvard University Press.

———. (1986). *Thought and language* (A. Kozulin, ed.). Cambridge, MA: MIT Press.

Zinchenko, V. (1994, September). *The zone of proximal development and beyond.* Paper presented at the Opening Plenary Session of the International Conference on L. S. Vygotsky and the Contemporary Human Sciences, Moscow, Russia.

CHAPTER 8

Aaron, I. E., J. S. Chall, D. Durkin, K. Goodman, and D. S. Strickland. (1990). The past, present, and future of literacy education: Comments from a panel of distinguished educators, part II. *The Reading Teacher* 43: 370–380.

Alverman, D. A., and J. T. Guthrie. (1993). Themes and directions of the National Reading Research Center. *Perspectives in reading research* (Tech. Report No. 1). National Reading Research Center, University of Georgia and University of Maryland.

Au, K. H. (1993). *Literacy instruction in multicultural settings.* Ft. Worth, TX: Harcourt Brace Jovanovich College Publishers.

Bayer, A. S. (1990). *Collaborative-apprenticeship learning: Language and thinking across the curriculum, K-12.* Mountain View, CA: Mayfield.

Blank, J. P. (1984, June). The triumph of Guadalupe Quintanilla. *Reader's Digest,* pp. 77–81.

Budoff, M. (1987). The validity of learning potential assessment. In C. S. Lidz (ed.), *Dynamic assessment: An interactional approach to evaluating learning potential,* pp. 52–81. New York: Guilford Press.

Campione, J. C., and A. L. Brown. (1985). *Dynamic assessment: One approach and some initial data* (Tech. Report No. 361). Urbana: University of Illinois Center for the Study of Reading. (ERIC Document Reproduction Service No. ED 269 735).

Chenet, R. (1994). *Intercultural collaboration: Developing skills at the interpersonal and inter-group level.* Unpublished manuscript. A training workbook of the Intercultural Community Leadership Project. Santa Fe, NM: Santa Fe Community College.

Collier, C. (1988). *Assessing minority students with learning and behavior problems.* Lindale, TX: Hamilton Publications.

Dixon [Krauss], L. A. (1985). An investigation of the zone of proximal development for reading placement. *Dissertation Abstracts International* 47–01A: 0136A.

Edmonds, P. (1994, May 12). Many argue separate can still be equal. *USA Today,* pp. 1–2.

Feuerstein, R., Y. Rand, M. R. Jensen, S. Kaniel, and D. Tzuriel. (1987). Prerequisites for assessment of learning potential: The LPAD model. In C. S. Lidz (ed.), *Dynamic assessment: An interactional approach to evaluating learning potential,* pp. 35–51. New York: Guilford Press.

Goodman, K. S. (1985). Commentary. *Journal of Reading* 28: 389–392.

Jefferson, T. (1776). Declaration of independence. Reprinted (1992) in G. Colombo, R. Cullen, and B. Lisle (eds.), *Rereading America: Cultural concepts for critical thinking and writing,* pp. 608–611. New York: St. Martin's Press.

Kletzien, S. B., and M. R. Bednar. (1990). Dynamic assessment for at-risk readers. *Journal of Reading* 33: 528–533.

Kragler [Newman], S. K. (1986). Static versus dynamic assessment: The impact of reading placement on reading underachievers. *Dissertation Abstracts International* 86: 18648.

Lidz, C. S. (ed.). (1987). *Dynamic assessment: An interactional approach to evaluating learning potential.* New York: Guilford Press.

Manzo, A. V., and U. C. Manzo. (1993). *Literacy disorders: Holistic diagnosis and remediation.* New York: Harcourt Brace Jovanovich College Publishers.

Meyers, J. (1987). The training of dynamic assessors. In C. S. Lidz (ed.), *Dynamic assessment: An interactional approach to evaluating learning potential,* pp. 403–425. New York: Guilford Press.

Minick, N. (1987). Implications of Vygotsky's theories for dynamic assessment. In C. S. Lidz (ed.), *Dynamic assessment: An interactional approach to evaluating learning potential,* pp. 116–140. New York: Guilford Press.

Morrison, T. (1970). *The bluest eye.* New York: Simon & Schuster.

Powell, W. R. (1989, May). *The reading program of the future.* Paper presented at the annual meeting of the International Reading Association, New Orleans, LA. (ERIC Document Reproduction Service No. ED 316 829).

Rodriquez, R. F. (1982). *The Mexican American child in special education.* (ERIC Document Reproduction Service No. ED 212 437).

Rogoff, B., and J. V. Wertsch (eds.). (1984). *Children's learning in the "zone of proximal development."* San Francisco: Jossey-Bass.

Salvia, J., and J. E. Ysseldyke. (1991). *Assessment.* Boston: Houghton Mifflin.

Schwartz, H. J. (1990, December). *Pricing literacy: The ethics of access.* Paper presented at the annual meeting of the Modern Language Association, Chicago, IL. (ERIC Document Reproduction No. ED 333 343).

Skuy, M., S. Kaniel, and D. Tzuriel. (1988). Dynamic assessment of intellectually superior Israeli children in a low socioeconomic status community. *Gifted Education International* 5: 90–96.

Smith, C. (1990). *Trends and issues in reading education.* Learning package No. 11, Indiana University School of Education, Bloomington, IN. (ERIC Document Reproduction Service No. ED 333 377).

Smith, E. B., K. Goodman, and R. Meredith. (1976). *Language and thinking in school.* New York: Holt.

Stanley, N. V. (1986). A concurrent validity study of the emergent reading level. *Dissertation Abstracts International* 47: 1675A.

———. (1988). Optimizing reading placement. *New Mexico Journal of Reading* 13: 19–21.

———. (1992). *Are standardized tests culturally biased?* Unpublished manuscript.

———. (1993). Gifted and the zone of proximal development. *Gifted Education International* 92.

———. (1994). The future of reading education, the next millennium. In M. Shaughnessy (ed.), *The future of education.* Portales: Eastern New Mexico University Press.

Stanley, N. V., J. Siegle, L. Cooper, and K. Marshall. (in press). Identification of gifted with the dynamic assessment procedure (DAP). *Gifted Education International.*

Tannenbaum, A. J. (1988). *The gifted movement—forward or on a treadmill.* West Lafayette, IN: Purdue University. (ERIC Reproduction Service No. ED 315 949).

Taylor, C. (1992). The politics of recognition. In A. Gutman (ed.), *Multiculturalism,* pp. 25–73. Princeton, NJ: Princeton University Press.

Vygotsky, L. S. (1962). *Thought and language* (E. Hanfmann and G. Vakar, eds. and trans.). Cambridge, MA: MIT Press.

———. (1978). *Mind in society: The development of higher psychological processes.* (M. Cole, V. John-Steiner, S. Scribner, and E. Souberman, trans.). Cambridge, MA: Harvard University Press.

CHAPTER 9

Allington, R. (1983). The reading instruction provided readers of differing reading abilities. *The Elementary School Journal* 83: 548–559.

———. (1990). Effective literacy instruction for at-risk readers. In M. Knapp and P. Shields (eds.), *Better schooling for the children of poverty,* pp. 9–30. Berkeley, CA: McCutchan Publishing.

Allington, R., H. Steutzel, M. Shake, and S. Lamarch. (1986). What is remedial reading? A descriptive study. *Reading Research and Instruction* 26: 15–30.

Anderson, R., and P. Freebody. (1981). Vocabulary knowledge. In J. Flood (ed.), *Comprehension and teaching: Research reviews,* pp. 77–117. Newark, DE: International Reading Association.

Anderson, R., and R. Kulhavy. (1972). Learning concepts from definitions. *American Educational Research Journal* 9: 385–390.

Athey, I. (1983). Language development factors related to reading development. *Journal of Educational Research* 76: 197–202.

Au, K. (1979). Using the experience-text-relationship method with minority children. *The Reading Teacher* 32: 677–679.

Barr, M. (1990). The Primary Language Record: Reflections of issues in evaluation. *Language Arts* 67: 244–253.

Baumann, J., L. Jones, and N. Seifert-Kessell. (1993). Using think alouds to enhance children's comprehension monitoring abilities. *The Reading Teacher* 47: 184–193.

Beck, I., C. Perfetti, and L. McKeown. (1982). Effects of long term vocabulary instruction on lexical access and reading comprehension. *Journal of Educational Psychology* 74: 506–521.

Bednar, M., and S. Kletzien. (1990). *Dynamic assessment procedure: A validation.* Paper presented at the 40th annual meeting of the National Reading Conference, Miami, FL. (ERIC Document Reproduction Service No. ED 329 921).

Braun, C., B. Rennie, and C. Gordon. (1987). An examination of contexts for reading assessment. *Journal of Educational Research* 80: 283–289.

Brophy, J. (1990). Effective schooling for disadvantaged students. In M. Knapp and P. Shields (eds.), *Better schooling for the children of poverty,* pp. 211–234. Berkeley, CA: McCutchan Publishing.

Brown, A., and R. Ferrara. (1985). Diagnosing zones of proximal development. In J. V. Wertsch (ed.), *Culture, communication, and cognition: Vygotskian perspectives,* pp. 273–305. Cambridge, MA: Cambridge University Press.

Brozo, W. (1990). Learning how at-risk readers learn best: A case for interactive assessment. *Journal of Reading* 33: 522–527.

Budoff, M. (1972). Measuring learning potential: An alternative to the traditional intelligence test. (*Studies in Learning Potential,* 3). Cambridge, MA: Research Institute for Educational Problems. (ERIC Document Reproduction Service No. ED 085 962).

Campione, J., and C. Brown. (1985). *Dynamic assessment: One approach and some initial data* (Tech. Report No. 361). (ERIC Document Reproduction Service No. ED 269 735).

Cazden, C. (1980). Toward a social educational psychology with Soviet help. *Contemporary Educational Psychology* 5: 196–201.

Clark, M. (1975). Language and reading research trends. In A. Davies (ed.), *Problems of language and learning,* pp. 89–112. London: Heinemann Educational Books Ltd.

Clay, M., and C. Cazden. (1990). A Vygotskian interpretation of Reading Recovery. In L. Moll (ed.), *Vygotsky and education: Instructional implications and applications of sociohistorical psychology,* pp. 206–222. New York: Cambridge University Press.

Coiffi, G., and J. Carne. (1983). Dynamic assessment of reading disabilities. *The Reading Teacher* 36: 764–768.

Cole, M., and P. Griffin. (1986). A sociohistorical approach to remediation. In S. Castell, A. Lube, and K. Egan (eds.), *Literacy society and schooling: A reader,* pp. 111–131. New York: Cambridge University Press.

Cornbleth, C., and W. Korth. (1980). Context factors and individual differences in pupil involvement in learning activity. *Journal of Educational Research,* 73: 318–323.

Dale, E. (1969). *Audiovisual methods in teaching* (3d ed.). New York: Holt, Rinehart & Winston.

Delpit, L. (1986). Skills and other dilemmas of a progressive black educator. *Harvard Educational Review* 56: 379–398.

DeStafano, J., H. Pepinsky, and T. Sanders. (1982). Discourse rules for literacy learning in a classroom. In L. C. Wilkinson (ed.), *Communicating in the classroom,* pp. 101–129. New York: Academic Press.

Duffy, J., and M. Fedner. (1978). Educational diagnosis with instructional use. *Exceptional Children* 44: 246–251.

Duffy, G., L. Roehler, and B. Herrmann. (1988). Modeling mental processes helps poor readers become strategic readers. *The Reading Teacher* 41: 762–767.

Elliot, S., and S. Piersel. (1982). Direct assessment of reading skills: An approach which links assessment to intervention. *Psychological Review* 11: 267–280.

Feuerstein, R. (1980). *The dynamic assessment of retarded performers: The learning potential assessment device, theory, instruments, and techniques.* Baltimore: University Park Press.

Gamblin, P., and M. Bountrogianni. (1985). *The assessment of the potential to learn: A multicultural perspective.* Paper presented at the 69th annual meeting of the American Educational Research Association, Chicago, IL. (ERIC Document Reproduction Service No. ED 262 105).

Gambrell, L. (1986). Reading in the primary grades: How often, How long? In M. Sampson (ed.), *The pursuit of literacy,* pp.102–107. Dubuque, IA: Kendall/Hunt Publishing.

Gambrell, L., R. Wilson, and W. Gantt. (1981). Classroom observations of task-attending behaviors of good and poor readers. *Journal of Educational Research* 74: 400-404.

Garcia, G., and P. Pearson. (1990). Modifying reading instruction to maximize its effectiveness for all students. In M. Knapp and P. Shields (eds.), *Better schooling for the children of poverty,* pp. 31–59. Berkeley, CA: McCutchan Publishing.

Gelzheiser, L., and J. Meyers. (1991). Reading instruction by classroom, remedial, and resource room teachers. *Journal of Special Education* 24: 512–526.

Glazer, S., and L. Searfoss. (1988). Reexamining reading diagnosis. In S. Glazer, L. Searfoss, and L. Gentile (eds.), *Reexamining reading diagnosis: New trends and procedures,* pp. 1–11. Newark, DE: International Reading Association.

Goodman, Y., and K. Goodman. (1990). Vygotsky in a whole-language perspective. In L. Moll (ed.), *Vygotsky and education: Instructional implications and applications of sociohistorical psychology,* pp. 223–250. Cambridge, MA: Cambridge University Press.

Harker, W. (1990). Testing reading: We need a new perspective. *Reading Horizons* 30: 309–319.

Haywood, H. (1990). Dynamic approaches to psychoeducational assessment. *School Psychological Review* 19: 411–422.

Hilliard, A. (1982). *The learning potential assessment device and instrumental enrichment as a paradigm shift.* Paper presented at the 66th annual meeting of the American Educational Research Association. (ERIC Document Reproduction Service No. ED 223 674).

Homan, S., C. Hines, and J. Kromrey. (1993). An investigation of varying reading level placement on reading achievement of Chapter I students. *Reading Research and Instruction* 33: 29–38.

Hymes, D. (1972). Introduction. In C. Cazden, V. John, and D. Hymes (eds.), *Functions of language in the classroom,* pp. xi-lvii. New York: Teachers College Press.

Indrisano, R., and J. Paratore. (1992). Using literature with readers at risk. In B. Cullinan (ed.), *Invitation to read: More children's literature in the reading program,* pp. 138–149. Newark, DE: International Reading Association.

Jennings, J. (1990). You can't afford not to read aloud. *Phi Delta Kappan* 71: 568–571.

John-Steiner, V., and P. Tatter. (1983). An interactionist model of language development. In B. Bain (ed.), *The sociogenesis of language and human conduct,* pp. 79–97. New York: Plenum Press.

Kletzien, S., and M. Bednar. (1990). Dynamic assessment for at-risk readers. *Journal of Reading* 33: 528–533.

Kragler, S. (1991). Mediated reading levels of Chapter I third grade students. *Reading Improvement* 28: 121–125.

Lidz, C. (1987). *Dynamic assessment: An interactional approach to evaluating learning potential.* New York: Guilford Press.

Manzo, A. (1969). Request procedure. *Journal of Reading* 13: 123–126.

Marlow, L., and D. Reese. (1992). Strategies for using literature with at-risk readers. *Reading Improvement* 28: 130–132.

McClelland, D. (1973). Testing for competence rather than for "intelligence." *American Psychologist* 28: 1–14.

Nagy, W. (1988). *Teaching vocabulary to improve comprehension.* Urbana, IL: National Council for Teachers of English.

Palinscar, A., and A. Brown. (1984). Reciprocal teaching of comprehension-fostering and comprehension-monitoring activities. *Cognition and Instruction* 1: 117–175.

Perfetti, C. (1983). Reading, vocabulary and writing: Implications for computer based instruction. In A. C. (ed.), *Classroom computers and cognitive science,* pp. 145–163. New York: Academic Press.

Powell, W. (1984). Mediated (emergent) reading levels: A construct. In J. Niles (ed.), *Thirty-third yearbook of the National Reading Conference,* pp. 247–251. Rochester, NY: National Reading Conference.

Putnam, L. (1994). Reading instruction: What do we know now that we didn't know thirty years ago. *Language Arts* 71: 362–366.

Quirk, T., D. Trismen, K. Nalin, and K. Weinberg. (1975). The classroom behaviors of teachers during compensatory reading. *Journal of Educational Research* 68: 185–192.

Roser, N., J. Hoffman, and C. Farest. (1990). Language, literature, and at-risk readers. *The Reading Teacher* 43: 554–559.

Royer, J., and D. Cunningham. (1981). On the theory and measurement of reading comprehension. *Contemporary Educational Psychology* 6: 187–216.

Stahl, S. (1983). Differential word knowledge and reading comprehension. *Journal of Reading Behavior* 15: 35–50.

Stahl, S., and S. Vancil. (1986). Discussion is what makes semantic maps work in vocabulary instruction. *The Reading Teacher* 40: 62–67.

Stanovich, K. (1986). Matthew effects in reading: Some consequences of individual differences in the acquisition of literacy. *Reading Research Quarterly* 15: 10–29.

Tough, J. (1983). Learning to represent meaning. In B. Hutson (ed.), *Advances in reading/language,* Vol. 2, pp. 55–81. Greenwich, CT: JAI Press.

Valencia, S., and P. Pearson. (1987). Reading assessment: Time for a change. *The Reading Teacher* 40: 726–732.

Vygotsky, L. S. (1978). *Mind in society: The development of higher psychological processes* (M. Cole, V. John-Steiner, S. Scribner, and E. Souberman, eds.). Cambridge, MA: Harvard University Press.

Walker, B. (1986). *Diagnostic lessons as assessment.* Paper presented at the 14th annual meeting of the Plains Regional Conference of the International Reading Association, Rapid City, SD. (ERIC Document Reproduction Service No. ED 277 976).

Walmsley, S., and T. Walp. (1990). Integrating literature and composing into the language arts curriculum: Philosophy and practice. *The Elementary School Journal* 90: 251–272.

Wertsch, J. (1983). Role of semiosis in L. S. Vygotsky's theory of human cognition. In B. Bain (ed.), *The sociogenesis of language and human conduct,* pp. 17–31. New York: Plenum Press.

———. (1984). The zone of proximal development: Some conceptual issues. In B. Rogoff and J. Wertsch (eds.), *Children's learning in the zone of proximal development,* pp. 7–30. San Francisco: Jossey-Bass.

Wilkinson, L., and F. Spinnelli. (1982). Conclusion: Applications for education. In L. C. Wilkinson (ed.), *Communication in the classroom,* pp. 323–327. New York: Academic Press.

Wozniak, R. (1975). Psychology and education of the learning disabled child in the Soviet Union. In W. Cruickshank and D. Hallahan (eds.), *Perceptual and learning disabilities in children,* pp. 407–479. Syracuse, NY: Syracuse University Press.

———. (1980). Theory, practice and the "zone of proximal development" in Soviet psychoeducational research. *Contemporary Educational Psychology* 5: 175–183.

CHAPTER 10

Arter, J., and V. Spandel. (1992). Using portfolios of student work in instruction and assessment. *Educational Measurement: Issues and Practice,* pp. 36–44.

Hansen, J. (1992, August). *Literacy portfolios.* Paper presented at the meeting of the Gulf Coast Conference on the Teaching of Writing, Point Clear, AL.

Kieffer, R., and L. Morrison, (1994). Changing portfolio process: One journey toward authentic assessment. *Language Arts* 71(6): 411–418.

Paulsen, F. L., P. R. Paulsen, and C. A. Meyer. (1991). What makes a portfolio a portfolio? *Educational Leadership* 48(5): 60–63.

Valencia, S. (1990). A portfolio approach to classroom reading assessment: The whys, whats, and how. *The Reading Teacher* 43: 338–340.

Wagner, C., D. Brock, and A. Agnew. (1994). Developing literacy portfolios in teacher education courses. *Journal of Reading* 37(8): 668–674.

Wertsch, J. V. (1984). The zone of proximal development: Some conceptual issues. In B. Rogoff and J. V. Wertsch (eds.), *Children's learning in the zone of proximal development,* pp. 7–18. San Francisco: Jossey-Bass.

Wolf, K. (1991). The school teacher's portfolio: Issues in design, implementation, and evaluation. *Phi Delta Kappan* 73(2): 129–136.

CHAPTER 11

Au, K. H., and A. J. Kawakami. (1984). Vygotskian perspectives on discussion processes in small-group reading-lessons. In P. L. Peterson, L. C. Wilkinson, and M. Hallinan (eds.), *The social context of instruction,* pp. 209–225. New York: Academic Press.

Bolter, J. D. (1990). *Writing space: The computer, hypertext, and the history of writing.* Hillsdale, NJ: Lawrence Erlbaum & Associates.

Carver, S. M., R. Lehrer, T. Connell, and J. Erickson. (1992). Learning by hypermedia design: Issues of assessment and implementation. *Educational Psychologist* 27(3): 385–404.

Crook, C. (1991). Computers in the zone of proximal development: Implications for evaluation. *Computers and Education* 17(1): 81–91.

Cuban, L. (1986). *Teachers and machines: The classroom use of technology since 1920.* New York: Teachers College Press.

Davies, I., and H. Shane. (1986). Computers and the educational program. In J. A. Culbertson and L. L. Cunningham (eds.), *Microcomputers and education. Eighty-fifth yearbook of the National Society for the Study of Education,* pp. 1–19. Chicago: University of Chicago Press.

Eisenhart, M. A., and K. Cutts-Dougherty. (1991). Social and cultural constraints on student's access to school knowledge. In E. H. Hiebert (ed.), *Literacy for a diverse society: Perspectives, practices, and policies,* pp. 28–43. New York: Teachers College Press.

Emihovich, C. (1989). Learning through sharing: Peer collaboration in Logo instruction. In C. Emihovich (ed.), *Locating learning: Ethnographic perspectives on classroom research,* pp. 289–310. Norwood, NJ: Ablex Publishing.

Fleming, R. (1989). Technological literacy: Implications for instruction. In C. K. Leong and B. S. Randhawa (eds.), *Understanding literacy and cognition: Theory, research, and application,* pp. 255–268. New York: Plenum Press.

Gardner, H. (1985). *The mind's new science.* New York: Basic Books Inc.

Gentry, C. G. (1991). Educational technology: A question of meaning. In G. Anglin (ed.), *Instructional technology: Past, present, and future*, pp. 1–10. Englewood, CO: Libraries Unlimited.

Goodman, Y. M., and K. S. Goodman. (1990). Vygotsky in a whole language perspective. In L. C. Moll (ed.), *Vygotsky and education: Instructional implications and applications of sociohistorical psychology*, pp. 223–250. New York: Cambridge University Press.

Gotkin, L. G., and J. F. Sweeney. (1967). Learning from teaching machines. In P. Lange (ed.), *Programmed Instruction. The sixty-sixth yearbook of the National Society for the Study of Education (Part 2)*, pp. 255–283. Chicago: University of Chicago Press.

Harel, I. (1991). *Children designers*. Norwood, NJ: Ablex Publishing.

Harel, I., and S. Papert. (1990). Software design as a learning environment. *Interactive Learning Environments* 1: 1–32.

Heap, J. L. (1989). Collaborative practices during word processing in a first grade classroom. In C. Emihovich (ed.), *Locating learning: Ethnographic perspectives on classroom research*, pp. 263–288. Norwood, NJ: Ablex Publishing.

Heinich, R., M. Molenda, and J. D. Russell. (1993). *Instructional media and the new technologies of instruction*. New York: Macmillan Publishing.

Lehrer, R. (1993). Authors of knowledge: Patterns of hypermedia design. In S. Lajoie and S. Derry (eds.), *Computers as cognitive tools*, pp. 197–228. Hillsdale, NJ: Lawrence Erlbaum & Associates.

Male, M. (1994). *Technology for inclusion: Meeting the special needs of all students* (2d ed.). Needham Heights, MA: Allyn & Bacon.

McCulloch, W., and W. Pitts. (1943). A logical calculus of the ideas immanent in nervous activity. *Bulletin of Mathematical Biophysics* 5: 115–133.

McLane, J. B. (1990). Writing as a social process. In L. C. Moll (ed.), *Vygotsky and education: Instructional implications and applications of sociohistorical psychology*, pp. 304–318. New York: Cambridge University Press.

Moeller, B. (1993). *Literacy and technology*. College of Education, Center for Children and Technology, Center for Technology Education, Bank Street, New York. (ERIC Document Reproduction Service No. ED 366 316).

Olson, D. R., and J. S. Bruner. (1974). Learning through experience and learning through media. In D. R. Olson (ed.), *Media and symbols: The forms of expression, communication, and education. The seventy-third yearbook of the National Society for the Study of Education*, pp. 125–150. Chicago: University of Chicago Press.

Papert, S. (1980). *Mindstorms: Children, computers, and powerful ideas*. New York: Basic Books.

Peters, J. M. (1991, March). *The use of HyperStudio in science teacher training and science instruction*. Paper presented at the annual meeting of the National Science Teachers Association, Houston, TX.

Peters, J. M., G. O'Brien, C. Briscoe, and S. Beightol. (1994). *Technology in the classroom: Successful activities for teacher preparation*. Paper presented at the annual meeting of the National Science Teachers Association, Anaheim, CA.

Ravitch, D. (1987). Technology and the curriculum: Promise and peril. In M. A. White (ed.), *What curriculum for the information age*, pp. 25–40. Hillsdale, NJ: Lawrence Erlbaum & Associates.

Routman, R. (1988). *Transitions from literature to literacy*. Portsmouth, NH: Heinemann.

Salomon, G. (1993). Pedagogical computer tools. In S. Lajoie and S. Derry (eds.), *Computers as cognitive tools*, pp. 179–196. Hillsdale, NJ: Lawrence Erlbaum & Associates.

——. (1994). *Interaction of media, cognition, and learning.* Hillsdale, NJ: Lawrence Erlbaum & Associates.

Schurman, K. (1994). Today's schools: Three R's . . . and one T (technology). *PC Novice* 5(9): 28–32.

Scott, T., M. Cole, and M. Engel. (1992). Computers and education: A cultural constructivist perspective. In G. Grant (ed.), *Review of research in education,* Vol. 18, pp. 191–251. Washington, DC: American Educational Research Association.

Simonson, M. R., and A. Thompson. (1994). *Educational computing foundations* (2d ed.). New York: Merrill.

Spiro, R. J., and J. C. Jehng. (1990). Cognitive flexibility and hypertext: Theory and technology for the nonlinear and multidimensional traversal of complex subject matter. In D. Nix and R. J. Spiro (eds.), *Cognition, education, and multimedia,* pp. 163–205. Hillsdale, NJ: Lawrence Erlbaum & Associates.

Spoehr, K. T. (1993, April). *Profiles of hypermedia authors: How students learn by doing.* Paper presented at the annual meeting of the American Educational Research Association, Atlanta, GA.

Teale, W. H. (1986). Home background and young children's literacy development. In W. H. Teale and E. Sulzby (eds.), *Emergent literacy: Writing and reading,* pp. 173–206. Norwood, NJ: Ablex Publishing.

U.S. Congress, Office of Technology Assessment. (1993). *Adult literacy and new technologies: Tools for a lifetime.* OTA-SET-550. Washington, DC: U.S. Government Printing Office.

Vygotsky, L. S. (1978). *Mind in society: The development of higher psychological processes* (M. Cole, V. John-Steiner, S. Scribner, and E. Souberman, eds.). Cambridge, MA: Harvard University Press.

Waggoner, M. D. (ed.). (1992). *Empowering Networks: Computer conferencing in education.* Englewood Cliffs, NJ: Educational Technology Publications.

Wedemeyer, D. J. (1991). The new age of telecommunication: Setting the context for education. In *The educational technology anthology series. Vol. 3: Telecommunications for learning,* pp. 5–11. Englewood Cliffs, NJ: Educational Technology Publications.

Wertsch, J. (1985). *Vygotsky and the social formation of the mind.* Cambridge, MA: Harvard University Press.

White, M. A. (1987). Information and imagery education. In M. A. White (ed.), *What curriculum for the information age,* pp. 41–66. Hillsdale, NJ: Lawrence Erlbaum & Associates.

Wiener, N. (1961). *Cybernetics, or control and communication in the animal and machine* (2d ed.). Cambridge, MA: MIT Press.

Wisnudel, M., and V. Spitulnik. (1994). *Students designing hypermedia instructional materials as a means to becoming better learners.* Paper presented at the annual meeting of the National Science Teachers Association.

Contributors

Lisbeth Dixon-Krauss, Department of Elementary and Middle Level Education, University of West Florida, Pensacola, Florida

Patricia Ashton, Department of Educational Foundations, University of Florida, Gainesville, Florida

Dana Brock, Department of Special, Primary, and Vocational Education, University of West Florida, Pensacola, Florida

Martha Combs, Department of Curriculum and Instruction, University of Nevada-Reno, Reno, Nevada

Xu Di, Department of Educational Foundations, Secondary, and Technology, University of West Florida, Pensacola, Florida

Clara M. Jennings, College of Education, Youngstown State University, Youngstown, Ohio

Sherry Kragler, Department of Elementary Education, Ball State University, Muncie, Indiana

Marian Matthews, Department of Reading Education, Eastern New Mexico University, Portales, New Mexico

Susan I. McMahon, Department of Curriculum and Instruction, University of Wisconsin-Madison, Madison, Wisconsin

Joe M. Peters, Department of Elementary and Middle Level Education, University of West Florida, Pensacola, Florida

Nile V. Stanley, Department of Reading Education, Eastern New Mexico University, Portales, New Mexico

Lyn Rothwell Wagner, Kid's Discovery Days Preschool, Arvada, Colorado

Index